*Iliad*
Book Nine

# HOMER

*Iliad* Book Nine

edited by
JASPER GRIFFIN

CLARENDON PRESS · OXFORD
1995

Oxford University Press, Walton Street, Oxford OX2 6DP
Oxford   New York
Athens   Auckland   Bangkok   Bombay
Calcutta   Cape Town   Dar es Salaam   Delhi
Florence   Hong Kong   Istanbul   Karachi
Kuala Lumpur   Madras   Madrid   Melbourne
Mexico City   Nairobi   Paris   Singapore
Taipei   Tokyo   Toronto
and associated companies in
Berlin Ibadan

Oxford is a trade mark of Oxford University Press

Published in the United States
by Oxford University Press Inc., New York

British Library Cataloguing in Publication Data
Data available

Library of Congress Cataloging in Publication Data
Iliad, Book nine / Homer: edited by Jasper Griffin.
Includes bibliographical references.
1. Achilles (Greek mythology)—Poetry.   2. Trojan War—Poetry.
3. Epic poetry, Greek.   I. Griffin, Jasper.   II. Title.
PA4020.P9   1995      883'.001—dc20      94-44516
ISBN 0-19-814078-9.
ISBN 0-19-814130-0

1 3 5 7 9 10 8 6 4 2

Typeset by Regent Typesetting, London
Printed in Great Britain
on acid-free paper by
Biddles Ltd., Guildford and King's Lynn

# PREFACE

This commentary on one of the masterpieces of ancient literature has the modest aim of helping the reader to understand and appreciate the text. It contains a short account of the salient features of Homeric style and composition; the Introduction makes clear the sort of view I take of the poem, its composition, its subject, and its significance. The large and valuable Commentary on the whole of the *Iliad* in six volumes edited by G. S. Kirk, (Cambridge, 1985-93), leaves room for the sort of smaller and perhaps more manœuvrable work of which Colin Macleod's Commentary on Iliad 24 is a distinguished example. I have tried to give some help to beginning Homerists, but I hope more advanced readers will also find some of the discussions interesting.

I am grateful to Mrs Susan McCann, who, with accuracy and good humour, typed most of the manuscript, and to Oxford University Press, which showed its usual urbane efficiency. It is a special pleasure to record my thanks to Sir Hugh Lloyd-Jones for help and encouragement over many years: τοῦ καὶ πρόσθεν ἀρίστη φαίνετο βουλή.

J. G.

# CONTENTS

# INTRODUCTION

## I. THE ILIAD AND HEROIC POETRY

The *Iliad* was composed a very long time ago. It is the beginning of European literature, although, as we shall see, it is set in what is now Asia, and it draws upon a long tradition of Eastern writing. In the nineteenth and twentieth centuries we have rediscovered many other languages and works of literature composed in the Near East and in Egypt before the birth of Christ: all of them lay lost to sight, undeciphered and mostly unheard of, for many centuries. Only the Greeks and the Hebrews produced works which survived in an unbroken tradition, always read, studied, and taught in schools. Among the Greeks the *Iliad*, even more than the *Odyssey*, always held an unchallenged position as the supreme work of their literature. It underlay Greek Tragedy, and it inspired the career and conquests of Alexander the Great; it was the challenge which the Roman poet Virgil aspired to meet with his *Aeneid*, the supreme masterpiece of the literature of Rome; it was a model and a rival for Milton's *Paradise Lost*. It is the ultimate source of the Western conceptions of heroism and of the grand style. Apart from the Bible, it is hard to think of a work comparable in its influence on the later world.

The earliest people to speak what we now call an Indo-European language—one of that great family of languages which includes Sanskrit, Old Persian, Greek, Latin and the Romance languages (French, Spanish, Italian), the Germanic languages (including English), and the languages of the Celts and the Slavs—had a long tradition of song about the exploits and doom of heroes. The Irish Cuchulainn, the Germanic Siegfried and Beowulf, the Indian heroes of the Mahabharata, move in a world of battle, the quest for honour, and the claim that in song glory can outlast death.[1] The ancestors of the Greeks, too, even before they reached Greece from

---

[1] C. M. Bowra, *Heroic Poetry* (London, 1952); H. M. Chadwick, *The Heroic Age* (Cambridge, 1912); R. Schmitt, *Dichtung und Dichtersprache in indogermanischer Zeit*

the north, shared that ancestral tradition, and it lies behind the *Iliad* (see note on line 413).

But the *Iliad* came into being from a fusion of that Indo-European tradition with other forms of literature: the poetry and mythology of the ancient cultures of the Near East, older than Greece, known to Greeks from centuries of interaction, both commercial and war-like. The epic of Gilgamesh told of a hero, son of a goddess, who caused the death of his dearest friend, kept his body unburied in passionate mourning, roared like a lion in his grief; it told of the goddess of love being taunted by a hero and complaining to her unsympathetic divine father (cf. *Il.* 5. 348 ff.). That poem seems to have begun in Sumer, and to have been widespread in differing versions and in several languages from *c.*2000 to *c.*600 BC. Its resemblances to the *Iliad*, from this summary, are obvious; although it should be added that the story of some of it does not resemble Homer, and all of it, as far as we can tell, was told in a considerably less sophisticated style.

Other Mesopotamian poems can be seen to have influenced the *Iliad*. The division of the world by casting lots between three gods, one taking the heavens, one the earth, and one the sea, was told at the beginning of *Atrahasis* (*c.*1700 BC) (cf. *Il.* 15. 187-93). The Homeric picture of the gods all living together on Mount Olympus, feasting and quarrelling, is not that which Greeks actually held, or which they implied in their ritual and worship. In Athens Athena was the great deity, at Delphi Apollo, at Argos Hera, and so on, and gods were invoked as perfectly able to grant prayers themselves, not as needing to get the consent of Zeus at a general divine gathering. The Iliadic picture, so lively and amusing for poetry, unmistakably resembles the divine gatherings of Hittite and Babylonian and Canaanite literature.[2]

To the ancestral songs of legendary heroism and doom, and the influence of the developed literatures of the East, must be added historical memories and traditions of the Greeks once they had reached the Aegean from the north. The places which are promi-nent in the heroic myths[3]—Mycenae, Tiryns, Thebes, Pylos,

(Wiesbaden, 1967); G. Nagy, *The Best of the Achaeans* (Johns Hopkins, 1979) (specu-lative); M. L. West in *Journal of Hellenic Studies*, 108 (1988), 154-5.

[2] *Myths from Mesopotamia: Creation, the Flood, Gilgamesh, and Others*, trans. S. Dalley (Oxford, 1991); W. Burkert, 'Oriental Myth and Literature in the *Iliad*', in *The Greek Renaissance of the Eighth Century B.C.* , ed. R. Hägg (Stockholm, 1981), 51-6.

[3] M. P. Nilsson, *Mycenaean Origins of Greek Mythology* (Berkeley, Calif., 1932).

Troy—are places which were powerful and conspicuous in the second millennium BC. 'Mycenae rich in gold' (*Il.* 7. 180, 11. 46) and 'Tiryns with its walls' (2. 559) are epithets notably apter before 1000 BC than after; on Orchomenos see note on 381. Troy, too, was a great fortress, on one occasion (it seems) levelled by an earthquake, on another sacked by men.[4] There must have been many raiding expeditions, to Asia Minor and to Egypt, by marauding Greeks: stories told in the *Odyssey* reflect a world in which such things were common, and to be a successful pirate was no disgrace (e.g. *Od.* 3. 69–74, the naïve question 'Are you traders or are you pirates?'; 14. 21 ff., 'I was illegitimate but a brave and fortunate leader of raids, and I preferred piracy to staying at home'; 17. 42 ff., 'I went raiding in Egypt, but it turned out disastrously'). Much of that probably reflects the unquiet world of the eighth and seventh centuries BC, but things will not have been so different three or four hundred years earlier.[5] Chance discoveries in the records of the Hittites have introduced to the modern world a thirteenth-century kingdom called (by the Hittites) Ahhiyawa; a ruler called Attarissiyas; a man called Alaksandus, ruler of Wilusa. We do seem to hear echoes of Achaea, Atreus, and Alexandros, prince of Wilios (older form of Ἴλιος, Troy). A sixteenth-century BC text in Luwian seems to have begun with the words 'When the men came from steep Wilusa', a startling coincidence with the Homeric 'steep Ilios', Ἴλιος αἰπεινή (3 times) and Ἴλιος αἰπή (5 times). There are traces in Homer and in Greek myth of various facts and stories of past history. But for reasons beyond discovery, the story of an expedition against Troy became *the* story of overseas adventure for Greece.[6]

We can see some hints of the way in which the Trojan story grew. As with the court of King Arthur, to which originally unconnected characters like Tristan eventually became attached, Troy drew in other heroes. Diomedes is an obvious example. He belonged in the Theban cycle: stories about his terrible father Tydeus, one of the Seven against Thebes, are always being told to

[4] *Cambridge Ancient History*, 3rd edn., ii. 1. 683–5; ibid. ii. 2. 160 ff.
[5] K. Latte, 'Zeitgeschichtliches zu Archilochos', *Hermes*, 92 (1964), 385–90 = *Kleine Schriften* (Munich 1968), 457–63; M. I Finley, *The World of Odysseus*[2] (Penguin 1973): to be used with caution; L. Foxhall and J. K. Davies (eds.), *The Trojan War: Its Historicity and Context* (Bristol, 1984).
[6] C. Watkins, 'The Language of the Trojans', in *Troy and the Trojan War*, ed. M. J. Mellink (Bryn Mawr, 1986), 58 f.

his son (4. 370-400, 5. 800-13, cf. 10. 284-91), who was one of the Epigoni, the Successors, who in the generation after their fathers' disastrous failure succeeded in taking Thebes (4. 403-10). Somehow he became part of the Trojan cycle, too, and in the *Iliad* he is firmly fixed and has a function, as a foil to Achilles: brave and high-spirited, he is not so easily nor so implacably offended by a slight as Achilles: see notes on 34ff., 57.

Another important person whom it is surprising to find at Troy is Nestor, a member of an older generation, who enables the poet to introduce stories from the battle poetry of the Peloponnese (1. 259-73, 7. 124-60, 11. 655-762, 23. 624-45). We may have our suspicions about Idomeneus the Cretan, too, who at Troy kills several heroes with Cretan-sounding names: Phaestos (5. 43), who has the name of a Cretan town, and Othryoneus.[7] Those killings, it has been conjectured, originally took place on Crete, far from Troy. Sarpedon the Lycian, who comes from the south of Asia Minor, kills a Greek from Rhodes, the island opposite his homeland (5. 628ff.) The presence of Lycians so far from home is an unexplained fact in the *Iliad*, and again one can guess that originally Sarpedon did his fighting in Lycia;[8] but in our *Iliad* he is an important figure, the greatest warrior to be killed by Patroclus in Book 16. Such examples give an idea of the way in which the poem has grown to its great size, and also of the way in which the Trojan expedition has come to be a representative one, the united action of all Greece against the foreign enemy. It is as if all the foreign wars were rolled into one, promoted in status, and dignified by the personal interest and participation of the gods.

## 2. THE ILIAD

### The Tradition and the Poem

The *Iliad* is the earliest poem to survive from what was clearly a rich tradition in Greece of heroic verse. It contains allusions to other stories than that of Troy: we have seen that Diomedes brings in episodes from the Theban cycle, and Nestor episodes from

---

[7] Cf. R. Janko, *Commentary on the Iliad*, ed. G. S. Kirk, iv (Cambridge, 1992), on 13. 363 and 16. 603-7.

[8] A. Heubeck, *Archaeologica Homerica 10: Schrift* (Göttingen, 1979), 131.

heroic battles in the Peloponnese. The poem is also pervaded by allusions to the career of the supreme hero, Heracles: his birth, (19. 95-133); his sacking of Troy, (5. 638-51, 14. 249-61); his battles with gods, (5. 392-404), and with monsters, (20. 144-8); his descent to the lower world and return with Cerberus the hellhound, (8. 362-9); his slaying of the brothers of Nestor, (11. 690-5). We hear in passing also of Zeus' father Cronos and his grandfather Uranus, and of the Titans (5. 887-8; 14. 279; 15. 187-93), whose gruesome and exotic stories were told at length, also in hexameter verse, in the almost contemporary *Theogony* of Hesiod. Other heroes with exciting adventures are known to the *Iliad* poet, such as Bellerophon (6. 152-95) who slew the Chimaera and fought the Amazons; and Jason (7. 469; 21. 41), and Perseus (14. 320), and Theseus (1. 265), and the Cretan princess Ariadne who helped him kill the Minotaur (18. 292). No doubt much of this, and much else, existed in heroic song.

The poet of the *Iliad* is of course acquainted with the whole story of the Trojan War. The name '*Iliad*' means 'Poem of Troy (Ilios)', and it is crucial to the poem that in its own way it tells or alludes to the whole of that story. In Book 2 we are told of the assembling of the expedition at Aulis, ten years ago (2..299-332), and the contingents are listed as they then embarked (2. 486-779): leaders who have since been killed or are not present are still listed, (2. 698-710, 718-28). Book 3 presents a duel between Paris and Menelaus for Helen, who is present on the wall to watch and to be the visible prize; Paris appears looking glamorous but not armed for proper Homeric battle. All this, it is clear, 'belongs' to the first encounter of Greeks and Trojans, as it does that Priam is unfamiliar with the Greek leaders and has to have them identified for him by Helen (3. 161-243). We see the beginning of the fighting, with Menelaus the typical Greek warrior and Paris the typical Asiatic playboy, rescued by Aphrodite and taken off from defeat to bed with Helen.[9] We see the effect of the Judgement of Paris, still further back, in the insatiable hostility of Hera and Athena to Troy (esp. 4. 20-61; 8. 457-69; 20. 310-17); there is one actual

[9] H. Fränkel, *Wege und Formen frühgriechischen Denkens* (Munich, 1955), 3f.; E. Bethe, *Homer I: die Ilias* (Leipzig, 1914), 65-7; J. T. Kakridis, 'Problems of the Homeric Helen', in *Homer Revisited* (Lund, 1971), 25-53. H. Erbse gives a rationalizing explanation: hitherto the Trojans have not dared to fight in the plain (*Studi Classici e Orientali*, 28 (1978), 16). That disregards what is said at 2. 786 ff., where again it is made clear that this is the *first* onset of the Achaeans.

glance at the story (24. 25-30).[10] We hear also of the end of the war. Immediately after he kills Hector, Achilles must die; and Troy must fall. The death of Achilles is predicted with increasing detail (1. 417; 9. 410-14; 18. 95-6; 22. 359-60), and although he is still alive at the end of the poem, he knows and accepts that he is on the verge of death (22. 365-6). The fall of Troy is predicted and described with touching fullness by Hector (6. 447-65), by Priam (22. 59-76), and by Andromache (24. 729-38; cf. also 22. 408-11).

To say this is to say that the *Iliad*, early as it is from our point of view, is by no means primitive or unsophisticated in its conception. It narrates a short part of the story of the war, an episode not as obviously vital as the Judgement of Paris or the Sack of Troy, but one which is made to be the key to the whole war by dextrous management (when Hector falls, Troy is doomed); while the rest of the story is brought in indirectly and by implication. Thus it is that the *Iliad* possesses a real but subtle unity, which the straightforward narration of the whole Trojan tale would not necessarily possess. It is noteworthy that the *Odyssey*, a poem clearly influenced by the *Iliad*, proceeds in a rather similar way, but that the poems of the so-called Epic Cycle, now lost but known from fragments and summaries, seem to have been much more simply composed in terms of 'and the next thing was . . .' αὐτὰρ ἔπειτα. The conception embodied in the *Iliad* was not easy to imitate.[11]

Another striking feature of the *Iliad* is its great length. With the exception of the *Odyssey*, which is just over three-quarters of the length of the *Iliad* and which is clearly influenced by it, no early Greek epic known to us approached it in size: most are far shorter (the *Little Iliad* consisted of four books, the *Aethiopis* of five, the *Iliu Persis* of two, the *Nosti* of five, the *Telegony* of two; the longest, the *Cypria*, had eleven). The picture given of the singer's position in the *Odyssey* (in the *Iliad* there are no professional singers, see note on 189) is of a performer whose audience may suggest his subject and feels free to interrupt him when dissatisfied:

Δημόδοκος δ' ἤδη σχεθέτω φόρμιγγα λίγειαν,
οὐ γάρ πως πάντεσσι χαριζόμενος τάδ' ἀείδει, (*Od.* 8. 537-8)

---

[10] K. Reinhardt, *Das Parisurteil* (Frankfurt, 1938) = *Tradition und Geist* (Göttingen, 1960), 16-36.

[11] J. Griffin, 'The Epic Cycle and the Uniqueness of Homer', *JHS* 97 (1977), 39-53.

Let Demodocus check his tuneful lyre, for what he is singing is not to the liking of everyone.

The one song (out of three) which the bard Demodocus is allowed to finish, a spicy tale of adultery and high spirits on Olympus, is a mere hundred lines in length (*Od.* 8. 266-369). That situation, one with the audience and not the singer in control, is perhaps what we naturally expect to find, and it is not easy to imagine the *Iliad* coming into existence in such a state of affairs. The existence of the *Iliad*, in fact, proves the existence of an audience prepared to listen to it—if the singer were interrupted at the end (say) of Book 20, the audience would have wasted all the time spent listening up to that point, as the lack of a conclusion would deprive the song and the experience of its sense and point.

It seems natural to infer that these two great decisions—the creation of a poem enormous in length, and organized and unified in a new and subtle way—went together, and that they were the decisions of a single mind. There is nothing 'natural' or inevitable about either of them; and the *Iliad* did not arise spontaneously from the mere existence of an epic tradition. It must have been the creation, essentially, of a singer of great powers, ambition, and reputation, whose ascendancy over his audience was such that they were prepared to trust him as he took them through a story highly original both in scale and in conception. He emerged from the oral tradition and composed in the oral style: we shall go on to discuss what that means. He also, it is reasonable to assume, took a third decision, which enabled him both to extend his song in length and to give it a specific moral character. That was the decision, which will be discussed in the next section, to develop and complicate the simple plot pattern by which a hero, slighted and dishonoured, withdraws from battle until his comrades are forced to beg for his return. That is the story up to Book Nine, where the poem takes another turn: the hero cannot bring himself to accept the offered compensation, causes the death of his dearest friend, and instead of triumphing finishes in remorse and despair, accepting death. The new complexity of plot implies also a new complexity of moral atmosphere: no one is simply right. That, too, must have been the conception of the great singer whom the people of later antiquity, who knew nothing about him, called Homer.

Some scholars refuse to accept the existence of this poet. There is an ancient tradition that the sixth century Athenian statesman Solon (according to the earliest source), or the tyrants who followed him at Athens, arranged for the Homeric poems to be recited at the festival of the Panathenaea by relays of rhapsodes. Some late sources (the earliest is the Roman writer Cicero in the first century BC,) add that this was the first time the poems, which up to then had not been arranged in a definite order, were brought into the order and shape in which they are familiar. This tradition seems to offer a means of escape from believing in a great poet as the creator of the *Iliad*.

To take a recent example, R. Seaford, in his book *Reciprocity and Ritual* (Oxford, 1994), 152-4, thinks it was essentially social institutions which were responsible for the extended size and the final shape of the epics:

'Of course there may have been a master-poet more influential than the others . . . Of the exceptional circumstances pointed out by Griffin, some at least are also susceptible to a historical explanation . . .'; he rejects any explanation in terms of 'Homer's "exceptional genius"'. It was 'sixth-century institutional practice (such as we find at Athens) that allowed the final fixation and predominance of the *Iliad* and *Odyssey* and not . . . an eighth century genius'.

This is surely very hard to believe. We have seen some reason to think that the whole conception and structure of the *Iliad* are extraordinary, more easily imaginable as the result of a set of linked decisions by a single singer than the result of any process of gradual accretion or shared creation. Another difficulty presents itself. It was the *Iliad* and *Odyssey* that the Athenians of the sixth century wanted to hear; Solon, or the tyrant Pisistratus, aimed to please by meeting a demand for them, not for the numerous other epic poems which existed at the time. It is a puzzle how this can have happened, if the two epics did not have the qualities which made them supreme—if in fact they did not really exist in definite form—until their performance at Athens finally brought them into shape.

Romantic scholars used to believe that the epics were created by the whole people (Volkspoesie); now institutions and rituals get the credit. It is as if we argued that the plays of Shakespeare were the product of the circumstances of his time: of course the artist is influenced by his period and himself influences it, but we are left with the question why (if we have ruled out individual genius) the plays of Shakespeare are so much better than those of his contemporaries.

## Gods and Men

At Troy we are in a heroic age. Heroes are not simply big brave warriors, taller and stronger than we are (5. 304, 12. 449, 20. 287): they are closer to the gods than later men and women, sons and daughters of gods and goddesses. Zeus sits on Mount Ida to keep a close watch on the Trojan fighting (11. 183, 337; 14. 157), and all the gods gaze down at it and argue and support their favourites with passionate partisanship[12] (4. 1–67; 8. 1–40; 20. 1–66); almost all except Zeus intervene at some point on the battlefield, and Zeus himself grieves for the death of his beloved Hector and causes bloody rain to fall to mark the death of his son Sarpedon (22. 166–85; 16. 459f.). The audience enjoys the privilege of seeing and following the divine interventions, which the characters in the poem only partly and intermittently understand. We know what Zeus intends, and what will come of Agamemnon's excessive self-confidence. Achilles, who is the son of a goddess, has some access to the divine workings. He knows more than other mortals of his own destiny (note on 410), and through his mother's influence with Zeus he starts the machinery which causes the Achaean defeats (1. 348–427, 493–530). But even Achilles does not really understand. When his refusal to return to battle has led to the death of Patroclus, he says to his mother 'It is true that Olympian Zeus has granted my prayers—but what joy do I have of it, since my dear friend Patroclus is dead . . . I caused his death' (18. 79–82). The plan of Zeus was fulfilled (1. 5), and it was more complex and more bitter than even a great and privileged mortal could discern.

$$\mathrm{\mathring{a}}\lambda\lambda' \ a\mathring{\iota}\epsilon\acute{\iota} \ \tau\epsilon \ \varDelta\iota\grave{o}s \ \kappa\rho\epsilon\acute{\iota}\sigma\sigma\omega\nu \ \nu\acute{o}os \ \mathring{\eta}\acute{\epsilon} \ \pi\epsilon\rho \ \mathring{a}\nu\delta\rho\widehat{\omega}\nu \quad (16. \ 688)$$

But the mind of Zeus is always more powerful than that of men.

True heroic verse is not just lively entertainment but gives a picture of the world and of what it is to be human in it. That involves the gods, without whom, as controllers of events and also as radiant foil to the weakness and fragility of even the greatest of mortals, human life is unintelligible. The subject matter of the epic singer is defined as 'actions of men and gods', ἔργ' ἀνδρῶν τε θεῶν τε (*Od.* 1. 338). It is part of the importance of the heroic myths, and it was vital in permitting them to be the vehicle of serious

---

[12] J. Griffin, *Homer on Life and Death* (Oxford, 1980) ch. 6, 'The Divine Audience'.

thought for the Greeks, that in them human actions and sufferings are transparent: we can see behind what happens the plans and interventions of the gods. In ordinary life those workings are concealed, and we see only what happens on the human plane. In epic, and later on in tragedy too, the actions and sufferings of the heroes and heroines of myth involve the divine, and so illuminate for us the limits, high and low, of human existence.

We have seen that it was, in all probability, from the East that the Greek epic derived the idea of all the gods living together and struggling for dominance in mortal affairs. Such a picture was to present problems for later Greeks who tried to take their gods seriously and to accept their poets as moral and religious authorities, as did the whole notion that the gods had love-affairs, rivalries, and jealousies—that they were, in fact, all too human. It did, however, offer exhilarating possibilities for an epic poet. First, it made available a second cast of characters and a second set of places: Mount Olympus, Mount Ida, the house of Zeus. Variety was thus immediately increased. More important, it made it possible to present the human actions in a particular perspective. The gods are, of course, grand and imposing; they are bigger and stronger than we (and heavier: the axle of Diomedes' chariot groans beneath the weight of Athena, 5. 838-9). Above all, they are exempt from age and death. There are moments when a god is presented as numinous, but usually they seem no more spiritual, or even more moral, than mortals.[13]

Not all gods are equal. Aphrodite, goddess of love, and Ares, god of war in its aspect of bloodshed and mayhem (Athena is goddess of war in its aspect of skill and, above all, of winning), adulterous paramours according to the song of Demodocus in the *Odyssey* (*Od.* 8.), are fair game for humiliation: 5. 318-430, 835-905; 21. 391-433. Like them, the great god Apollo is on the Trojan side; but he cannot be treated in such a way, and he always keeps his dignity (cf. 21. 435-67). Athena, dynamic and alert, is the patron of favoured heroes and assists them in their battles. She gets into Diomedes' chariot, shoving out his driver, and drives it herself (5. 835 ff.); she always came to the aid of Heracles in his distresses, (8. 362-9); she helps Achilles in his final duel with

[13] W. F. Otto, *The Homeric Gods* (English trans. by M. Hadas, London and New York, 1954); J. Griffin, *Homer on Life and Death*, 144-78; W. Burkert, *Greek Religion*, tr. J. Raffan (Cambridge, Mass., 1985), 119-90.

Hector (22. 214-305). In the *Odyssey* she will play a similar role for Odysseus and his son Telemachus. She, too, is a god who cannot be humiliated or lose her dignity. Hera, wife of Zeus, is pretty consistently presented as angry and suspicious (1. 517-69). She and Athena do not simply want the success of their protégés, as other gods do: they are implacably determined on the destruction of Troy (4. 1-67; 20. 309-17). That reflects the Judgement of Paris, who foolishly slighted them and the gifts which they represented—respectively the life of kingly rule and the life of a great warrior—in favour of Aphrodite and erotic pleasure. Hera's one 'loving' scene with Zeus is a trick, distracting his attention from events on the plain of Troy (14. 153-360).

These gods and goddesses interact with each other and with mortals in a most lively way, but they do not seem to fulfil all the demands which mortals make of their gods, either in awesomeness or in concern for justice. It is important to recognize that there is another side to Homeric religion, sometimes overlooked, which has much more of those properties. It is also important that the poem feels no need to keep these two sides separate: on the contrary, they are repeatedly juxtaposed. Thus, at the beginning of the *Iliad*, Thetis goes to Olympus to ask Zeus to bring defeat on the Greeks and so forward the plan of her son. For twelve days all the gods have been away at the edge of the world, feasting with the Ethiopians; the world has apparently got on without them. Now they are back, and Thetis finds Zeus alone, on a topmost peak. She begs him to aid her scheme, reminding him delicately that he owes her a considerable favour (1. 498-510, cf. 1. 394-407). Zeus sits in silence. Thetis repeats her plea, and Zeus replies that this a grievous business: 'You will set me at odds with Hera, when she stings me to anger with her taunts. Even without this she is always carping at me among the immortal gods. Now, you must leave, so that Hera shall not notice. . . .' and then he nods his head to confirm his promise: 'So spoke the son of Cronos and nodded his dark brows. The god's immortal hair streamed forward from his deathless head: and he made mighty Olympus shake.' Then he goes to join the others, and immediately Hera begins to nag him. That sequence of events combines the all-too-human god worried about his wife, subject to moral pressure from Thetis, capable of taking a twelve-day holiday, with the dread god whose gesture is described in grand style: it was said to have been this passage which inspired Phidias when he created his great statue of Olympian Zeus, one of the wonders of the world, the grandest of all Greek representations of the divine.

That extraordinary combination can be paralleled repeatedly. In Book Five Diomedes is allowed to attack and rout the disliked gods Ares and Aphrodite: he also attacks Apollo, who thrusts him back with the solemn command 'Think! Reflect on the difference between gods and men' (5. 436-42, cf. 16. 705 ff.). As Apollo was to say at his shrine of Delphi: Know Yourself. Amid the farcical indignities of the 'Battle of the Gods', in which Aphrodite is knocked down by Athena, who simply shoves her over, while Artemis has her ears boxed by Hera, we still find the hills shaking and the god of the dead leaping from his throne in anxiety lest the earth should split open and his hateful realm of decay be revealed (20. 54-66), and Apollo declining to fight Poseidon with the crushing words: 'Earthshaker, you would never call me sensible again if I fight you on account of mortals, wretched creatures, who one moment flourish like the leaves, eating the fruits of the earth, and at another fade into lifelessness' (21. 462-6). The grandiose scale of even a frivolous divine battle is for a moment present, and the crushing divine perspective in which nothing human is really serious (cf. 1. 573-6). Even in the almost comic story of Hera seducing Zeus, as the god embraces his wife 'Beneath them the holy earth set up fresh growing grass, and dewy lotus, and saffron, and hyacinth thick and soft . . . On that bed they lay, wrapping themselves in cloud, golden and beautiful: drops of dew fell glistening from it' (14. 346-51). The union of these two is still the cosmic marriage of heaven and earth which makes the whole world fruitful. And at times, too, Zeus does show some care for justice: despite the intrigues of selfish gods, Troy started it, and it is right that Troy should fall.

The poet of the *Iliad* preserves that difficult balance of frivolity and sublimity with extraordinary panache. Already in the *Odyssey* the picture is different: Zeus defends himself against human criticism (*Od.* 1. 32-43), the gods no longer have such rowdy and full-blooded gatherings, nor such direct clashes: Athena would not dream of opposing the will of her uncle Poseidon (*Od.* 13. 341-3), and generally speaking the divine is on its best behaviour in the *Odyssey*. The *Iliad* presents human life against that extraordinary back-cloth, and it is vital to the poem that it depicts the greatest of humankind, heroes akin to gods, and even Achilles himself, in a light which emphasizes both their greatness and their fragility. 'Godlike', 'equal to Ares', 'sprung from Zeus', are common epithets for the heroic characters, and their doings, especially their duels to the death, command the excited attention of the gods (e.g. 4 *init.*, all the gods 'pledged each other in golden goblets, gazing on the city of Troy'; 7. 58–62, Athena and Apollo sit in a lofty oak-tree, in the form of birds, to watch the duel between Hector and Ajax, 'taking delight in the men'; 22. 166, as Achilles chases Hector, 'all the gods looked on').

But at the same time men are, as Apollo crushingly says, creatures of a day, here today and gone tomorrow. Sarpedon was the son of Zeus, a mighty hero: when he is dead, and the armies fight over his body, 'Then not even a knowledgeable man would have recognized godlike Sarpedon, as he was covered from head to foot with weapons and blood and dirt. And they swarmed about the corpse, like flies around milk-pails . . .' (16. 638–42); flies, blood, an unrecognizable corpse—that is now the godlike Sarpedon; and still 'Zeus did not turn his shining eyes away from the battle', (16. 644–5). The horror of death in battle is not concealed or minimized, and every warrior must face it. So it is that when kind-hearted Patroclus is to be sent by Achilles to find out what is happening to the defeated Achaeans, Achilles calls him out of his hut, 'And he came out, the equal of Ares; and that was the beginning of his doom' (11. 604): ἔκμολεν ἶσος Ἄρηι, κακοῦ δ' ἄρα οἱ πέλεν ἀρχή. We share the privileged view of the gods and see him, at the same moment, as godlike and as marked for death. That is the light in which the poem also presents Achilles.

One further step remains. As Sarpedon lay dead, Zeus did not look away; but we have seen that for twelve days the gods were taking no interest in Troy or anything near it. We can add that at another time only the horrid deity Eris, 'Strife', was there to take pleasure in the sight of the fighting, fierce as it was: 'The other gods were not present but sitting at their leisure in their houses, as each had a fine house on the glens of Olympus' (11. 73–7). And as for Zeus, when he had brought the Trojans and Hector right up to the Achaean ships, 'He left them there to suffer toil and pain unceasingly, but for his part he turned away his shining eyes, gazing far away to the land of the horsemen of Thrace, and the Mysians who fight at close quarters, and the haughty Hippemolgi

("Horse-milkers") who live on milk, and the Abii, most righteous of mankind. To Troy he did not turn his shining eyes at all' (13. 1–7). The Trojan War was important, splendid, fascinating; the gods themselves dignified it by their interest, and they glorify us as an audience when we hear that their keen attention is directed in the same way as ours, that as we watch Hector hunted to death 'all the gods were looking on', too; but in the end even the Trojan War was not inexhaustibly interesting, not to the gods who live at ease (θεοὶ ῥεῖα ζώοντες), to whom nothing human is, in the end, wholly serious.[14] That forces the audience to see the tragedy of Achilles in a very special light: the gods are used to show that it both is and is not truly significant. That is the characteristic and very particular viewpoint of the *Iliad*.

### Atmosphere

The characters of the *Iliad* are aristocrats in more than being of noble birth and fighting prowess. It is of incalculable importance for the whole history of manners in the West that the heroes are courteous and civilized in their dealings with each other.[15] Nobody insults a woman; Helen, even, is never reproached by anyone but herself (3. 161–80; 6. 342–68; 24. 761–75). Achilles tells us that he 'loved from his heart' the captive woman who has been taken from him—as 'every good man loves his wife and cares for her' (9. 340–3).

Heroes speak to each other with tact, on the whole; Nestor's speeches in Book 9 are a good example (see notes on 70, 96ff.). The brutal frankness with which Achilles speaks is thus all the more striking (309ff. cf. 1. 140–60; 225–32). Leading characters have a whole line formula of address in the vocative case: 'Son of Laertes, sprung from Zeus, Odysseus of the many plans'; 'Father Zeus, who rulest from Ida, most glorious, most great'; 'Most glorious son of Atreus, Agamemnon king of men'—διογενὲς Λαερτιάδη, πολυμήχαν' Ὀδυσσεῦ (9. 308, etc.); Ζεῦ πάτερ, Ἴδηθεν μεδέων, κύδιστε μέγιστε (2. 412, etc.); Ἀτρεΐδη κύδιστε, ἄναξ ἀνδρῶν Ἀγάμεμνον (9. 96, etc.). That is a mark of the high formality of Homeric society—as well as providing an unstressed and regularly

---

[14] K. Reinhardt coined the phrase 'erhabener Unernst', sublime frivolity, for the gods of the *Iliad* (*Das Parisurteil*, 9).

[15] I. M. Hohendahl-Zoetelief, *Manners in the Homeric Epic* (Leiden, 1980).

repeated verse, which allowed the singer a moment of respite in his work of improvisation and the audience a moment to catch up on what they had just heard.

The civility of social life becomes in the *Odyssey* a central theme in its own right. Young Prince Telemachus is sent to the palaces of Nestor (*Od.* 3) and Menelaus (*Od.* 4 and 15) in part to be shown how to mix with his equals, with older men (*Od.* 3. 13–28), heroes of his father's generation (*Od.* 4. 69 ff.), and the glamorous *grande dame* Helen (*Od.* 4 and 15). In the *Iliad* it is important that Hector is courteous to the ladies of Troy (*Il.* 6; 24. 767–75), and that Achilles, through most of the poem so savage, used to be different, civilized and generous even towards a dead enemy (*Il.* 6. 414–20). In the last two books he regains that character, first with his comrades and then with his enemy, the father of the man who slew Patroclus, King Priam.[16] This is no mere tale of brutal killers.

An extraordinary feature of the Homeric poems is that a sort of heroic courtesy and urbanity can at times be seen between heroes and gods. When Achilles has half decided to kill Agamemnon, in their great quarrel, Athena comes down from heaven to stop him. She says 'I have come to check your fury, if you will listen to me', and the hero, addressing the goddess in a tone not much different from that in which heroes converse with each other, says 'One should heed what you say, goddess, however angry at heart: that is the better course; he who listens to the gods, they truly listen to him' (1. 205–18). The intimacy and reasonableness of the scene is only underlined by the impressive, intense way in which her coming is described: 'She stood behind him and seized him by his fair hair, visible to him alone—none of the others could see her; and Achilles was startled, and turned, and at once he recognized Pallas Athena: terrible was the flashing of her eyes' (1. 198–200). The whole scene makes a very strong contrast with the way in which relations of men and God are described in the Old Testament. In the *Odyssey* Athena and Odysseus become at moments really close associates (*Od.* 13. 287–332). The *Iliad* never goes quite that far, but it is part of the character and significance of Achilles that Athena takes such trouble over him, and that she comes again to help him in his final duel with Hector (22. 214 ff.). He is a person of the stature to win such divine support.

---

[16] The distinguished commentary of C. W. Macleod on *Iliad* 24 deserves special recommendation (Cambridge, 1982).

The position of Achilles rests on his being the greatest warrior in the Achaean camp. That is what establishes the difficult relationship with Agamemnon, the leader, which we detect in their quarrel in Book 1. That dispute implies previous resentment on both sides. Agamemnon tells Achilles not to try trick him, ἀγαθός περ ἐών, 'good fighter though you are' (1. 131); 'If you are very strong, it was surely a god who gave it to you' (1. 178); 'If the gods have made him a fighter, is that a reason for abuse to flow from his lips?' (1. 290-1). We seem to see in these words a history of anxiety in Agamemnon about his over-mighty subordinate, while Achilles' words betray a long-hoarded contempt for the commander who helps himself to the spoils but who is no fighting man—'You could never endure to arm for battle with the army . . . that feels like death to you' (1. 226); 'It is my hands which do the fighting, but when the distribution comes, you get the lion's share' (1. 165-7). That lack of liking is present in the poem until the end (23. 889-97, silence of Agamemnon in response to a generous gesture by Achilles).

Fighting is the supreme test: it is in battle that men win glory (μάχην κυδιάνειραν). It is his prowess which makes Hector supreme in Troy. The *Iliad* keeps its most intense narrative for the scenes, so many in the course of the poem, in which two heroes face each other in single combat, risking that terrible transition from godlike splendour to helpless corpse, which is the moment of truth for Homer. The similes which are one of the great glories of the *Iliad* cluster unmistakably about the duels and the killings: they are the points in the poem which the poet is above all concerned to make vivid to the mind of the audience.

But it is not in the battle alone that men win fame, and to be quarrelsome and fond of a fight is loathsome (1. 175f. 5. 890f. note on 64). The epithet κυδιάνειρα is used also of the ἀγορή, the assembly where speeches are made; and old Phoenix says that Achilles' father sent him with his son 'to teach you all this: to be a speaker of words and a doer of deeds' (9. 438-43), cf. note on 443). Each of the three envoys of Book 9 makes an effective speech, the three being in very different styles, and Achilles replies with a long speech of unrivalled power.[17] He is at the opposite extreme from the inarticulate hero of the traditional western movie, and the

[17] A. Parry, 'The Language of Achilles', *TAPA* 87 (1956) 1-7, repr. in *The Language of Achilles and Other Papers* (Oxford, 1989), 1-7; J. Griffin, 'Homeric Words

heroism of the *Iliad* has an intellectual side in this mastery of effective and elaborate speech. His outburst of anger, scorn, and hurt pride is overwhelming, and he is the most inventive coiner of similes of all Homeric speakers (note on 323–4). That does not mean that he is a model of eloquence for other heroes to follow: his great speech does not convince his hearers in the poem and so is, in rhetorical terms, a failure. Achilles himself says ruefully, when it is too late, that he is unequalled in fighting, but others excel him in (prudent) speech (18. 106 ἀγορῇ δέ τ' ἀμείνονές εἰσι καὶ ἄλλοι). His great speech in Book 9 is one of self-expression, and it reveals to the audience that he possesses a capacity for passionate feeling, different from that displayed by any other hero, which will explain his conduct in the rest of the poem.

## Book 8 and Book 9

We speak familiarly of the Homeric poems as consisting of twenty-four books each, and of the books as separate unities, but in the early period the epics were not thought of in that way. There is no evidence that the division into numbered books is earlier than the activity of the Alexandrian scholars of the third century BC.[18] It enabled people to refer to each book by one of the letters of the (Attic) Greek alphabet: *A* for Book 1, and so on. The division, whoever made it, was on the whole sensibly done, especially in the *Iliad*.

With the striking exception of Book 10, which in antiquity was alleged not to have been originally part of the *Iliad* at all (Σ in 10. 1), Homeric books are not self-contained. The epic connects events backward and forward. That is true of Book 9, too. The previous day of fighting ended with Zeus bringing the Achaeans to defeat and rout, forbidding their patron gods to help them. Zeus predicts to the gods, and to the audience, that Hector will continue to be victorious until Achilles returns to battle after Patroclus' death (8. 469–83). The sun sets, and darkness ends the fighting, to the disappointment of the Trojans but the relief of the Achaeans (8. 484–8).[19]

and Speakers', *JHS* 106 (1986), 36–57; R. P. Martin, *The Language of Heroes* (Ithaca, NY, 1989), a very full and subtle analysis—sometimes, in my view, too subtle.

[18] O. Taplin, *Homeric Soundings* (Oxford, 1992), 285–93; N. J. Richardson, *Commentary on the Iliad*, ed. G. S. Kirk, vi (Cambridge, 1993), 20f.

[19] Karl Lachmann put the beginning of a new 'lay' at 8. 487.

There follows a Trojan council of war, clearly designed as a contrast and foil to the Achaean assembly which opens (our) Book 9. Out on the battlefield, 'where a clear space appeared among the corpses' (8. 491), not in a peaceful setting, Hector harangues his troops; in his hand he holds his great spear, its point glittering in the gloom. That is, he does not hold the sceptre which is the symbol of orderly debate (1. 234 ff.). The mood is triumphant. The only question is how to prevent the demoralized Achaeans from slipping away before morning: fires must burn all night, and at dawn the Achaeans will suffer a complete defeat. Hector speaks as commander. There is no discussion, simply a roar of approbation; the Trojan watchfires cover the plain like stars on a cloudless night (8. 489-565). Great is the contrast with the scene by the Achaean ships. There Agamemnon weeps, the mood is one of defeatism, and the commander-in-chief must accept open discussion and some frank criticism. The Achaean assembly is compared to a storm-tossed sea (9. 4-8), in answer to the serene night sky simile used of the Trojans (8. 555 ff.).

This last part of (our) Book 8 thus forms a structure with the opening of (our) Book 9.[20] But the Achaean meeting which opens Book 9 also forms a symmetrical structure with the Achaean gathering which closes the book, two dark scenes of anxious waiting by firelight, the parallel being made inescapable by the reappearance of Diomedes in the same role (9. 29-51, 695-711). Such overlapping structures are important to the poem, which is not meant to be capable of being chopped up into clearly separate sections. It is of course part of every good story-teller's technique to carry his audience smoothly forward into the next part of his tale, not allowing sharp breaks to suggest a termination.

---

[20] Book 8 has been very variously regarded. Good scholars have thought it early (K. Reinhardt, *Die Ilias und ihr Dichter*, ed. U. Hölscher (Göttingen, 1961), 138 ff.); late (W. Schadewaldt, *Iliasstudien*, (3rd edn., Darmstadt, 1966), 95 ff., H. Erbse, *Rh. Mus.* 104 (1961), 181 ff.); not a unity (H. Diller, *Hermes*, 93 (1965), 137–47 = *Kleine Schriften* (Munich, 1971), 3-15); left 'unrefined' at the time of the death or retirement of Homer (*Commentary on the Iliad*, ed. Kirk, ii. 294).

### 3. BOOK NINE AND THE ILIAD

The plot of the *Iliad* can be described in outline very briefly. The greatest Achaean hero is insulted by the leader of the expedition, who takes away a captive woman who has been allotted to him from the booty; the hero withdraws from the fighting, rejects offers of compensation, relents so far as to allow his closest friend to return, and, when the friend is killed by the leading Trojan hero, returns to avenge his death by killing his slayer. That summary does less than justice to a poem whose great length is inseparable from its effect, and which has a divine level—and a cast of divine characters—in addition to the straightforwardly human one. It is, for instance, vital to the poem that Achilles, when he returns to battle and kills Hector, knows from his goddess mother that by doing so he seals his own fate, and that his own death will be next. Such knowledge is essential to the tragic effect of the last quarter of the *Iliad*.

But simple as the basic pattern of events is, it still contains a development which was not foreseen by the audience at the opening of the poem. Insulted and wronged by Agamemnon, Achilles was in two minds about killing him on the spot. The goddess Athena dissuaded him, promising that 'In time you shall have three times the quantity of splendid gifts to make up for this insult' (1. 212–14). That seems to envisage a clear and simple pattern: the hero by his withdrawal forces his enemy to climb down and substitute honour, in tangible form, for the dishonour he has inflicted. In Book 9 the wise old Phoenix, Achilles' tutor, tells us that 'This is what we have heard about the heroes of the old days, too, when furious anger came on one of them: they could be won over with presents and talked round with speeches' (9. 524–6). Until this point in the poem that is the story-line we have been expecting, and the Achaean heroes are at a loss to understand why this time it doesn't happen (9. 515 ff., Phoenix; 9. 628 ff., Ajax).

The ninth book is the vital hinge of the plot. It is here that Achilles finds himself unable, now that it has come to the pinch, to accept the 'threefold gifts' originally promised by Athena, or the lavish offerings now made by Agamemnon, which in the opinion of good judges are above criticism for generosity (9. 164, Nestor; 9. 515–19, Phoenix; 9. 636–9, Ajax). It is not, in fact, a matter of quantity at all. Not all the treasures of Delphi and of Egypt, not all the wealth that Agamemnon will ever have, not gifts as numerous as the sand or the dust, will satisfy Achilles' burning anger (9. 379–87). And so, although he is forced to admit to Ajax that 'All that you have said is much to my way of thinking' (9. 646), he cannot bring himself to accept it.

We thus have an important change in the situation. Up to now, Achilles has been purposeful and in control. His own absence from the battlefield, and his mother's influence with Zeus, push Agamemnon to a point where he must climb down and sue for peace. After Book 9, however, Achilles too has lost his freedom. He is shown to us standing on the stern of his beached ship and eagerly watching the fighting, from which he has barred himself (11. 599 f.). Unable to find a way back, he falls into the mistake of sending Patroclus into battle without him. Patroclus' death overwhelms him with despair and guilt (18. 1–137, especially 98 ff.), and now the rich gifts duly produced by Agamemnon are of no interest (19. 145–53), and all that Achilles wants is to kill Hector, accepting that this means speedy death for himself (18. 98 'Let me die at once, since I failed to save my friend . . .').

Thus the plot turns from simple to complex. The old and evidently familiar story-pattern of the hero's withdrawal and triumphant return takes on a new intensity and a darker atmosphere: nobody emerges triumphant at the end of the *Iliad*, and guilt, responsibility, and tragedy have invaded and transformed a tale of heroic adventure. It has been argued that Achilles' very name meant 'grief for (his) people', from ἄχος and λαός, and that the figure of Achilles was always that of a hero who brought suffering on his people.[21] Even if that is so, it may have meant no more than that his early death grieved them:[22] cf. Penthesilea the Amazon, slain by Achilles, whose name more obviously means the same thing (from πένθος and λαός). Making Achilles into an ambiguous and tragic figure may possibly have been suggested by his name, but it was surely achieved by the change of myth which is at the heart of the creation of the *Iliad*.

We saw in the first part of Section 2 that there is good reason to believe that the poet of the *Iliad* created his great poem in line

[21] Nagy, *The Best of the Achaeans*, 69 ff.
[22] So e.g. Ed. Hermann, *Sprachwissenschaftlicher Kommentar* (Heidelberg, 1914), 51, citing P. Kretschmer, *Glotta*, 4 (1913), 307.

with a set of basic decisions: to create, in the tradition of the oral epic, a work of exceptional length, narrating a part of the Trojan story but by ingenious means including or implying the rest, and complicating the simple traditional plot pattern of a hero's angry withdrawal and triumphant return with a darker and less manageable story, tragic in its colouring and its outcome.

If such an account is close to the truth, then some consequences follow from it for Book 9. Scenes of quarrelling between hero and chieftain no doubt existed in the poetic tradition, but it is much less easy to suppose that there existed extensive scenes in which a hero was offered satisfaction but rejected it. If that was the special contribution of the *Iliad*, then here, more perhaps than anywhere else, the singer will have been forced to go beyond his tradition in creating a scene of an original character. Especially the great speech in which Achilles replies to Agamemnon's offer must have posed a challenge to its composer. It must not only set out the reasoning which makes the hero reject the compensation which all regard as satisfactory in terms of the heroic code; it must, even more importantly, display the emotional nature, the depth of hurt and anger, which drives Achilles into a position which neither he nor anybody else in the poem wholly understands. It is no coincidence, then, that lines 307–429 contain what is by general consent the most powerful and extraordinary speech in Homer, a speech which has been the subject of much detailed scholarly writing. If that speech had been a failure, the whole of the *Iliad* would have been gravely damaged: it is the point at which we see how extraordinary a hero Achilles is, and at which we judge his fatal decision not to come to terms with Agamemnon.

Achilles' great speech is the high point of Book 9. But it forms part of a scene containing six speeches, contrasted in length and style, and forming a whole with a satisfying shape and development. First Odysseus, the intelligent and reliable envoy, sets out Agamemnon's offer with eloquence and clarity. It is a lavish offer, and Achilles will be well advised to accept. The speech is ably delivered, but it fails to reach the emotional level on which Achilles now lives and broods; no apology, and no sense of the outrageous wrong which he feels that he has suffered. Achilles' reply is passionate. He has been insulted and injured; no conceivable compensation will suffice; the whole business of being a hero is a cheat, if one is to be treated like this; he will give it up and sail home in the morning to a peaceful and domestic old age. It seems that an impasse has been reached, and this explosion is followed by a long silence. Finally old Phoenix, Achilles' tutor, speaks on a quite different line. His speech, the third long one, is emotional and personal, delivered with tears. He tells the story of his own life, blighted by anger and stubbornness, and of his devotion to Achilles: 'I fed you on my lap when you were little (485ff.), you are the son I never had.' In this vein he appeals to the hero to return. Achilles is partly shaken, partly resentful: 'Don't try to break down my resolution with your tears and moans, all to curry favour with Agamemnon' (612f.). His answer is short, and it ends with a considerable concession: 'In the morning we'll decide whether to go or to stay' (618f.).

That seems to be the end of the scene, and Achilles starts arranging for a bed to be made up for Phoenix. Ajax, the third envoy, will apparently not have a chance to make a speech at all. He turns to Odysseus and says that they had better be on their way: Achilles will not yield to the prayers of his friends in their hour of need. How can he be so unreasonable? Then, with a marvellously effective turn to the man himself: 'We are offering you full compensation, and we are your best friends: don't turn us down!' (636-42). A short, bluff speech, it strikes the right manly note: Achilles finds it hard to dissent from the appeal to comradeship. It is just that he can't bring himself to do what he sees to be right (644ff.). But he makes a second concession: 'When Hector reaches *my* ship, I fancy he will have to stop' (654f.).

The scene has a powerful and convincing movement and shape, with two long speeches and one short one aimed by the three heroes at Achilles, each different from the others in tone; and three replies, one long and two short, marking a progressive softening of Achilles' position.

The difficulties begin when we look at the setting of the scene; and they are very serious. Both the introduction and the consequence of the great appeal to Achilles present problems. The latter, though not trivial, is the less grave. We have seen that the hero twice modified his original threat that in the morning he will sail home, finally saying that he will be encamped at Troy when Hector reaches his ship and finds that he has his hands full. Yet Odysseus reports to the Achaean commanders, who are anxiously waiting for Achilles' answer, that 'He declared that he will sail away in the morning' (682f.), a message which understandably fills the gathering with gloom (693f.). That report does little credit to Odysseus' reputation for intelligence, and ever since antiquity scholars have struggled to explain it.

The problems with the introduction are far more serious.[23] Agamemnon's proposal is: 'Let Phoenix lead the way, and then Ajax and Odysseus; and let two heralds go with them' (168-170). Nestor gives them some coaching, 'glancing at each of them, and mostly at Odysseus' (179f.), a passage which seems to imply more than two envoys. But when they set out for Achilles' hut, no less than a dozen grammatical forms are used of them which are not plural but dual, implying that they are two in number (182-98). These dual forms have been called 'probably the most serious stumbling-block in the whole Iliad'.[24] In addition, there is a difficulty about Phoenix: Achilles' devoted tutor and attendant, he apparently is with Agamemnon, not with Achilles, who has to invite him specifically to spend the night in his camp, and who gives instructions for a bed to be got ready for him (617-19). There is a third oddity: when the envoys are about to speak, 'Ajax nodded to Phoenix; but Odysseus saw, and he filled his cup' and he began to speak. That is not like the rather formal good manners which Homeric heroes normally observe towards one another, and it seems pointless, too.

Various attempts have been made to meet these difficulties (cf. Appendix), the most suggestive being that originally, or alternatively, there existed a version of the episode in which there were only two envoys, Phoenix being added to expand the scene and vary its emotional range (see notes on 182, 223). We cannot, however, recapture an earlier form by simply cutting out Phoenix from the text as we have it. At 167ff. and at 222ff his name is impossible to remove without producing a hiatus in the text; and, even more important, the whole episode is now conceived as including a substantial and pathetic speech, which enables Achilles to begin to change his stance from absolute non-co-operation to the more opaque position (not fighting, but still there) which he will in fact occupy in Books 11-15.

In general I think it important to observe that there is a certain family resemblance between the problems posed by the text before

---

[23] See the Appendix, pp. 51-4.
[24] Schadewaldt, *Iliasstudien*, 137.

and after the central scene. The wooden report made by Odysseus of Achilles' decision is necessary, because the Achaeans are to be made to fight on in desperation, without the comfortable knowledge that Achilles will, sooner or later, return to the fray: that is vitally important for the following books. That, ultimately, must be the reason why Odysseus cannot report the hero's more encouraging later utterances. The audience are free, if they wish, to improvise psychological explanations for Odysseus' conduct; and scholars have done so, from antiquity to our own time (see note on 682). The fact that it is possible to do it has some importance, as it often has in Attic tragedy, too: we need not be simply at a complete loss to understand how this could possibly have happened. If we were, we might be alienated and unsympathetic. But the poet does not show much interest in the question.

In the case of the duals, it is significant that it would not have been difficult to replace them with plurals. It would not be difficult now. Evidently it was felt in antiquity that even in such a difficulty the text should be respected. I think it likely that this, the turning point of the plot and a masterpiece of Homeric poetry, was sometimes asked for and performed separately. It might be performed in a longer or shorter version, to fit the exigencies of time and the mood of the audience. It may be a partial parallel that in the *Odyssey* 'the Muse invited the singer Demodocus to sing of the glorious tales of men, that path of song whose glory at that time reached heaven: the quarrel of Odysseus and Achilles, how they strove with one another at a feast of the gods, with violent language. . . .' (*Od*. 8. 73 ff.). That suggests that a dispute, even one with no deadly consequences, could be exciting enough to be the theme of an heroic lay; and we also observe that the song is soon interrupted by the audience, on the ground that not everybody is happy with it (ibid. 94–100). In such a setting a singer might well have more than one way of narrating a favourite scene. The text of *Iliad* and *Odyssey* which reached us must ultimately go back to a performance of each poem, and in this case the performance was one which showed a high-handed indifference to punctiliousness about factual details. The great scene of Achilles and the envoys has been developed with its own logic and shape, so that it runs away with the main plot, and Achilles says things which must not be reported to the Achaeans: the text simply back-pedals to reach the point it wants. At the beginning there is a lack of clarity about the envoys: two or three? The text disregards the difficulty and sails on to what really interests it, the six speeches and the unfolding of the soul of Achilles. Some parallels to this technique are suggested in the notes on 17, 168, 223-4.

A final difficulty has been seen in the omission of any mention of the embassy at a couple of places later in the *Iliad* where it might have been expected. At 11. 608-10, Achilles says to Patroclus, 'Now I think the Achaeans will cluster round my knees in supplication: their need is insupportable.' At 16. 72, he says that the Trojans would be fleeing in rout and massacre, 'if Agamemnon were kindly towards me'. In neither case is there a real contradiction. At 11. 608 Achilles can be said to be thinking of *all* the Achaeans: he has repeatedly said that his quarrel is with them all for taking Agamemnon's side (1. 240f., 299; 9. 316, answering Odysseus' appeal at 9. 301f.), and he may demand that all shall come to beg his pardon.[25] In Book 16 he may well feel that Agamemnon's forced and unapologetic offer of Book 9 did not count as 'feeling kindly', ἤπια εἰδέναι. That is not to say that the poem was actually composed in so straightforward and unproblematic a way as these arguments seem to suggest: only that there need, for us, be no real difficulty in reading it in that way.

## The Choice of Achilles and the Meaning of the 'Iliad'

We expected Achilles to accept the offerings of Agamemnon; so do the heroic characters of the poem. Zeus indeed predicts implicitly that he will not, declaring that Hector will prevail 'until swift Achilles rises up beside the ships, on the day when they are fighting at the stern of the ships, in desperate confinement, over the body of Patroclus. Thus it is decreed' (8. 473-7). The two lines referring to Patroclus' death were excised by some ancient scholars as not an exact prophecy of what will happen, but a certain vagueness can be said to be *de rigueur* for prophecies, and this one is effective enough.[26] ὣς γὰρ θέσφατόν ἐστιν implies that all this is part of the Διὸς βουλή, the plan of Zeus, announced in general terms at 1. 5. The hint about Achilles is however a

[25] A. Roemer, *Homerische Aufsätze* (Berlin, 1914), 50f.
[26] U. von Wilamowitz-Moellendorff, *Die Ilias und Homer*[2] (Berlin, 1920), 41f.; Schadewaldt, *Iliasstudien*, 110f.

quickly passing one, which will not, to an audience not already familiar with the *Iliad*, suggest anything like Book 9.

The refusal of Achilles to yield is the central fact in the creation of the *Iliad* from the traditional plot of the hero's withdrawal and triumphant return. In the poem it is made intelligible by the extraordinary vehemence of his speech, 225–306. Scholars have added particular reasons: the Achaean plight was not yet bad enough,[27] Agamemnon's apology not sufficiently heart-felt.[28] The audience are at liberty to invoke such psychological subtleties, or to ignore them. It is worth noticing that the pattern of Achilles' partial relenting in the course of Book Nine—'I shall sail home in the morning!' (9. 356 f.); 'In the morning we shall decide whether to stay or to go' (9. 618 f.); 'I will not fight until Hector reaches my ships' (9. 650 f.)—is perfectly in line with his behaviour elsewhere in the poem. In the original quarrel with Agamemnon he said 'Now I shall sail home' (1. 169 f.), and he actually has his sword half out to kill the king (1. 188 f.); but in the event he stays and even allows Briseis to be taken from him ('I will not fight over the girl', 1. 297 f.). So too he first denies Hector burial and threatens that carrion beasts shall devour his body (22. 354 f.), but in the end he gives it up for the family funeral which he had threatened to prevent, in return for the ransom which he had vowed to refuse (22. 348 f.). That is in his consistent character—a first violent response, subsequently toned down.[29]

In the embassy scene of Book 9 Achilles responds to the overtures of Agamemnon with the same volcanic violence. As the scene develops he recedes to some extent from that first stand, but only for the future, not for the present: for the present, he will not fight. His anger comes from the *thumos* which every hero must have, and which as the greatest hero he possesses in fullest measure. Hainsworth says in his Commentary that 'Akhilleus is wrong but from an excess of rectitude. He rejects a fair offer, but does so from the highest heroic motives.'[30] That seems a little strange, and 'rectitude' and 'the highest motives' sound more Wykehamist than heroic. The disastrous mistake of Achilles comes from a paradox at the heart of heroism itself. To be a hero a man

---

[27] So Hentze, Anhang zu Ameis-Hentze, *Homers Ilias* (Leipzig, 1913).

[28] So Taplin, *Homeric Soundings*, 69 f.

[29] Schadewaldt, *Iliasstudien* 135; D. Lohmann, *Die Komposition der Reden in der Ilias* (Berlin, 1970), 279.

[30] *Commentary on the Iliad*, ed. Kirk, iii. 57.

must be a fighter, and that means being quick to anger, the possessor of great *thumos*: μεγάθυμος, μεγαλήτωρ, are regular epithets of heroes. θυμὸς δὲ μέγας ἐστὶ διοτρεφέων βασιλήων, 'the spirit of kings is great', is a proverbial line (2. 196). He must resist the blandishments of women and old men, who try to lure him away from the perils of the battlefield: 6. 258 ff. (Hecuba), 6. 354 ff. (Helen), 6. 429 ff. (Andromache); 11. 717 ff. (Nestor's father); 22. 37-92 (Priam and Hecuba); cf. *Od.* 2. 357 f., 373 f. (Penelope); 4. 271-89 (Helen); 5. 203-24 (Calypso).

The difficulty is to reconcile that high spirit and self-assertion with serving the good of the community as a whole. Carried to an excess, heroic qualities become worse than useless. Achilles can be called αἰναρέτης (16. 31),[31] one whose prowess is a disaster. Nestor contrasts his own socially valuable youthful exploits with Achilles' selfishness—οἷος τῆς ἀρετῆς ἀπονήσεται (11. 763); 'he is the only one who will get any benefit from his heroism'. Achilles is a good warrior, but he has no care for his community, and he will see us all killed—ἐσθλὸς ἐὼν Δαναῶν οὐ κήδεται οὐδ' ἐλεαίρει (11. 665 f.). In this excess of angry *thumos* and self-will, Achilles is not alone. It was 'giving way to his great heart' that Agamemnon disregarded advice and first insulted him (9. 109), with all the disastrous consequences; Hector, too, refuses to listen to prudent counsels and insists, first on camping out on the plain rather than withdrawing to the protection of the city (18. 249 ff.), and then on staying to face Achilles and his own death (22. 90 f.). Even in that less heroic poem the *Odyssey*, we find Odysseus, on occasion, getting himself and his companions into ruinous trouble by following his 'great-hearted spirit', ignoring prudent advice, and telling the Cyclops his real name (*Od.* 9. 491-536).

The relation of the warrior to his society, the tension between self-assertion and the common good: this is one of the central themes of the *Iliad*, shown in the crime of Paris (a disaster to his people: *Il.* 3. 39-57), and in the mistakes of Achilles, Agamemnon, and Hector. Achilles, greatest of heroes, makes the greatest mistake, which he lives to repent with no less passion (18. 98-111). It is hard to be a hero, to fight and kill and yet remain tractable. Diomedes shows how it can be done; but were Diomedes the greatest hero, there would be no *Iliad*. See note on 109.

[31] A. Lesky, 'Zur Eingangssene der Patroklie', *Serta Philologica Aenipontana*, 7-8 (Innsbruck, 1961) 19-26 = *Kleine Schriften* (Bern, 1966), 72-82.

The anger of Achilles and his mistake thus have a moral on the social, human level. The poet Horace draws it explicitly: Homer, says Horace, is the best of all moral philosophers at teaching the bad consequences of the passions (*Epistles* 1. 2). But it also has another aspect, at least equally important. Achilles is a supremely great hero, handsome, invincible, the beloved son of a goddess. He has, through his mother, privileged access to Zeus, and he is able to take a hand in the shaping of events (1. 493-530), bringing about the Achaean defeat which he needs. In Book 9 he insists that Zeus is showing him honour (9. 607-8). But even Achilles cannot really understand the divine plan. His stubbornness in Book 9, and his enjoyment of his own anger (18. 107-10), bring about the death of his dearest friend and the ruin of his own life. So far is even the greatest of mortals from being a god. That, too, is part of the lesson of the *Iliad*.

## 4. LANGUAGE AND STYLE

### Dialect

It is one of the striking features of ancient Greek that it had not one but several literary dialects. Latin, like English and French, had really only one dialect in which serious works could be composed. There have been some poets who wrote in non-standard dialects of English, like the Lowland Scots of Robert Burns and the West Country poems of William Barnes, and Tennyson wrote a few poems in Lincolnshire dialect. But on the whole serious English writers, in prose and verse, have not, since the Middle Ages, differed in the dialect forms they use.

Greek was very different. The branches of the Greek people— Ionic, Aeolic, Doric—spoke in dialects which could differ from each other (as we see from some inscriptions) as much as, say, Italian and Spanish. The choral lyric was a Dorian invention, and so its words had a Doric colouring. That is why non-Dorians like Bacchylides of Ceos (Ionian) and Pindar of Thebes (Aeolian) in their lyric poems write, notionally at least, in Doric; and why the choral songs of Attic tragedy have a Doric veneer, with α for η. The Ionians gave its standard form and colouring to dactylic verse, hexameters and elegiac couplets. Later on it was to be the

Athenians, an Ionian people but with a local dialect of marked local character, who would establish the dialect felt to be appropriate for philosophy, oratory, and history, in fact for literary prose in general. So keen was the Greeks' feeling for literary form that they continued to demand that epics should be written in something based on the Homeric dialect, as they demanded that the lyrics and the spoken passages of tragedy should have the colouring of two different dialects. If this was not respected, the work felt wrong.

The dialect of the Homeric poems, as we have them, is basically Ionic. It excludes, in principle, Doric forms. It also tries to exclude mention of Dorians—in the heroic age they did not exist; but such revealing slips as mention of a place called Dorion, a sea-nymph called Doris, and the Dorians of Crete (*Il.* 2. 594, 18. 45; *Od.* 19. 177—once only each) show that they were perfectly familiar to singer and audience. But 'while the language of Homer is basically Ionic, it has incorporated elements of widely different date and dialect reaching back into the Mycenaean age'.[32] We find some phrases which seem to go far back into the second millennium BC, such as ξίφος ἀργυρόηλον, 'sword inlaid with silver', and δέπας ἀμφικύπελλον, 'cup with two handles'. Archaeological evidence suggests that objects answering to these descriptive phrases were in use before rather than after 1200 BC,[33] and the words, too, are ancient, occurring on the Linear B tablets. Other phrases, too, may be of great antiquity: e. g. κλέος ἄφθιτον, 'deathless glory' (see note on 413); λιποῦσ' ἀνδροτῆτα καὶ ἥβην, 'leaving its manliness and youth', of the soul of a dying man, *Il.* 16. 857, 22. 362;[34] νωμῆσαι βῶν ἀζαλέην, 'wield my parched cow' (a warrior claiming skill in the brandishing of his leather-covered shield), *Il.* 7. 238. Such a person, too, as Ajax 'the son of Telamon', conspicuous for his mighty archaic tower-shield, when most fighting is done with the later round, wielding shield—and whose father's name perhaps was originally a misunderstanding: τελαμώνιος, 'Ajax with the τελαμών', the broad strap which supported his great shield, interpreted as Τελαμώνιος, 'son of Telamon'—has an air of great antiquity. Ajax, or 'the two Ajaxes',

---

[32] L. R. Palmer, *The Greek Language* (London, 1980), 83.

[33] J. B. Hainsworth, Commentary on *Odyssey* 8. 89 and 11. 632-5; Kirk, *Commentary on the Iliad*, i. 45.

[34] M. L. West, 'The Rise of the Greek Epic', *JHS* 108 (1988), 158.

Αἴαντε, originally Ajax and Teucer, may well go back to 1500 BC or so.[35]

Other elements in the Homeric dialect are very early: a striking example is the fact that Homer still makes free use of the very archaic Indo-European practice—(found in the Vedas) of separating prepositional preverbs from the verb: ἂν δ' Ἀγαμέμνων ἵστατο (9. 13 f.), ἐγὼ δ' ἐπὶ μεῖλα δώσω (9. 147), ἐν δ' ἄρα νῶτον ἔθηκε (207), for classical Greek ἀνίστατο, ἐπιδώσω, ἐνέθηκε. This is already antiquated by the time of the Mycenaean Linear B tablets, which regularly treat such compounds as single words. It must therefore be a great archaism, preserved both for its metrical convenience and also, doubtless, for its venerable air. Also probably archaic is the licence, shared with the Linear B tablets, of omitting the augment in past tenses of the verb, as 9. 1 ἔχον, 10 φοίτα, 12 πονεῖτο, 21 βουλεύσατο.[36]

We find features which are not Ionic but Aeolic: metrically useful words, scanning differently from their Ionic equivalents, like πίσυρες 'four'; πτόλις 'city', πτόλεμος 'war' (for πόλις, πόλεμος: useful for lengthening a vowel at the end of the preceding word); ζάθεος 'holy'; adjectives in -ννός: ἀργεννός ἐραννός ἐρεβεννός. Also the very convenient pronouns and pronominal adjectives ἄμμες, ἄμμε, 'we'; ὔμμες, ὔμμε, ὔμμιν 'you'; ἁμός 'our/my'; ὑμός 'your'. There are also forms which look like Attic rather than general Ionic, notably the handy short dative plural forms in -αις and -οις (not -ῃσι and -οισι), e. g. *Il.* 12. 484 ἀκταῖς; contracted forms like ποντοπορούσης, *Od.* 11. 11 (not ποντοπορεούσης).

The archaic consonant *vau*, digamma (ϝ), which disappeared early in the Ionic dialect, is not found in the written text of Homer but—as Richard Bentley saw—the verse constantly presupposes it. ἄνδρα ἕκαστον (9. 11) presents a hiatus between vowels which originally did not occur, the second word being ϝέκαστον; ἐγὼ εἴπω (9. 26) was originally ϝείπω. It has been calculated[37] that digamma is observed in the text of Homer some 3,354 times,

---

[35] Wackernagel's explanation of Αἴαντε as 'Ajax and his companion' (*Kleine Schriften* i. 538 ff.) is set out with characteristic verve by D. L. Page, *History and the Homeric Iliad* (Berkeley, Calif., 1959), 235-8.

[36] Important works on the Homeric dialect include P. Chantraine, *Grammaire homérique* (Paris, 1958); M. Leumann, *Homerische Wörter* (Basel, 1950); K. Meister, *Die homerische Kunstsprache* (Leipzig, 1921); J. Wackernagel, *Sprachliche Untersuchungen zu Homer* (Göttingen, 1916); E. Risch, *Wortbildung der homerischen Sprache*² (Berlin, 1973). There is a good introduction by L. R. Palmer in Wace and Stubbings (eds.), *Companion to Homer*, 75-178.     [37] *Companion to Homer*, 101.

ignored 617 times. Clearly it was widely present in the tradition, and the singers made a point of trying to maintain it: its presence was one of the many features of Homeric verse which made it different from ordinary language, and so traditional and impressive. The same motive must have been powerful in keeping alive words which felt grand and appropriate, although their actual meaning was obscure or unknown: such highly 'poetical' epithets as ἀκάκητα, δασπλῆτις, ἑλίκωπες, ἰόμωροι, τανηλεγής, τριχάϊκες; and such phrases as νυκτὸς ἀμολγῷ and πτολέμοιο γέφυραι.

It is a feature of the Homeric dialect which shows its artificiality that it contains so many coexisting forms of the same word or case or person. Nouns of the second declension, like δόμος, have the genitive singular forms δόμοιο and also δόμου; and a number of phrases survive which require, in order to be metrical, a third form, in -οο. Thus ὁμοιίου πτολέμοιο of our texts was once ὁμοιίοο πτολέμοιο—the form in our texts is a mere attempt to produce something that looks as if it scans, once the old form in -οο had become unintelligible and been rewritten as -ου. So too Ἰλίου προπάροιθεν (Ἰλίοο), ἀδελφειοῦ κταμένοιο (ἀδελφεόο), Αἰόλου κλυτὰ δώματα (Αἰόλοο).

The Homeric hexameter is, by the standard of the epic metres of the world, a long line, and also it imposes severe discipline on the composer by the strictness of its rules. It is no doubt partly in response to its difficulty that the Homeric poems admit so many alternative forms of words. We have already seen some examples; others include the Aeolic form προτί alongside the Ionic πρός; the two forms of the modal particle, κεν and also ἄν, respectively Aeolic and Ionic.[38] These are among the commonest words in the Greek language, as are μέν, for which the Aeolic μάν and the Attic μήν both also appear, and σύν, sometimes replaced by the Attic form ξύν. A common word like ἀνήρ has a range of forms from two different declensions: ἀνέρα ἀνέρος ἀνέρι: ἄνδρα ἀνδρός ἀνδρί, and dative plural forms ἄνδρεσσι and ἀνδράσι. υἱός, son, is even more various, with three possible forms of the nominative plural: υἱέες, υἱεῖς, υἷες. The verb 'to be', among a wide range of alternative forms, exhibits no fewer than five for the infinitive: εἶναι, ἔμμεναι, ἔμεναι, ἔμμεν, ἔμεν. Their wide range of metrical values is clearly the point.[39]

[38] See Chantraine, *GH* ii. 345 ff.
[39] υἱός: Chantraine, *GH* i. 227 f. εἶναι: ibid. i. 286-91.

All this, and much more, makes an implicit claim that Homeric verse is not just the creation of one fraction of the Greek people but more of a national possession. It also shows the singers helping themselves to compose by claiming the freedom to choose from an extraordinary range of dialect forms, and to invent more. The language of the poems is not that which anybody ever spoke. As the German scholar K. Witte put it, 'the language of the Homeric poems is a creation of the epic verse'.[40] We can see how metrical exigencies created special forms which never existed outside verse: purely metrical duplicates like πτολιπόρθιος (πτολίπορθος), Αἰτώλιος (Αἰτωλός), δαφοινέος (δαφοινός), and such purely 'poetical' forms as οἰνοχοεύειν, Δαρδανίωνες, εὐτειχέα, εὐρέα (πόντον), for εὐρύν, created on the model of the dative εὐρέϊ πόντῳ (see note on 72). Such names as Achilles and Odysseus have two forms: Ἀχιλλεύς/Ἀχιλεύς, Ὀδυσσεύς/Ὀδυσεύς, to facilitate versification.

## Formulaic Composition

It was obvious in antiquity that the style of the Homeric poems differed from other poetry by its constant verbal repetitions. Later epic poets like Apollonius of Rhodes and, in Latin, Virgil, while evoking Homer at every turn, felt that they could not imitate his repetitiveness. There are four repeated lines in the *Argonautica* of Apollonius, just enough to remind the reader of Homer; Virgil uses such phrases as *pius Aeneas* and *fidus Achates* to give a distant echo of the Homeric mannerism of providing the name of each hero with a fixed descriptive phrase.

It was not until the twentieth century that this aspect of Homeric verse was investigated systematically. The American Milman Parry,[41] carrying much further the work of scholars like Witte and Murko, was able to show in great detail how the style worked and the function in it of the fixed, recurrent, formulaic expression. He took as the most striking example the proper-name-plus-epithet formulae for the heroes. He was able to show that there existed, with startlingly few exceptions, one phrase for each hero, in each grammatical case, to fit each metrical length to the end of the line (11): δῖος Ὀδυσσεύς and ἐσθλὸς Ὀδυσσεύς, as the

---

[40] K. Witte in *RE* s.v. Homeros, viii. 2214. 4.
[41] His articles are now published in one volume: *The Making of Homeric Verse*, ed. A. Parry (Oxford, 1971).

preceding word ended with a vowel or a consonant; πολύμητις
'Οδυσσεύς and πτολίπορθος 'Οδυσσεύς (single and double initial con-
sonant); πολύτλας δῖος 'Οδυσσεύς to fill the whole of the second half
of the line; and so on. We find also, in the genitive case, 'Οδυσσῆος
θείοιο and Λαερτιάδεω 'Οδυσῆος (∪ − − − − − −‖ and − − ∪∪ − ∪∪ − −‖
respectively); in the middle of the line, 'Οδυσεὺς δουρίκλυτος, before
− ∪∪ − −‖. Similar systems can be shown to exist for other often
mentioned characters. It is clear from this that the precise mean-
ing of the epithet is of secondary importance: whether Odysseus is
'of many schemes' or 'famed for his spear', on each occasion,
depends more on metrical considerations than any others. It was
probably the most striking of Parry's findings that to a remarkable
extent there is only one formulaic phrase for each hero in each
metrical position (his principle of 'thrift'). Similar systems can be
shown to apply to ships (which may be 'swift', 'black', 'well-
balanced', 'well-decked', according to the metrical need), and also
to spears, the earth, the sea, and other features of the world which
receive frequent mention in the poems.

Parry's discussion of the name-epithet phrase attracted atten-
tion, only slowly in German-speaking countries but soon and over-
whelmingly in Britain and North America. It came to be assumed
by sanguine Homerists that the whole of Homer was formulaic in
composition: that is to say, composed in blocks of words rather
than single words, and in blocks which were unchanging, offered
no alternatives, and served their purpose—to allow the singer to
improvise within the closely set limits of traditional style—by an
appropriateness which was general and loose rather than specific
to a particular passage. This, it was rather hastily assumed, meant
that Homer was not like other poetry and required a new 'oral
poetics' to criticize it properly: it was inept to concentrate on
particular words, when the Homeric style had only one way of
saying each thing. And besides, the great range of the formulae, so
numerous and also so economical, meant that it must have been
the work of generations of singers, each adding a little to the
stately structure.

Two points are important here. One is that the Homeric poems
emerge from a long tradition of heroic song. In this the results of
the oralists and the detailed work done on the Homeric formulae
fit in with the results of archaeological and linguistic research, both
of which agree that the text of Homer contains elements from

different points over an extensive range of time. The second is that we need to be careful about ascribing originality or specific purpose to words and phrases in Homer (cf. notes on 447, 478, 486, 494). Recent work has, however, tended to move away from the assumption that the text is completely formulaic. It has, for example, been shown that there are considerable differences between the vocabulary and style of the narrative and of the speeches; that the name of Odysseus occurs more frequently with no epithets than with them; that many 'formulaic' expressions, far from being available to describe any action of a given person or thing, are regularly used in one single context, thus sharply limiting their 'utility'; that some names (Telemachus, Priam) have no discernible set of epithets; that Parry's account of the 'formulaic system' for referring to Achilles is badly flawed by his neglecting to notice that the poet constantly uses, besides Achilles' own name, phrases meaning 'the son of Peleus'—$\Pi\eta\lambda\acute{\epsilon}os$ $\upsilon\acute{\iota}\acute{o}s$, $\Pi\eta\lambda\epsilon\acute{\iota}\delta\eta s$, $\Pi\eta\lambda\eta\epsilon\acute{\iota}\omega\nu\alpha$, and even $\Theta\acute{\epsilon}\tau\iota\delta os$ $\pi\acute{a}\ddot{\iota}s$ $\mathring{\eta}\upsilon\kappa\acute{o}\mu o\iota o$ and $A\mathring{\iota}\alpha\kappa\acute{\iota}\delta\alpha o$ ('son of Thetis' and 'grandson of Aeacus') and a whole range of other possibilities: 'the hero', 'the chieftain', 'the shepherd of the people', and so on.[42] And the name-plus-epithet system is much the clearest instance in Homeric poetry of what could be thought to be a thoroughgoing formulaic system. Verbs do not, on the whole, lend themselves so neatly to tabulation in columns of exact repetitions.[43] Some recent writers have estimated that the proportion of the Homeric text which can plausibly be called formulaic is at most some two thirds;[44] and even that judgement is far from secure, as the fraction of the Homeric text which consists of actually repeated phrases or lines is about a third.[45]

That means that a considerable portion of the text consists of expressions which are, at least for us, unique or unusual. It will seem reasonable to think that the singers had to do more inventing when they dealt with a subject-matter rarely depicted, or rarely depicted at such length, in the tradition. The utterances of Achilles,

[42] J. Griffin, *JHS* 106 (1986), 36–57; N. Austin, *Archery at the Dark of the Moon* (Berkeley, Calif., 1975), ch. 1; David M. Shive, *Naming Achilles* (Oxford, 1987).

[43] An interesting example of the application of this approach to a group of verbs: M. Finkelberg, 'Formulaic and Non-formulaic Elements in Homer', *CP* 84 (1989), 179–97.

[44] See J. B. Hainsworth in *BICS* 9 (1962) 66; Finkelberg, loc. cit. 196.

[45] See R. B. Rutherford, Commentary on *Odyssey* 19 and 20 (Cambridge, 1992), 49.

a hero who needed to have a very particular character to make the peculiar plot of the *Iliad* work, are not surprisingly such an area. The Homeric poems are not like snowballs, the same texture all the way through: they are more like Christmas puddings, some parts containing much more and others much less of similes, speeches, and innovative language. Much of Book 9 belongs to the most highly wrought and, surely, most original part of Homer.

Another important aspect of the oral style is the typical scene. Life itself, of course, contains many recurrent scenes: going to school, eating dinner, giving a lecture, making love. Homer can be seen to have an extensive repertoire in which such recurrent scenes are presented with set elements and exactly repeated lines in a set order, going well beyond the repetitiveness of life.[46] Such scenes as: a warrior arriving for battle, visitors arriving and being entertained to a meal, the launching of a ship, prayers and sacrifice, a duel on the battlefield. These scenes can be presented in a very short form or enlarged and developed at great length. Agamemnon arms for battle in 30 lines (11. 15-46). Paris enlarges the theme by wearing the wrong armour and having to change and borrow before putting the right armour on (3. 15-37, 328-38); but when he puts it on, that is described in the same lines in the same order. The arming of Achilles, whose armour is lost, is enormously expanded, first by his intervention in the battle without armour, and then by the commissioning, creating, and description of a new set of armour for him, especially the marvellous shield (18. 130-7, 178-238, 369-617; 19. 1-23, 349-424); but here too the actual donning of the armour is described in the identical words (19. 369-73).

In Book Nine we have examples of the scene of assembling a meeting (1-13, cf. 1. 54—the minimum form—2. 85-100, 8. 489ff., 14. 27ff.); the final scene of the Book, Odysseus' report of Achilles' reply to the Achaean chiefs, echoes the meeting at the beginning, the echo being made unmistakable by the two morale-raising speeches of Diomedes (29-51, 693-711). There are also such set scenes as the eating of a meal (89-92, 174-7, 199-221) and going to bed (658ff.).

---

[46] W. Arend, *Die typischen Szenen bei Homer* (Berlin, 1933); Mark W. Edwards, *Homer: Poet of the Iliad* (Johns Hopkins, 1987), ch. 7, with refs.; J. I. Armstrong, 'The Arming Motif in the *Iliad*', *AJP* 79 (1958), 337-54.

*Style: General*

Matthew Arnold said of the Homeric style: 'He is eminently rapid; he is eminently plain and direct, both in the evolution of his thought and in the expression of it, that is, both in his syntax and in his words; he is eminently plain and direct in the substance of his thought, that is, in his matter and ideas; and finally he is eminently noble.'[47] Any Homeric connoisseur will recognize that account, general as it is, and agree with the implied statement that Homer is not slow or impacted in movement, not tortuous in connection of thought, not precious in expression, and not low or crude or inconsistent in tone and level. Few poets can have been less like Homer in speed of movement or directness of expression than his greatest professed imitator, Virgil; as indeed the style of Virgil seems in many respects almost the exact opposite of that of his greatest professed follower, Dante. Nobility, in very varied styles, is perhaps what most unites them.

The poet ascribes his narrative not to his own invention but to the Muse, or Muses, invoked at 1. 1, 2. 484, 11. 218, 14. 508, 16. 112. The Muses know everything, and their utterance gives— appropriately enough—its unwearying and objective manner to the narrative. Comparison with Virgil shows the difference: Homer avoids making explicit moral judgements or siding with his characters. We are able to see Troy as both doomed by its own wrongdoing and also as the pathetic home of such attractive characters as Hector and his family. We can see fighting as both 'battle where men win glory' and 'war which brings tears' ($\mu\acute{\alpha}\chi\eta\nu$ $\kappa\nu\delta\iota\acute{\alpha}\nu\epsilon\iota\rho\alpha\nu$, $\pi\acute{o}\lambda\epsilon\mu o\nu$ $\delta\alpha\kappa\rho\nu\acute{o}\epsilon\nu\tau\alpha$). Men are god-like and also marked down for death. The actions of Agamemnon and Achilles speak for themselves, and the poet is as far from naïve moralizing ('So you see that it is bad to lose your temper') as from naïve nationalism— Hector is a great hero and an appealing man, and we are left in no doubt that the national victory over Troy means loss and disaster for both sides. Homer describes hundreds of killings in battle, many of them in pitiless detail, without sliding either into sadism or into sentimentality. The use of fixed 'formulaic' language has something to do with this extraordinary achievement. Things and people are presented as they always, regularly, are; they are not presented in a quite different or special way when something

[47] M. Arnold, *On Translating Homer* (1861).

special is happening, but in an expansion or development of their ordinary manner of appearance. The climactic duel between Achilles and Hector in Book 22 is like a regular Homeric duel, except that it is expanded and ornamented with additional scenes, themselves made up of familiar sorts of material: a hero ponders whether to stand or run (cf. 11. 401ff., 17. 892ff., 21. 550ff.), gods look on and intervene (cf. 4 *init.*, 7. 58ff., 1. 194ff., 4. 86ff., 21. 596ff.). Priam is constrained to eat with his deadly enemy Achilles in Book 24: that takes up and carries to its highest power the motif of eating together which has been important at other high points of the poem (cf. note on 221-2; 19. 154ff.).

The narrative, then, is in manner objective, which does not mean that it is supposed to leave its audience unmoved. But nearly half the text, some 45 per cent, is not narrative by the poet but actual speech by the characters; in the case of Book 9, 82 per cent is speech. The characters do not observe the restraint and objectivity of the narrator's manner. On the contrary, they express emotion with the utmost vividness and power. We also observe such qualities as tact (note on 96ff.), irony (note on 348-50), pathos (485ff.). We see also a wide range of style and pace: the competent Odysseus and the passionate Achilles, the transition from abrupt utterance almost choking with fury to a long drawn out and crushing climax (365-77, 378-83).

## *Style: Particular*

The style of Homer is in general paratactic rather than periodic. That means that instead of complex sentences with clauses subordinated to one another, in the formal manner of Cicero or Milton, we mostly find simple clauses added on to each other, sometimes with less than complete grammatical smoothness, as in unselfconscious speech (see notes on 73, 167, 191, 324, 496-7). 'Achilles, subdue your great passion; you ought not to have a heart without pity; even the gods can be prevailed on. . . .' That is not only true of reported speeches, either: 'Sing, Muse, the wrath of Achilles, that accursed wrath which brought countless woes on the Achaeans, and it sent many doughty souls to Hades, souls of heroes, and made the men a feast for the dogs and birds; and the will of Zeus worked itself out' (1. 1-5). Such a manner contributes greatly to the rapidity which Arnold identifies as one of Homer's chief characteristics. It is also helped by the fact that Homer prefers concrete and particular to abstract modes of expression (see note on 700).

Another feature which is visible in the lines just quoted from the opening of the *Iliad* is the tension between composition in units of a single line and run-on from one line to the next. The hexameter, a long line which normally has from 15 to 17 syllables, is seen to divide naturally into separate rhythmical units ('cola'), the commonest number being four.[48]

> εἰ μὲν δὴ | νόστον γε ‖ μετὰ φρεσί, | φαίδιμ' Ἀχιλλεῦ
> βάλλεαι, | οὐδέ τι πάμπαν ‖ ἀμύνειν | νηυσὶ θοῆσι
> πῦρ | ἐθέλεις ἀίδηλον, ‖ ἐπεὶ χόλος | ἔμπεσε θυμῷ,
> πῶς ἄν ἔπειτ' | ἀπὸ σεῖο, ‖ φίλον τέκος, | αὖθι λιποίμην
> οἶος· | σοὶ δε μ' ἔπεμπε ‖ γέρων ἱππηλάτα Πηλεὺς
> ἤματι τῷ | ὅτε σ' ἐκ Φθίης | Ἀγαμέμνονι πέμπε
> νήπιον.   (434-40)

Lines 438 and 439 do not fall into four but into three cola, the last being the longest: for this quite common type of line G. S. Kirk has coined the name 'rising three-folders'.[49] It may be that originally most lines were separate units in terms of grammar and sense. Enjambment is very rare in many epic traditions. We find that pattern tending to emerge in unstressed narrative passages like 656-68, where only once, at 666-7, is there a real run on of construction from one line to the next, or at 25-31. Another instance among many in which a perceptible pause follows each line:

> ὣς εἰπὼν τοὺς μὲν λίπεν αὐτοῦ, βῆ δὲ μετ' ἄλλους.
> εὗρε δὲ Τυδέος υἱόν, ὑπέρθυμον Διομήδεα,
> ἑσταότ' ἔν θ' ἵπποισι καὶ ἅρμασι κολλητοῖσι·
> πὰρ δέ οἱ ἑστήκει Σθένελος, Καπανήιος υἱός.
> καὶ τὸν μὲν νείκεσσεν ἰδὼν κρείων Ἀγαμέμνων,
> καί μιν φωνήσας ἔπεα πτερόεντα προσηύδα·
> Ὦ μοι, Τυδέος υἱὲ δαΐφρονος ἱπποδάμοιο,
> τί πτώσσεις, τί δ' ὀπιπεύεις πολέμοιο γεφύρας;
> οὐ μὲν Τυδέι γ' ὧδε φίλον πτωσκαζέμεν ἦεν,
> ἀλλὰ πολὺ πρὸ φίλων ἑτάρων δηΐοισι μάχεσθαι . . .
>                      (*Il.* 4. 364-73)

---

[48] Fränkel, 'Der homerische und der kallimachische Hexameter', in *Wege und Formen*, 100-56; id., *Early Greek Poetry and Philosophy*, 30-4; Kirk, *Commentary on the Iliad*, i. 17-37, 'The structural elements of Homeric verse'.
[49] *Commentary on the Iliad*, i. 20.

This end-stopped manner is enlivened and varied by the deployment of 'run on', a device which enables the singer to move smoothly forward in his subject.

μῆνιν ἄειδε, θεά, Πηληιάδεω Ἀχιλῆος   (Il. I. 1)

Sing, Muse, of the wrath of of Achilles, Peleus' son.

The wrath is then given an epithet:

οὐλομένην, ἥ . . .

the accursed wrath which . . .

πολλὰς δ᾽ ἰφθίμους ψυχὰς Ἄϊδι προΐαψεν   (1. 3)

and it sent many doughty souls to Hades—

ἡρώων,

souls of heroes . . .

The alternation of end-stopped and run-on lines is in fact one of the great beauties of Homeric verse.

There are passages, not least in Book 9, in which this regular feature is developed with special effectiveness. Thus the furious anger of Achilles is conveyed at moments by a staccato delivery, repeatedly overrunning the verse end: 'Of all the spoils I have won in hard fighting and handed in to Agamemnon for distribution',

> ἄλλα δ᾽ ἀριστήεσσι δίδου γέρα καὶ βασιλεῦσι,
> τοῖσι μὲν ἔμπεδα κεῖται, ἐμεῦ δ᾽ ἀπὸ μούνου Ἀχαιῶν
> εἵλετ᾽, | ἔχει δ᾽ ἄλοχον θυμάρεα· τῇ παριαύων
> τερπέσθω. | τί δὲ δεῖ πολεμιζέμεναι Τρώεσσιν
> Ἀργείους; | τί δὲ λαὸν ἀνήγαγεν ἐνθάδ᾽ ἀγείρας
> Ἀτρεΐδης; | ἦ οὐχ Ἑλένης ἕνεκ᾽ ἠυκόμοιο; |
> ἦ μοῦνοι φιλέουσ᾽ ἀλόχους μερόπων ἀνθρώπων
> Ἀτρεῖδαι; | ἐπεὶ ὅς τις ἀνὴρ ἀγαθὸς καὶ ἐχέφρων
> τὴν αὐτοῦ φιλέει καὶ κήδεται, | ὡς καὶ ἐγὼ τὴν
> ἐκ θυμοῦ φίλεον, | δουρικτήτην περ ἐοῦσαν. |   (9. 334–43)

The grammar repeatedly overruns the verse, showing that the poet is not composing line by line; and he gives ferocious emphasis to the words εἵλετο 'from me alone he has taken her away!' τερπέσθω 'let him sleep with her—I hope he enjoys himself!' and, twice, 'son of Atreus', 'sons of Atreus'—my hated enemy, proud of his rank (cf. 392, 'I am not fit to marry the daughter of so great a man'). Another striking example of word positioning: Phoenix asking pathetically 'How can I stay here without you, *alone*'—

πῶς ἂν ἔπειτ᾽ ἀπὸ σεῖο, φίλον τέκος, αὖθι λιποίμην
οἶος;

In marked contrast with the passage just quoted from Achilles, staccato and insistent, is a passage later in the same speech, in which Achilles produces a long and elaborate crescendo: 'Not if he offered me ten times and twenty times as much, all that he has and all that he could get; even all the wealth that flows to Orchomenus, and to Thebes, in Egypt, where the vastest treasures are, the city of 100 gates, with 200 men driving through each with chariots and horses; even if he offered me gifts as numberless as the sand and the dust—even so Agamemnon would not prevail on me, before he has paid me back for all my grievous hurt' (9. 379–87). Here the rhythm is smooth, with a slight pause at the end of each line in an inexorable build-up. Such extreme instances can serve to illustrate the range and suppleness of this aspect of Homeric versification. The very high proportion of the Homeric epics which is in direct speech is unusual as epic traditions go, a mark of the ripeness of the Greek tradition at this date.

We have remarked on the courtesy and urbanity which normally mark the dealings of Homeric heroes with each other and with women. That is partly a stylistic matter. The formulaic lines in which heroes are addressed—Ἀτρεΐδη κύδιστε, ἄναξ ἀνδρῶν Ἀγάμεμνον, and διογενὲς Λαερτιάδη, πολυμήχαν᾽ Ὀδυσσεῦ, and the rest—themselves add a stateliness to the pace and the atmosphere of the dialogue. Even an enemy is referred to in similar style: Achilles says it is 'the might of man-slaying Hector' which Agamemnon is failing to repel (9. 351), as it is 'Hector of the flashing helmet' whom Agamemnon urges his men not to attack, as he proposes a truce and a duel (3. 83). The transition from that manner to the dehumanizing rage of Achilles after Patroclus' death, when he calls Hector 'You dog', refuses him burial, and defiles his body (22. 345ff.) is meant to be felt as shocking; and it is important that Achilles used to be chivalrous (6. 414–20), and that he returns to his humanity before the end of the poem (Book 24).

The epithets, so often patronized as meaningless, have a great part to play in establishing the level of the Homeric style. They tend to come at the end of the line, and things or persons mentioned at the end of the line have a strong tendency to receive epithets—it is no coincidence that most 'formulaic' phrases for heroes are metrically shaped for the line end. That additional weight slowed down the movement of the verse and marked the lines as units. A special instance is the line which consists of a list of three things, the last being extended:

> ἢ Αἴας ἢ Ἰδομενεὺς ἢ δῖος Ὀδυσσεύς    (1. 145)
> Ἄργος τε Σπάρτη τε καὶ εὐρυάγυια Μυκήνη    (4. 52)
> Καρδαμύλην Ἐνόπην τε καὶ Ἱρὴν ποιήεσσαν    (9. 150: see note)

and so on: cf. note on 150. The style is tolerant of epithets which conveyed little in the way of definite meaning (ἐριούνιος, Γερήνιος) if they had the right feel; and the names of important characters, human or divine, no more expect to lack some attendant pomp than their bearers did in life, where a lord or lady did not appear unaccompanied. Even in her haste to rush 'like a maenad' to see if her husband has been slain, Andromache does not omit to take two maidservants; and such important men as the envoys to Achilles must go with two 'heralds', useless as they seem to be in practical terms (22. 449–61, 9. 170). Thus 'ox-eyed lady Hera', and 'Lord Apollo, son of Zeus', and 'silver-footed Thetis, daughter of the Old Man of the Sea', are stylistically just like 'Agamemnon King of men' and 'swift-footed Achilles'. So the Achaeans speak of capturing πόλιν Τροίην εὐτείχεον, 'the well-walled town of troy' (1. 129), and Hera says that Zeus may, when he chooses, sack 'Mycenae of the broad streets', and Agamemnon says that 'there shall be a day when holy Troy shall fall, and Priam, and the people of Priam of the good ashen spear' (4. 164–6).

Places, like people, are not lightly to be deprived of their epithets and their dignity. So the River Scamander is εὔρροος and βαθυδινήεις and δινήεις, 'fair-flowing' and 'with deep eddies' (7. 329; 21. 603; 22. 148), and also, less naturalistically, δῖος and διοτρεφής, 'noble' and 'nurtured by Zeus' (12. 21; 21. 223) like a heroic figure—and indeed he does intervene in the action (Book 21), and he receives cult like a god (5. 77). Lions are 'well bearded', ἠϋγένειος (15. 275 etc.); the sea is 'ever-roaring', πολύφλοισβος; 'unharvested', ἀτρύγετος; 'of broad paths', εὐρύπορος; (1. 34 etc., 14. 204, 15. 381); it is the sounding sea (ἠχήεσσα, 1. 157), the sparkling sea (γλαυκή, 16. 34), the 'divine', 'deep', 'glittering', 'grey', 'heaving', (πορφυρέη), 'wine-dark' (οἴνοπα: perhaps 'sparkling like wine') 'violet' (ἰοειδέα); it has countless paths, it teems with fish (ἰχθυόεντα), in fact it has 'fishy pathways'

(*Od.* 3. 177). It is not surprising that the sea contains deities: the Old Man of the Sea and his daughters, of whom Thetis the silver-footed is one, and the dark-eyed goddess Amphitrite, who herds the creatures of the deep (*Od.* 5. 422), and the great god Poseidon, who can pass over the sea in his golden chariot, drawn by horses with hooves of bronze, while the sea monsters recognize their king and frisk about him (*Il.* 13. 23-31).

*Psychology and Speech*

We have observed that the Homeric epics contain an extra-ordinarily high proportion of direct speech by the characters. That goes with the conception of Homeric people as articulate and complex. We are far from the monosyllabic heroes of Western movies, or from the Nordic Sagas, where (in the caricature of W. H. Auden) a hero will suddenly break silence with 'That was an ill word', and strike at somebody with a sword. Even Ajax, though laconic, speaks effectively. To be a speaker was a vital part of heroism (note on 443), and Homeric people are connoisseurs, appreciating different styles of public speech (3. 204-24). In Book 9 both Achilles and Phoenix speak at length and powerfully about their feelings, in strongly contrasting styles; and if Agamemnon does not, that is in line with the fact that his feelings are, throughout the poem, of a crasser kind.

It is a paradox that Homeric verse, emerging as it does from a tradition of oral song with many fixed and formulaic elements, provides the most elaborate and convincing representations of individual psychology to be found in classical literature. Virgilian epic was not so much interested or so successful in creating persons interesting in themselves and well contrasted with each other. It is noteworthy that conversation worthy of the name can occur in Homer (e. g. Hera's series of encounters, (14. 188-345; Thetis and Achilles, 18. 70-137; Odysseus and Eumaeus, *Od.* 14; Odysseus and Penelope, *Od.* 19). That never happens in the *Aeneid*. The original quarrel between Agamemnon and Achilles is shown developing in a series of convincingly realistic and deftly psychologized speeches (1. 59-305). Hector and Andromache have a dialogue which encapsulates the whole polar contrast between the softer world of the woman, domestic and tempting to the fighting man, and the hard compulsion of heroism, which must drive him away from its allurements to the battle-field: this is what, ultimately, it is to be a woman and to be a man (6. 390–502). But it is also a vivid and memorable conversation between two people.

Nestor and Odysseus are particularly famous for their ability to make good speeches, and the long set piece in which Odysseus presents Agamemnon's offer to Achilles (9. 225–306) is a fine example of a competent, 'professional' speech with an elegant shape, deft transitions, and a judicious mixture of personal material (see note on 225–61)—'Remember what your father said!' along with the more formal contents. It is the contrast with Achilles' vehement outburst which makes it look thin and emotionally uncommitted, as Achilles deploys such standard rhetorical devices as rhetorical questions (337–41), irony (348–50), and a long build-up to a crushing climax (379–91), but uses them in the course of a speech which seems improvised and passionate rather than rhetorical and calculated. That shows great sophistication on the part of the poet.

It is Achilles who makes most frequent and effective use of changes of pace and changes of perspective (on his sudden wide vistas, see note on 360), and who more than any other hero coins similes (note on 323–4) as a device to express with vividness his emotional reactions. Another very individual speaker, old Phoenix, constantly addresses Achilles as 'dear child'; he tells a story from his own life, but a story of unhappiness and disastrous error, very different from the straightforwardly nostalgic and self-glorifying memories of old Nestor ('Those were the days, when I slew X . . .' cf. 7. 132–60, 11. 668–762). Forced to produce arguments of an unusually abstract or general kind in face of Achilles' stubborn resistance, Phoenix uses allegory (502–14) with an elaboration unknown elsewhere in Homer (on Phoenix' speech, see note on 434 ff). Also in Book 9 we find the designed contrast, made explicit at 9. 52–62 (cf. 14. 109–28), between the manly and spirited speech of Diomedes and the wilier proceedings of Nestor, 9. 29 ff: the uncomplicated young warrior *versus* the man of long experience, longer views, and more tact (notes on 63 and 96 ff).

In the speeches Homer departs from his normal 'objective' manner of presenting the world and events.[50] The speakers express

---

[50] On this cf. J. Griffin, *Homer on Life and Death*, ch. 4, but with the reservations suggested by the narratological approach of I. J. F. de Jong, *Narrators and Focalisers: The Presentation of the Story in the Iliad* (Amsterdam, 1987).

every kind of emotion, hatred and fear and love and exultation, and they also use a vocabulary importantly different from that of the main narration: the speeches are hospitable to superlatives, emotional adjectives, negative expressions, value-loaded words like δίκη, θέμις, κακός, ἀγαθός, ὕβρις, τιμή, ἔλεος—in fact, all the elements that explicitly pass a judgement on events. The austerity with which the poet keeps out of his own narrative such explicit valuations (the narrative does indeed implicitly judge events, leaving no doubt for instance that Achilles in rejecting the embassy makes a disastrous mistake) is perhaps connected with a feeling that the utterance of the Muse would be above such moralizing.

The vividness of the speeches goes with the liveliness and spontaneity with which Homeric people react to events. Homeric men weep freely (note on 14-16), and indeed roll about on the ground in extreme grief (24. 165, cf. the Odyssean line 'when I had my fill of weeping and rolling about', *Od.* 4. 541, 10. 499). Achilles in his mourning for Patroclus is thought likely to cut his own throat; he refuses to eat, he sleeps out on the sea-shore (18. 33-4, 19. 205 ff., 23. 59 f.). In mourning women beat their breasts and tear their cheeks, while Achilles lies on the ground and pours dust on his head (19. 284-6, 18. 22-31). When Achilles sees the envoys coming 'in amazement he leapt to his feet' (9. 193); in excitement or grief men smite their thighs (12. 162, 15. 113 etc.); they may strike themselves on the chest while arguing with their hearts (*Od.* 20. 17)—and a dialogue with one's own 'heart' is not uncommon, when a hero must bring himself to follow a painful or difficult course of action, as if one's 'heart' were a kind of second self (11. 403, 17. 90, etc.). Thus it is that Achilles can be asked to subdue his great heart (9. 496, see note on 109). Gods and men alike can be seized with inextinguishable laughter (1. 599 f., 23. 784); the suitors of Penelope, seeing the beggar Irus knocked out,'threw up their arms and died laughing', (*Od.* 18. 100). When the devoted retainer Eumaeus sees Telemachus returned safely from danger, 'He kissed his head and his two eyes and both his hands; a big tear fell from him' (*Od.* 16. 15 f.). But when Penelope learned that he had gone, (*Od.* 4. 715-18) 'she could not sit on her chair for grief, but she squatted on the floor whimpering pitifully, and all the women of the house, young and old, wailed round her'.

They inhabit a world of vivid gestures, both to express emotion

44

and to serve as ritual markers. Supplication[51] involves squatting at the feet of the person supplicated, clinging to his knees (1. 500-16, 21. 68-72, 24. 477-512, cf. 22. 219-21, Apollo said by Athena to 'roll about at the feet of Zeus' in supplication—a hostile exaggeration). When Achilles withdraws from participation with the Achaeans, he flings down the sceptre which is held by a speaker who 'has the floor' at a formal debate. The gesture is described at length; it is formal, as well as passionate (*Il.* 1. 234-46, cf. Od 2. 80-1). When a truce is made between the Achaean and Trojan armies, sheep are sacrificed and wine is poured out with the words: 'Zeus and all you other gods, whoever are the first to break this truce, may their brains be poured out on the earth like this wine, their own and their children's, and may their wives be possessed by other men' (3. 298-301). Menelaus accuses young Antilochus of cheating in the chariot race: he demands that Antilochus shall swear an oath 'as is the custom: stand in front of your horses and chariot, with your whip in your hand, touch your horses and swear by Poseidon that you did not deliberately foul my chariot' (23. 581-5). Antilochus prefers not to accept the dangerous challenge. Such gestures and tableaux make vivid the essence of what is happening.

The clarity and power of Homeric speech is part of a world which is clearly and vividly illuminated. We see the gods come down and intervene: to the people in the poem, perhaps like a falling star (4. 73-84), or a bird (7. 58-61, 13. 62-72), or a mist (1. 359), or indeed invisible to most observers altogether (1. 198), but to us, Homer's audience, identifiable and intelligible. We hear the rowdy discussions among the Olympian gods; we even follow Zeus when he sits alone, away from the rest of Olympus (1. 498, 5. 753, 15. 152f.). The world is shown to us with its seas, mountains, forests, wild beasts, agriculture, peace and war. And above all we see what it is to be human, neither god nor beast: capable of splendour, but doomed to death. The deepest reflections on that central theme are reserved for the greatest hero, Achilles, in Book 9 and Book 24.

---

[51] John Gould, 'Hiketeia', in *JHS* 93 (1973), 74-103.

## 5. THE TEXT

We know nothing about the first writing down of the *Iliad*. It seems likely that it was committed to writing soon after its composition, and before 600 BC. Even before the scholarly work done on the text in Alexandria in the third and second centuries BC,[52] the text of the Homeric poems seems to have been substantially the same all over the Greek world. That is in marked contrast with the situation of such epics as the *Nibelungenlied*, the *Chanson de Roland*, and the *Mahabharata*. The Ptolemies of Egypt collected manuscripts, and unprecedented quantities were at the disposal of the Alexandrian scholars Zenodotus, Aristophanes of Byzantium, and Aristarchus. As we see from the early papyri that survive, the characteristic fault which needed emendation was the presence in many of the early manuscripts of additions, passages expanded and increased in length by the mechanical re-use of lines from elsewhere in the poems; but there were also interpolations, omissions, variant grammatical forms, and long-standing corruptions.

After about 150 BC, thanks in part at least to the work of Aristarchus, in part to the activity of the book trade, the 'wild' texts disappear, and the text of Homer in papyrus texts of later antiquity differs little from that of the medieval manuscripts. Hence our modern printed editions vary surprisingly little. The text used here is essentially that of the Oxford Classical Text by (D. B. Monro and) T. W. Allen, 3rd edition, 1920. The drastically simplified apparatus roughly follows C. W. Macleod's procedure in his Commentary on *Iliad* 24.[53] I use the letter **a** to indicate variant readings of interest in one or more of the mediaeval manuscripts of the *Iliad*, **b** to indicate variants recorded in other ancient sources, and **p** to indicate readings found only in papyri (texts which survive from the ancient world, older than the medieval manuscripts). Conjectures and readings of ancient scholars are indicated with Al(exandrian); conjectures by later scholars are assigned simply to the century in which they were made. I have not listed variants or ancient suggestions which seem to me clearly wrong.

---

[52] See S. West, 'The Transmission of the Text', in *Commentary on the Odyssey* i. 33-48; Janko, 'The Text and Transmission of the *Iliad*', in *Commentary on the Iliad*, iv. 20-38. His verdict on Allen's text is severe; the verdict of N. G. Wilson is crushing: *PBA* 76 (1990), 316. But its universal accessibility leads one to use it perforce.

[53] *Commentary on Iliad Book 24*, 60.

# BIBLIOGRAPHY

It is possible to mention only a small fraction of the enormous modern bibliography on the *Iliad*. Survey articles can be found in *Classical World*: 49 (1955-6), 17-55 (F. M. Combellack); 66 (1972), 257-93 (J. P. Holoka); 79 (1986), 379-94 (M. E. Clark); 83 (1990), 393-461, and 84 (1990), 89-156 (J. P. Holoka). Also J. B. Hainsworth, *Greece and Rome Survey* 3, *Homer* (Oxford, 1969); A. Heubeck, *Die homerische Frage* (Darmstadt, 1974). Mark W. Edwards, *Homer, Poet of the Iliad* (Johns Hopkins, 1987) is arranged by topics, each chapter followed by a handy reading list. The chapter on Book 9 is on pp. 214-37. Adam Parry gives an interesting account of the work of his father Milman Parry as the Introduction to *The Making of Homeric Verse* (the collected papers of Milman Parry), edited by Adam Parry (Oxford, 1971).

## 1. TEXT

Oxford Classical Text (D. B. Monro and) T. W. Allen, 3rd edn., 1920. H. van Thiel is at work on a new text based on a fresh study of the manuscript tradition.

## 2. COMMENTARIES

W. Leaf, 2 vols. (London, 1900-2, reprinted): large, learned, in the 'analytical' tradition but still valuable. Contains a text.

G. S. Kirk and others, 6 vols. (Cambridge 1985-93). Book Nine is in vol. 3 by J. B. Hainsworth. No text; massive and thorough work of high standard.

M. M. Willcock, 2 vols. (London, 1978-84). Contains text; unpretentious and helpful.

M. M. Willcock, *Companion to the Iliad* (Chicago 1976).

K. F. Ameis, C. Hentze, and P. Cauer, *Homers Ilias* (Leipzig, 1868-1932, reprinted). Always worth consulting.

P. Von der Mühll, *Kritisches Hypomnema zur Ilias* (Basel, 1952). Old-fashioned but intelligent.

## 3. REFERENCE

### (a) Dictionaries

G. Authenrieth, *An Homeric Dictionary* (Eng. trans.: London, 1877, reprinted).

R. J. Cunliffe, *A Lexicon of the Homeric Dialect* (London, 1924). (Two helpful and modest works.)

C. Ebeling (and others), *Lexicon Homericum* (Leipzig 1885, repr.): in Latin; a substantial work of scholarship.

*Lexikon des frühgriechischen Epos*, ed. B. Snell (Göttingen, 1955–  ): on an enormous scale. So far it has reached καπνός.

Concordance: G. L. Prendergast, revised by B. Marzullo (Hildesheim, 1960).

### (b) Grammar

P. Chantraine, *Grammaire homérique*, 2 vols. (Paris 1958–63): the standard Homeric grammar (*GH*).

D. B. Monro, *A Grammar of the Homeric Dialect* (Oxford, 2nd edn. 1891).

A good short introduction to Homeric language: L. R. Palmer in A. J. B. Wace and F. H. Stubbings (eds.), *A Companion to Homer* (London, 1962).

### (c) Ancient Commentaries

*Scholia Graeca in Homeri Iliadem*, ed. H. Erbse, 7 vols. (Berlin, 1969–88).

### (d) Translations

Alexander Pope: the work which made Pope rich and famous; rhyming couplets. Brilliant, rhetorical, changes Homer considerably to make him resemble a proper eighteenth-century poet; well worth looking at.

A. Lang, W. Leaf, and E. Myers (London, 1914). In the idiom of the King James Bible.

R. Fitzgerald (New York, 1961). (Free) verse.

M. Hammond, *A New Prose Translation of the Iliad* (Harmondsworth, 1987)—replacing the unpoetical but very popular Penguin Classic by E. V. Rieu.

## 4. GENERAL

A. W. H. Adkins, *Merit and Responsibility* (Oxford, 1960): on moral ideas and values.

Ø. Andersen, *Die Diomedesgestalt in der Ilias* (Oslo, 1977).

W. Arend, *Die typischen Szenen bei Homer* (Berlin, 1933): a pioneering work.

Matthew Arnold, *On Translating Homer* (1861, often repr.).

*Archaeologia Homerica*, ed. F. Matz and H. G. Buchholz (Göttingen 1967– ).

E. Benveniste, *Le vocabulaire des institutions indo-européennes* (Paris, 1969).

C. M. Bowra, *Tradition and Design in the Iliad* (Oxford, 1930).

W. Burkert, *Greek Religion*, Eng. trans. by J. Raffan (Cambridge, Mass., 1985) of *Griechische Religion der archaischen und klassischen Epoche* (Stuttgart 1977).

F. Codino, *Introduzione a Omero* (Turin, 1965).

A. B. Cook, *Zeus* (Cambridge, 1914–1940).

S. Dalley, *Myths from Mesopotamia* . . . trans. with introduction and notes (Oxford, 1989).

I. J. F. de Jong, *Narrators and Focalisers: the Presentation of the Story in the Iliad* (Amsterdam, 1987).

D. E. Eichholz, 'The Propitiation of Achilles', *AJP* 74 (1953), 137–48.

R. Finnegan, *Oral Poetry* (London, 1977).

G. Finsler, *Homer* (Berlin, 1914).

L. Foxhall and J. D. Davies (eds.), *The Trojan War: Its Historicity and Context* (Bristol 1984).

H. Fränkel, *Die homerischen Gleichnisse* (Göttingen 1921, repr.).

—— *Early Greek Poetry and Philosophy* (trans. M. Hadas and J. Willis, Oxford, 1975). Eng. trans. of *Dichtung und Philosophie des frühen Griechentums* (2nd edn., Munich 1962). Contains an interesting account of Homer.

H. Friis Johansen, *The Iliad in Early Greek Art* (Copenhagen, 1967).

J. Griffin, *Homer* (Past Masters: Oxford, 1980): a short introduction.

—— *Homer on Life and Death* (Oxford, 1980).

—— 'Homeric Words and Speakers', *Journal of Hellenic Studies* 106 (1986) 36–57.

J. B. Hainsworth, *The Flexibility of the Homeric Formula* (Oxford, 1968).

R. Harder, *Kleine Schriften* (Munich, 1960).

A. T. Hatto (ed.), *Traditions of Heroic and Epic Poetry* (London. 1980–9).

A. Heubeck, 'Das Meleagros-Paradeigma in der Ilias', *Neue Jahrbücher* 118 (1943), 13–20 = *Kleine Schriften* (Erlangen, 1984), 128–35.

A. Hoekstra, *Homeric Modifications of Formulaic Prototypes* (Amsterdam, 1969).

I. M. Hohendahl-Zoetelief, *Manners in the Homeric Epic* (Leiden, 1980).

J. T. Kakridis, *Homeric Researches* (Lund, 1949).

H. C. King, *Achilles* (Berkeley, Calif., 1987).

G. S. Kirk, *The Songs of Homer* (Cambridge, 1962). Good general account.

—— (ed.), *The Language and Background of Homer* (Cambridge, 1964).

M. Leumann, *Homerische Wörter* (Basel, 1950) (*HW*).

H. Lloyd-Jones, *The Justice of Zeus* (2nd edn., Berkeley, Calif., 1983).

D. Lohmann, *Die Komposition der Reden in der Ilias* (Berlin, 1970).

C. W. Macleod, *Commentary on Iliad Book 24* (Cambridge, 1982).

R. P. Martin, *The Language of Heroes* (Ithaca, NY, 1989).

M. J. Mellink (ed.), *Troy and the Trojan War* (Bryn Mawr, 1986).

D. Motzkus, *Untersuchungen zum 9. Buch der Ilias* (Diss. Hamburg, 1964).

G. Nagy, *The Best of the Achaeans* (Johns Hopkins, 1979).

D. L. Page, *History and the Homeric Iliad* (Berkeley, Calif., 1959): with an Appendix on Book 9.

A. Parry, 'The Language of Achilles', *Transactions of the American Philological Association*, 87 (1956), 1–7: repr. in *The Language of Achilles and Other Papers* (Oxford, 1989), 1–7.

—— 'Have we Homer's *Iliad*?', *Yale Classical Studies*, 20 (1966), 177–216, repr., as above, 104–40.

M. Parry, *The Making of Homeric Verse* (collected papers), ed. A. Parry (Oxford. 1971).

R. Pfeiffer, *History of Classical Scholarship*. i: *To the End of the Hellenistic Age* (Oxford, 1968).

J. M. Redfield, *Nature and Culture in the Iliad*² (Chicago, 1992): an anthropological approach.

K. Reinhardt, *Die Ilias und ihr Dichter*, ed. U. Hölscher (Göttingen, 1961).

R. Renehan, 'The "Heldentod" in Homer', *CP* 82 (1987), 99–116.

W. Schadewaldt, *Iliasstudien* (3rd edn., Darmstadt, 1966).

W. Schulze, *Quaestiones Epicae* (Gutersloh, 1898).

E. Schwyzer, *Griechische Grammatik*, 4 vols. (Munich, 1939–1971).

David M. Shive, *Naming Achilles* (Oxford, 1987).

O. Taplin, *Homeric Soundings* (Oxford, 1992).

M. Ventris and J. Chadwick, *Documents in Mycenaean Greek*, 2nd edn., (Cambridge, 1973).

H. von Kamptz, *Homerische Personennamen* (Göttingen, 1982).

S. Weil, *The Iliad or the Poem of Force*, trans. M. McCarthy; also in her *Intimations of Christianity among the Ancient Greeks*, trans. E. Geissbuhler (London 1957).

M. L. West, 'The Rise of the Greek Epic', in *JHS* 108 (1988), 151–72.

# APPENDIX

## The Embassy to Achilles and the Duals, 182-98

'Surely the greatest problem in the whole of the *Iliad*' was the comment of Wolfgang Schadewaldt on the dual forms which are so uniquely numerous in 9. 182-98 (*Iliasstudien*, 137; cf. A. Lesky, *Geschichte der gr. Literatur*² (1963), 49). Nestor offers to nominate envoys to Achilles: 'First let Phoenix be leader (ἡγησάσθω), and then great Ajax and shining Odysseus; and of heralds let Odios and Eurybates follow with them' (9. 168-70). Nestor then 'gives them many instructions, glancing at each man, but most at Odysseus' (179-80). All seems clear: three envoys and two supernumeraries. But as soon as they set off they are described with a barrage of dual forms: τὼ δὲ βάτην . . . εὐχομένω . . . ἱκέσθην . . . τὼ δὲ βάτην προτέρω . . . τὼ . . . χαίρετον . . . ἱκάνετον . . . ἔστον.

The difficulty was of course felt in antiquity, and ancient scholars hit on an explanation still quite popular: Phoenix is not counted as a (full) envoy (Σ on 168, 169, 182, 197, 520). Thus the 'two' are Odysseus and Ajax: so, recently, A. Köhnken, *Glotta*, 53 (1975), 25-36, 56 (1978), 5-14, who argues that Phoenix' position in the army makes him clearly inferior. It must be said that neither 223 nor 311 suggests that the poet makes any such distinction. It is often alleged that Phoenix ('let him be leader', 168) is not with the others because he has gone ahead to prepare Achilles for their arrival: an expedient adopted by a surprisingly large number of scholars, including Ameis-Hentze and Chantraine (*GH*. ii. 28). It is surely an answer to this that Achilles is taken by surprise when they arrive (193-5).

Another approach is to argue that the duals refer to two *groups* among the envoys: on the one hand Phoenix, on the other the two heralds plus Odysseus and Ajax (A. Thornton, *Glotta*, 56 (1978), 1-4); or, perhaps, on the one hand the two heralds, on the other the three heroes (R. Gordesiani, *Philologus*, 124 (1980), 163-74). It is very hard to find a plausible parallel grammatically, and the oddity of Achilles greeting his visitors as 'you two groups, very dear to me' (197) is surely unacceptable.

G. Nagy tries a new line: Odysseus is such a bitter enemy of Achilles—there is an obscure story that they quarrelled at Delphi, *Od.* 8. 73-82—that he does not count him among the envoys, the two thus being Ajax

51

and Phoenix (*The Best of the Achaeans* (Johns Hopkins, 1979), 49–55). Apart from the very questionable myth, and the oddity of supposing that wise Nestor would select as envoy to Achilles a man whom he hated, or that Achilles would say of such a party that they are 'my dearest friends' (197f., 204, 521f.), it has been pointed out that at 9. 182f. the dual forms are used, not by Achilles, but by the poet (Solmsen, *AJP* 102 (1981), 82). To this R. P. Martin (*The Language of Heroes* (Ithaca, NY, 1989), 235–7) replies that the poet identifies himself so completely with Achilles that he, too, refuses to count his enemy Odysseus. Such a romantic subjectivity seems to me completely alien to the Homeric manner, and in any case so unexplained here as to be unintelligible.

It was suggested long ago by F. Boll (*Zeitschr. f. österr. Gymn.* 68 (1917), 1ff., 69 (1919–20), 414ff.) that the dual forms echoed the scene in Book 1 in which Briseis was taken away by two heralds: the poet accepted the grammatical irregularity as the price of that echo. That line is pursued by C. Segal (*GRBS* 9 (1968), 101–14), who thinks the two persons referred to by the duals are the two heralds, Odios and Eurybates; and D. Lohmann (*Die Komposition der Reden in der Ilias* (Berlin, 1970), 227ff., who thinks they are Ajax and Odysseus. The former suggestion, which leaves Achilles ignoring the great heroes and welcoming only the insignificant heralds, seems impossible; the second leaves Phoenix as a problem (why does Achilles ignore him?).

Two courses seem to remain: to say that the dual forms are not really distinct from plurals, or to say that they are survivors from a version of the story in which there really were two envoys: doubtless, Odysseus and Ajax, without Phoenix. The former view, popular in the nineteenth and early twentieth centuries (Wackernagel, *Vorlesungen über Syntax*, i (1920), 78f.; Debrunner, *Glotta*, 15 (1927), 17, etc.) has been shown to be impossible. Homer does on occasion offer plurals for duals, but not duals for plurals (M. Noé, *Phoinix, Ilias und Homer* (Leipzig, 1940), 14ff., W. Burkert, *Wiener Studien*, 10 (1976), 8 n. 12). And besides, there simply are too many dual forms in immediate succession for this account to be credible.

The second, supported with characteristic bravura by D. L. Page (*History and the Homeric Iliad* (Berkeley, Calif., 1959) 298ff.), was put forward by T. Bergk (*Griechische Literaturgeschichte*, i (Berlin, 1872), 595ff.), and accepted by W. Leaf and many others (listed: D. Motzkus, *Untersuchungen zum 9. Buch der Ilias* (Diss. Hamburg, 1964), 97). It seems, of all these views, the most likely to be, in some sense, right. The approach of the envoys is described in a way which clearly suggests that they are only two in number. The obvious difficulty is that the following scene, the six speeches, is so well and convincingly constructed; and that we cannot simply remove Phoenix from the text as we now have it. The transition from Achilles' utter rejection of the offers of Agamemnon (401–29) to his half-mollified reply to Ajax (643–55) would be unintelligibly abrupt: more time, and a change of emotional tone, is necessary—precisely what Phoenix provides. I am no more able to give a satisfactory answer to this problem than my predecessors. The reader is referred to Introduction pp. 22–4. It may be worth remarking that the earliest extant representation of the Embassy in art, a bronze relief from Olympia dated about 620 BC, shows Phoenix leading, looking back over his shoulder at Odysseus and Ajax (K. Friis Johansen, *The Iliad in Early Greek Art* (Copenhagen, 1967), figure 8); the next, a Caeretan hydria from *c.*520–510 BC, showed Nestor, Phoenix, Ajax, Odysseus, and the two heralds (figure 62). Several Attic vases from *c.*480 BC also show Phoenix as a member of the scene (figures 63–7). A version without Phoenix does not seem to have left a mark in the visual arts.

Ὣς οἱ μὲν Τρῶες φυλακὰς ἔχον· αὐτὰρ Ἀχαιοὺς
θεσπεσίη ἔχε Φύζα, Φόβου κρυόεντος ἑταίρη,
πένθεϊ δ᾽ ἀτλήτῳ βεβολήατο πάντες ἄριστοι.
ὡς δ᾽ ἄνεμοι δύο πόντον ὀρίνετον ἰχθυόεντα
Βορέης καὶ Ζέφυρος, τώ τε Θρήκηθεν ἄητον                5
ἐλθόντ᾽ ἐξαπίνης· ἄμυδις δέ τε κῦμα κελαινὸν
κορθύεται, πολλὸν δὲ παρὲξ ἅλα φῦκος ἔχευεν·
ὣς ἐδαΐζετο θυμὸς ἐνὶ στήθεσσιν Ἀχαιῶν.
Ἀτρεΐδης δ᾽ ἄχεϊ μεγάλῳ βεβολημένος ἦτορ
φοίτα κηρύκεσσι λιγυφθόγγοισι κελεύων                    10
κλήδην εἰς ἀγορὴν κικλήσκειν ἄνδρα ἕκαστον,
μηδὲ βοᾶν· αὐτὸς δὲ μετὰ πρώτοισι πονεῖτο.
ἷζον δ᾽ εἰν ἀγορῇ τετιηότες· ἂν δ᾽ Ἀγαμέμνων
ἵστατο δάκρυ χέων ὥς τε κρήνη μελάνυδρος
ἥ τε κατ᾽ αἰγίλιπος πέτρης δνοφερὸν χέει ὕδωρ·          15
ὣς ὁ βαρὺ στενάχων ἔπε᾽ Ἀργείοισι μετηύδα·
"ὦ φίλοι Ἀργείων ἡγήτορες ἠδὲ μέδοντες
Ζεύς με μέγα Κρονίδης ἄτῃ ἐνέδησε βαρείῃ
σχέτλιος, ὃς τότε μέν μοι ὑπέσχετο καὶ κατένευσεν
Ἴλιον ἐκπέρσαντ᾽ εὐτείχεον ἀπονέεσθαι,                 20
νῦν δὲ κακὴν ἀπάτην βουλεύσατο, καί με κελεύει
δυσκλέα Ἄργος ἱκέσθαι, ἐπεὶ πολὺν ὤλεσα λαόν.
οὕτω που Διὶ μέλλει ὑπερμενέϊ φίλον εἶναι,
ὃς δὴ πολλάων πολίων κατέλυσε κάρηνα
ἠδ᾽ ἔτι καὶ λύσει· τοῦ γὰρ κράτος ἐστὶ μέγιστον.        25
ἀλλ᾽ ἄγεθ᾽, ὡς ἂν ἐγὼ εἴπω, πειθώμεθα πάντες·
φεύγωμεν σὺν νηυσὶ φίλην ἐς πατρίδα γαῖαν·
οὐ γὰρ ἔτι Τροίην αἱρήσομεν εὐρυάγυιαν."
Ὣς ἔφαθ᾽, οἱ δ᾽ ἄρα πάντες ἀκὴν ἐγένοντο σιωπῇ.
δὴν δ᾽ ἄνεῳ ἦσαν τετιηότες υἷες Ἀχαιῶν·               30

5 βορρᾶς a          14 ἵστατο δάκρυ χέων μετὰ δ᾽ Ἀργείοισιν ἔειπεν Al.
21 ἀπάτην: ἄτην p

ὀψὲ δὲ δὴ μετέειπε βοὴν ἀγαθὸς Διομήδης·
"Ἀτρεΐδη, σοὶ πρῶτα μαχήσομαι ἀφραδέοντι,
ἦ θέμις ἐστίν, ἄναξ, ἀγορῇ· σὺ δὲ μή τι χολωθῇς.
ἀλκὴν μέν μοι πρῶτον ὀνείδισας ἐν Δαναοῖσι
φὰς ἔμεν ἀπτόλεμον καὶ ἀνάλκιδα· ταῦτα δὲ πάντα          35
ἴσασ' Ἀργείων ἠμὲν νέοι ἠδὲ γέροντες.
σοὶ δὲ διάνδιχα δῶκε Κρόνου πάϊς ἀγκυλομήτεω·
σκήπτρῳ μέν τοι δῶκε τετιμῆσθαι περὶ πάντων,
ἀλκὴν δ' οὔ τοι δῶκεν, ὅ τε κράτος ἐστὶ μέγιστον.
δαιμόνι', οὕτω που μάλα ἔλπεαι υἷας Ἀχαιῶν          40
ἀπτολέμους τ' ἔμεναι καὶ ἀνάλκιδας ὡς ἀγορεύεις;
εἰ δέ τοι αὐτῷ θυμὸς ἐπέσσυται ὥς τε νέεσθαι,
ἔρχεο· πάρ τοι ὁδός, νῆες δέ τοι ἄγχι θαλάσσης
ἑστᾶσ', αἵ τοι ἕποντο Μυκήνηθεν μάλα πολλαί.
ἀλλ' ἄλλοι μενέουσι κάρη κομόωντες Ἀχαιοὶ          45
εἰς ὅ κέ περ Τροίην διαπέρσομεν. εἰ δὲ καὶ αὐτοὶ
φευγόντων σὺν νηυσὶ φίλην ἐς πατρίδα γαῖαν·
νῶϊ δ', ἐγὼ Σθένελός τε, μαχησόμεθ' εἰς ὅ κε τέκμωρ
Ἰλίου εὕρωμεν· σὺν γὰρ θεῷ εἰλήλουθμεν."
"Ὣς ἔφαθ', οἱ δ' ἄρα πάντες ἐπίαχον υἷες Ἀχαιῶν          50
μῦθον ἀγασσάμενοι Διομήδεος ἱπποδάμοιο.
τοῖσι δ' ἀνιστάμενος μετεφώνεεν ἱππότα Νέστωρ·
"Τυδεΐδη, πέρι μὲν πολέμῳ ἔνι καρτερός ἐσσι,
καὶ βουλῇ μετὰ πάντας ὁμήλικας ἔπλευ ἄριστος.
οὔ τίς τοι τὸν μῦθον ὀνόσσεται, ὅσσοι Ἀχαιοί,          55
οὐδὲ πάλιν ἐρέει· ἀτὰρ οὐ τέλος ἵκεο μύθων.
ἦ μὲν καὶ νέος ἐσσί, ἐμὸς δέ κε καὶ πάϊς εἴης
ὁπλότατος γενεῆφιν· ἀτὰρ πεπνυμένα βάζεις
Ἀργείων βασιλῆας, ἐπεὶ κατὰ μοῖραν ἔειπες.
ἀλλ' ἄγ' ἐγών, ὃς σεῖο γεραίτερος εὔχομαι εἶναι,          60
ἐξείπω καὶ πάντα διΐξομαι· οὐδέ κέ τίς μοι
μῦθον ἀτιμήσει, οὐδὲ κρείων Ἀγαμέμνων.
ἀφρήτωρ ἀθέμιστος ἀνέστιός ἐστιν ἐκεῖνος
ὃς πολέμου ἔραται ἐπιδημίου ὀκρυόεντος.
ἀλλ' ἤτοι νῦν μὲν πειθώμεθα νυκτὶ μελαίνῃ          65
δόρπα τ' ἐφοπλισόμεθα· φυλακτῆρες δὲ ἕκαστοι
λεξάσθων παρὰ τάφρον ὀρυκτὴν τείχεος ἐκτός.
κούροισιν μὲν ταῦτ' ἐπιτέλλομαι· αὐτὰρ ἔπειτα,

36 ἠμὲν νέοι· ἠδὲ γέροντες: ἡγήτορες ἠδὲ μέδοντες Al.          44 line rejected Al.
59 line rejected C.19.          62 ἀτιμήσει' a

56

Ἀτρεΐδη, σὺ μὲν ἄρχε· σὺ γὰρ βασιλεύτατός ἐσσι.
δαίνυ δαῖτα γέρουσιν· ἔοικέ τοι, οὔ τοι ἀεικές.                    70
πλείαί τοι οἴνου κλισίαι, τὸν νῆες Ἀχαιῶν
ἠμάτιαι Θρήκηθεν ἐπ' εὐρέα πόντον ἄγουσι·
πᾶσά τοί ἐσθ' ὑποδεξίη, πολέεσσι δ' ἀνάσσεις.
πολλῶν δ' ἀγρομένων τῷ πείσεαι ὅς κεν ἀρίστην
βουλὴν βουλεύσῃ· μάλα δὲ χρεὼ πάντας Ἀχαιοὺς       75
ἐσθλῆς καὶ πυκινῆς, ὅτι δήϊοι ἐγγύθι νηῶν
καίουσιν πυρὰ πολλά· τίς ἂν τάδε γηθήσειε;
νὺξ δ' ἥδ' ἠὲ διαρραίσει στρατὸν ἠὲ σαώσει."
    Ὣς ἔφαθ', οἱ δ' ἄρα τοῦ μάλα μὲν κλύον ἠδ' ἐπίθοντο.
ἐκ δὲ φυλακτῆρες σὺν τεύχεσιν ἐσσεύοντο                    80
ἀμφί τε Νεστορίδην Θρασυμήδεα ποιμένα λαῶν,
ἠδ' ἀμφ' Ἀσκάλαφον καὶ Ἰάλμενον υἷας Ἄρηος,
ἀμφί τε Μηριόνην Ἀφαρῆά τε Δηΐπυρόν τε,
ἠδ' ἀμφὶ Κρείοντος υἱὸν Λυκομήδεα δῖον.
ἕπτ' ἔσαν ἡγεμόνες φυλάκων, ἑκατὸν δὲ ἑκάστῳ       85
κοῦροι ἅμα στεῖχον δολίχ' ἔγχεα χερσὶν ἔχοντες·
κὰδ δὲ μέσον τάφρου καὶ τείχεος ἷζον ἰόντες·
ἔνθα δὲ πῦρ κήαντο, τίθεντο δὲ δόρπα ἕκαστος.
    Ἀτρεΐδης δὲ γέροντας ἀολλέας ἦγεν Ἀχαιῶν
ἐς κλισίην, παρὰ δέ σφι τίθει μενοεικέα δαῖτα.             90
οἱ δ' ἐπ' ὀνείαθ' ἑτοῖμα προκείμενα χεῖρας ἴαλλον.
αὐτὰρ ἐπεὶ πόσιος καὶ ἐδητύος ἐξ ἔρον ἕντο,
τοῖς ὁ γέρων πάμπρωτος ὑφαίνειν ἤρχετο μῆτιν
Νέστωρ, οὗ καὶ πρόσθεν ἀρίστη φαίνετο βουλή·
ὅ σφιν ἐϋφρονέων ἀγορήσατο καὶ μετέειπεν·              95
"Ἀτρεΐδη κύδιστε, ἄναξ ἀνδρῶν Ἀγάμεμνον,
ἐν σοὶ μὲν λήξω, σέο δ' ἄρξομαι, οὕνεκα πολλῶν
λαῶν ἐσσι ἄναξ καί τοι Ζεὺς ἐγγυάλιξε
σκῆπτρόν τ' ἠδὲ θέμιστας, ἵνά σφισι βουλεύῃσθα.
τώ σε χρὴ πέρι μὲν φάσθαι ἔπος ἠδ' ἐπακοῦσαι,       100
κρηῆναι δὲ καὶ ἄλλῳ, ὅτ' ἄν τινα θυμὸς ἀνώγῃ
εἰπεῖν εἰς ἀγαθόν· σέο δ' ἕξεται ὅττί κεν ἄρχῃ.
αὐτὰρ ἐγὼν ἐρέω ὥς μοι δοκεῖ εἶναι ἄριστα.
οὐ γάρ τις νόον ἄλλος ἀμείνονα τοῦδε νοήσει,
οἷον ἐγὼ νοέω, ἠμὲν πάλαι ἠδ' ἔτι καὶ νῦν,               105
ἐξ ἔτι τοῦ ὅτε, διογενές, Βρισηΐδα κούρην
χωομένου Ἀχιλῆος ἔβης κλισίηθεν ἀπούρας
οὔ τι καθ' ἡμέτερόν γε νόον· μάλα γάρ τοι ἔγωγε

πόλλ' ἀπεμυθεόμην· σὺ δὲ σῷ μεγαλήτορι θυμῷ
εἶξας ἄνδρα φέριστον, ὃν ἀθάνατοί περ ἔτεισαν,　　110
ἠτίμησας, ἑλὼν γὰρ ἔχεις γέρας· ἀλλ' ἔτι καὶ νῦν
φραζώμεσθ' ὥς κέν μιν ἀρεσσάμενοι πεπίθωμεν
δώροισίν τ' ἀγανοῖσιν ἔπεσσί τε μειλιχίοισι."
　　Τὸν δ' αὖτε προσέειπεν ἄναξ ἀνδρῶν Ἀγαμέμνων·
"ὦ γέρον, οὔ τι ψεῦδος ἐμὰς ἄτας κατέλεξας·　　115
ἀασάμην, οὐδ' αὐτὸς ἀναίνομαι. ἀντί νυ πολλῶν
λαῶν ἐστὶν ἀνὴρ ὅν τε Ζεὺς κῆρι φιλήσῃ,
ὡς νῦν τοῦτον ἔτεισε, δάμασσε δὲ λαὸν Ἀχαιῶν.
ἀλλ' ἐπεὶ ἀασάμην φρεσὶ λευγαλέῃσι πιθήσας,
ἂψ ἐθέλω ἀρέσαι δόμεναί τ' ἀπερείσι' ἄποινα.　　120
ὑμῖν δ' ἐν πάντεσσι περικλυτὰ δῶρ' ὀνομήνω.
ἕπτ' ἀπύρους τρίποδας, δέκα δὲ χρυσοῖο τάλαντα,
αἴθωνας δὲ λέβητας ἐείκοσι, δώδεκα δ' ἵππους
πηγοὺς ἀθλοφόρους, οἳ ἀέθλια ποσσὶν ἄροντο.
οὔ κεν ἀλήϊος εἴη ἀνὴρ ᾧ τόσσα γένοιτο,　　125
οὐδέ κεν ἀκτήμων ἐριτίμοιο χρυσοῖο,
ὅσσα μοι ἠνείκαντο ἀέθλια μώνυχες ἵπποι.
δώσω δ' ἑπτὰ γυναῖκας ἀμύμονα ἔργα ἰδυίας,
Λεσβίδας, ἃς ὅτε Λέσβον ἐϋκτιμένην ἕλεν αὐτὸς
ἐξελόμην, αἳ κάλλει ἐνίκων φῦλα γυναικῶν.　　130
τὰς μέν οἱ δώσω, μετὰ δ' ἔσσεται ἣν τότ' ἀπηύρων
κούρη Βρισῆος· ἐπὶ δὲ μέγαν ὅρκον ὀμοῦμαι
μή ποτε τῆς εὐνῆς ἐπιβήμεναι ἠδὲ μιγῆναι,
ἦ θέμις ἀνθρώπων πέλει, ἀνδρῶν ἠδὲ γυναικῶν.
ταῦτα μὲν αὐτίκα πάντα παρέσσεται· εἰ δέ κεν αὖτε　　135
ἄστυ μέγα Πριάμοιο θεοὶ δώωσ' ἀλαπάξαι,.
νῆα ἅλις χρυσοῦ καὶ χαλκοῦ νηησάσθω
εἰσελθών, ὅτε κεν δατεώμεθα ληΐδ' Ἀχαιοί,
Τρωϊάδας δὲ γυναῖκας ἐείκοσιν αὐτὸς ἑλέσθω,
αἵ κε μετ' Ἀργείην Ἑλένην κάλλισται ἔωσιν.　　140
εἰ δέ κεν Ἄργος ἱκοίμεθ' Ἀχαιϊκὸν, οὖθαρ ἀρούρης,
γαμβρός κέν μοι ἔοι· τείσω δέ μιν ἶσον Ὀρέστῃ,
ὅς μοι τηλύγετος τρέφεται θαλίῃ ἔνι πολλῇ.
τρεῖς δέ μοί εἰσι θύγατρες ἐνὶ μεγάρῳ εὐπήκτῳ
Χρυσόθεμις καὶ Λαοδίκη καὶ Ἰφιάνασσα·　　145
τάων ἥν κ' ἐθέλῃσι φίλην ἀνάεδνον ἀγέσθω
πρὸς οἶκον Πηλῆος· ἐγὼ δ' ἐπὶ μείλια δώσω

119a ἢ οἴνῳ μεθύων ἤ μ' ἔβλαψαν θεοὶ αὐτοί b　　130 ἐξ ἑλόμην Al.

πολλὰ μάλ', ὅσσ' οὔ πώ τις ἑῇ ἐπέδωκε θυγατρί·
ἑπτὰ δέ οἱ δώσω εὖ ναιόμενα πτολίεθρα,
Καρδαμύλην Ἐνόπην τε καὶ Ἱρὴν ποιήεσσαν,                    150
Φηράς τε ζαθέας ἠδ' Ἄνθειαν βαθύλειμον,
καλήν τ' Αἴπειαν καὶ Πήδασον ἀμπελόεσσαν.
πᾶσαι δ' ἐγγὺς ἁλός, νέαται Πύλου ἠμαθόεντος·
ἐν δ' ἄνδρες ναίουσι πολύρρηνες πολυβοῦται,
οἵ κέ ἑ δωτίνῃσι θεὸν ὣς τιμήσουσι                         155
καί οἱ ὑπὸ σκήπτρῳ λιπαρὰς τελέουσι θέμιστας.
ταῦτά κέ οἱ τελέσαιμι μεταλλήξαντι χόλοιο.
δμηθήτω· Ἀΐδης τοι ἀμείλιχος ἠδ' ἀδάμαστος·
τοὔνεκα καί τε βροτοῖσι θεῶν ἔχθιστος ἁπάντων—
καί μοι ὑποστήτω, ὅσσον βασιλεύτερός εἰμι                  160
ἠδ' ὅσσον γενεῇ προγενέστερος εὔχομαι εἶναι."
    Τὸν δ' ἠμείβετ' ἔπειτα Γερήνιος ἱππότα Νέστωρ·
"Ἀτρεΐδη κύδιστε, ἄναξ ἀνδρῶν Ἀγάμεμνον,
δῶρα μὲν οὐκέτ' ὀνοστὰ διδοῖς Ἀχιλῆϊ ἄνακτι·
ἀλλ' ἄγετε, κλητοὺς ὀτρύνομεν, οἵ κε τάχιστα               165
ἔλθωσ' ἐς κλισίην Πηληϊάδεω Ἀχιλῆος.
εἰ δ' ἄγε, τοὺς ἂν ἐγὼ ἐπιόψομαι, οἱ δὲ πιθέσθων.
Φοῖνιξ μὲν πρώτιστα Διῒ φίλος ἡγησάσθω,
αὐτὰρ ἔπειτ' Αἴας τε μέγας καὶ δῖος Ὀδυσσεύς·
κηρύκων δ' Ὀδίος τε καὶ Εὐρυβάτης ἅμ' ἑπέσθων.             170
φέρτε δὲ χερσὶν ὕδωρ, εὐφημῆσαί τε κέλεσθε,
ὄφρα Διὶ Κρονίδῃ ἀρησόμεθ', αἴ κ' ἐλεήσῃ."
    Ὣς φάτο, τοῖσι δὲ πᾶσιν ἑαδότα μῦθον ἔειπεν.
αὐτίκα κήρυκες μὲν ὕδωρ ἐπὶ χεῖρας ἔχευαν,
κοῦροι δὲ κρητῆρας ἐπεστέψαντο ποτοῖο,                     175
νώμησαν δ' ἄρα πᾶσιν ἐπαρξάμενοι δεπάεσσιν.
αὐτὰρ ἐπεὶ σπεῖσάν τ' ἔπιόν θ' ὅσον ἤθελε θυμός,
ὁρμῶντ' ἐκ κλισίης Ἀγαμέμνονος Ἀτρεΐδαο.
τοῖσι δὲ πόλλ' ἐπέτελλε Γερήνιος ἱππότα Νέστωρ
δενδίλλων ἐς ἕκαστον, Ὀδυσσῆϊ δὲ μάλιστα,                  180
πειρᾶν ὡς πεπίθοιεν ἀμύμονα Πηλεΐωνα.
    Τὼ δὲ βάτην παρὰ θῖνα πολυφλοίσβοιο θαλάσσης
πολλὰ μάλ' εὐχομένω γαιηόχῳ ἐννοσιγαίῳ
ῥηϊδίως πεπιθεῖν μεγάλας φρένας Αἰακίδαο.
Μυρμιδόνων δ' ἐπί τε κλισίας καὶ νῆας ἱκέσθην,            185
τὸν δ' εὗρον φρένα τερπόμενον φόρμιγγι λιγείῃ,
καλῇ δαιδαλέῃ, ἐπὶ δ' ἀργύρεον ζυγὸν ἦεν,

τὴν ἄρετ' ἐξ ἐνάρων πόλιν Ἠετίωνος ὀλέσσας·
τῇ ὅ γε θυμὸν ἔτερπεν, ἄειδε δ' ἄρα κλέα ἀνδρῶν.
Πάτροκλος δέ οἱ οἶος ἐναντίος ἧστο σιωπῇ,                                     190
δέγμενος Αἰακίδην ὁπότε λήξειεν ἀείδων.
τὼ δὲ βάτην προτέρω, ἡγεῖτο δὲ δῖος Ὀδυσσεύς,
στὰν δὲ πρόσθ' αὐτοῖο· ταφὼν δ' ἀνόρουσεν Ἀχιλλεὺς
αὐτῇ σὺν φόρμιγγι, λιπὼν ἕδος ἔνθα θάασσεν.
ὣς δ' αὔτως Πάτροκλος, ἐπεὶ ἴδε φῶτας, ἀνέστη.                               195
τὼ καὶ δεικνύμενος προσέφη πόδας ὠκὺς Ἀχιλλεύς·
"χαίρετον· ἦ φίλοι ἄνδρες ἱκάνετον· ἦ τι μάλα χρεώ,
οἵ μοι σκυζομένῳ περ Ἀχαιῶν φίλτατοί ἐστον."
Ὣς ἄρα φωνήσας προτέρω ἄγε δῖος Ἀχιλλεύς,
εἶσεν δ' ἐν κλισμοῖσι τάπησί τε πορφυρέοισιν.                                 200
αἶψα δὲ Πάτροκλον προσεφώνεεν ἐγγὺς ἐόντα·
"μείζονα δὴ κρητῆρα, Μενοιτίου υἱέ, καθίστα,
ζωρότερον δὲ κέραιε, δέπας δ' ἔντυνον ἑκάστῳ·
οἱ γὰρ φίλτατοι ἄνδρες ἐμῷ ὑπέασι μελάθρῳ."
Ὣς φάτο, Πάτροκλος δὲ φίλῳ ἐπεπείθεθ' ἑταίρῳ.                                205
αὐτὰρ ὅ γε κρεῖον μέγα κάββαλεν ἐν πυρὸς αὐγῇ,
ἐν δ' ἄρα νῶτον ἔθηκ' ὄιος καὶ πίονος αἰγός,
ἐν δὲ συὸς σιάλοιο ῥάχιν τεθαλυῖαν ἀλοιφῇ.
τῷ δ' ἔχεν Αὐτομέδων, τάμνεν δ' ἄρα δῖος Ἀχιλλεύς·
καὶ τὰ μὲν εὖ μίστυλλε καὶ ἀμφ' ὀβελοῖσιν ἔπειρε,                            210
πῦρ δὲ Μενοιτιάδης δαῖεν μέγα ἰσόθεος φώς.
αὐτὰρ ἐπεὶ κατὰ πῦρ ἐκάη καὶ φλὸξ ἐμαράνθη,
ἀνθρακιὴν στορέσας ὀβελοὺς ἐφύπερθε τάνυσσε,
πάσσε δ' ἁλὸς θείοιο κρατευτάων ἐπαείρας.
αὐτὰρ ἐπεί ῥ' ὤπτησε καὶ εἰν ἐλεοῖσιν ἔχευε,                                 215
Πάτροκλος μὲν σῖτον ἑλὼν ἐπένειμε τραπέζῃ
καλοῖς ἐν κανέοισιν, ἀτὰρ κρέα νεῖμεν Ἀχιλλεύς.
αὐτὸς δ' ἀντίον ἷζεν Ὀδυσσῆος θείοιο
τοίχου τοῦ ἑτέροιο, θεοῖσι δὲ θῦσαι ἀνώγει
Πάτροκλον, ὃν ἑταῖρον· ὁ δ' ἐν πυρὶ βάλλε θυηλάς.                            220
οἱ δ' ἐπ' ὀνείαθ' ἑτοῖμα προκείμενα χεῖρας ἴαλλον.
αὐτὰρ ἐπεὶ πόσιος καὶ ἐδητύος ἐξ ἔρον ἕντο,
νεῦσ' Αἴας Φοίνικι· νόησε δὲ δῖος Ὀδυσσεύς,
πλησάμενος δ' οἴνοιο δέπας δείδεκτ' Ἀχιλῆα·
"χαῖρ', Ἀχιλεῦ· δαιτὸς μὲν ἐίσης οὐκ ἐπιδευεῖς                               225

197 ἦ τι μάλα χρεώ: ἡμέτερόνδε Al.    198 φιλτάτω a    212 αὐτὰρ ἐπεὶ πυρὸς
ἄνθος ἀπέπτατο παύσατο δὲ φλόξ b

ἠμὲν ἐνὶ κλισίῃ Ἀγαμέμνονος Ἀτρεΐδαο
ἠδὲ καὶ ἐνθάδε νῦν, πάρα γὰρ μενοεικέα πολλὰ
δαίνυσθ'· ἀλλ' οὐ δαιτὸς ἐπηράτου ἔργα μέμηλεν,
ἀλλὰ λίην μέγα πῆμα, διοτρεφές, εἰσορόωντες
δείδιμεν· ἐν δοιῇ δὲ σαωσέμεν ἢ ἀπολέσθαι                    230
νῆας ἐϋσσέλμους, εἰ μὴ σύ γε δύσεαι ἀλκήν.
ἐγγὺς γὰρ νηῶν καὶ τείχεος αὖλιν ἔθεντο
Τρῶες ὑπέρθυμοι τηλεκλειτοί τ' ἐπίκουροι
κηάμενοι πυρὰ πολλὰ κατὰ στρατόν, οὐδ' ἔτι φασὶ
σχήσεσθ', ἀλλ' ἐν νηυσὶ μελαίνῃσιν πεσέεσθαι.              235
Ζεὺς δέ σφι Κρονίδης ἐνδέξια σήματα φαίνων
ἀστράπτει· Ἕκτωρ δὲ μέγα σθένεϊ βλεμεαίνων
μαίνεται ἐκπάγλως πίσυνος Διί, οὐδέ τι τίει
ἀνέρας οὐδὲ θεούς· κρατερὴ δέ ἑ λύσσα δέδυκεν.
ἄραται δὲ τάχιστα φανήμεναι Ἠῶ δῖαν·                        240
στεῦται γὰρ νηῶν ἀποκόψειν ἄκρα κόρυμβα
αὐτάς τ' ἐμπρήσειν μαλεροῦ πυρός, αὐτὰρ Ἀχαιοὺς
δῃώσειν παρὰ τῇσιν ὀρινομένους ὑπὸ καπνοῦ.
ταῦτ' αἰνῶς δείδοικα κατὰ φρένα, μή οἱ ἀπειλὰς
ἐκτελέσωσι θεοί, ἡμῖν δὲ δὴ αἴσιμον εἴη                      245
φθίσθαι ἐνὶ Τροίῃ ἑκὰς Ἄργεος ἱπποβότοιο.
ἀλλ' ἄνα, εἰ μέμονάς γε καὶ ὀψέ περ υἷας Ἀχαιῶν
τειρομένους ἐρύεσθαι ὑπὸ Τρώων ὀρυμαγδοῦ.
αὐτῷ τοι μετόπισθ' ἄχος ἔσσεται, οὐδέ τι μῆχος
ῥεχθέντος κακοῦ ἔστ' ἄκος εὑρεῖν· ἀλλὰ πολὺ πρὶν          250
φράζευ ὅπως Δαναοῖσιν ἀλεξήσεις κακὸν ἦμαρ.
ὦ πέπον, ἦ μὲν σοί γε πατὴρ ἐπετέλλετο Πηλεὺς
ἤματι τῷ ὅτε σ' ἐκ Φθίης Ἀγαμέμνονι πέμπε·
'τέκνον ἐμόν, κάρτος μὲν Ἀθηναίη τε καὶ Ἥρη
δώσουσ' αἴ κ' ἐθέλωσι, σὺ δὲ μεγαλήτορα θυμὸν             255
ἴσχειν ἐν στήθεσσι· φιλοφροσύνη γὰρ ἀμείνων·
ληγέμεναι δ' ἔριδος κακομηχάνου, ὄφρα σε μᾶλλον
τίωσ' Ἀργείων ἠμὲν νέοι ἠδὲ γέροντες.'
ὣς ἐπέτελλ' ὁ γέρων, σὺ δὲ λήθεαι· ἀλλ' ἔτι καὶ νῦν
παύε', ἔα δὲ χόλον θυμαλγέα· σοὶ δ' Ἀγαμέμνων            260
ἄξια δῶρα δίδωσι μεταλλήξαντι χόλοιο.
εἰ δὲ σὺ μέν μευ ἄκουσον, ἐγὼ δέ κέ τοι καταλέξω
ὅσσα τοι ἐν κλισίῃσιν ὑπέσχετο δῶρ' Ἀγαμέμνων·

230 σαωσέμεν: σόας ἔμεν, σάους ἔμεν C.19.

ἕπτ' ἀπύρους τρίποδας, δέκα δὲ χρυσοῖο τάλαντα,
αἴθωνας δὲ λέβητας ἐείκοσι, δώδεκα δ' ἵππους        265
πηγοὺς ἀθλοφόρους, οἳ ἀέθλια ποσσὶν ἄροντο.
οὔ κεν ἀλήϊος εἴη ἀνὴρ ᾧ τόσσα γένοιτο,
οὐδέ κεν ἀκτήμων ἐριτίμοιο χρυσοῖο,
ὅσσ' Ἀγαμέμνονος ἵπποι ἀέθλια ποσσὶν ἄροντο.
δώσει δ' ἑπτὰ γυναῖκας ἀμύμονα ἔργα ἰδυίας,        270
Λεσβίδας, ἃς ὅτε Λέσβον ἐϋκτιμένην ἕλες αὐτὸς
ἐξέλεθ', αἳ τότε κάλλει ἐνίκων φῦλα γυναικῶν.
τὰς μέν τοι δώσει, μετὰ δ' ἔσσεται ἣν τότ' ἀπηύρα,
κούρη Βρισῆος· ἐπὶ δὲ μέγαν ὅρκον ὀμεῖται
μή ποτε τῆς εὐνῆς ἐπιβήμεναι ἠδὲ μιγῆναι,        275
ἣ θέμις ἐστίν, ἄναξ, ἤ τ' ἀνδρῶν ἤ τε γυναικῶν.
ταῦτα μὲν αὐτίκα πάντα παρέσσεται· εἰ δέ κεν αὖτε
ἄστυ μέγα Πριάμοιο θεοὶ δώωσ' ἀλαπάξαι,
νῆα ἅλις χρυσοῦ καὶ χαλκοῦ νηήσασθαι
εἰσελθών, ὅτε κεν δατεώμεθα ληΐδ' Ἀχαιοί,        280
Τρωϊάδας δὲ γυναῖκας ἐείκοσιν αὐτὸς ἑλέσθαι,
αἵ κε μετ' Ἀργείην Ἑλένην κάλλισται ἔωσιν.
εἰ δέ κεν Ἄργος ἱκοίμεθ' Ἀχαιϊκόν, οὖθαρ ἀρούρης,
γαμβρός κέν οἱ ἔοις· τείσει δέ σε ἶσον Ὀρέστῃ,
ὅς οἱ τηλύγετος τρέφεται θαλίῃ ἔνι πολλῇ.        285
τρεῖς δέ οἵ εἰσι θύγατρες ἐνὶ μεγάρῳ εὐπήκτῳ,
Χρυσόθεμις καὶ Λαοδίκη καὶ Ἰφιάνασσα·
τάων ἥν κ' ἐθέλῃσθα φίλην ἀνάεδνον ἄγεσθαι
πρὸς οἶκον Πηλῆος· ὁ δ' αὖτ' ἐπὶ μείλια δώσει
πολλὰ μάλ', ὅσσ' οὔ πώ τις ἑῇ ἐπέδωκε θυγατρί·        290
ἑπτὰ δέ τοι δώσει εὖ ναιόμενα πτολίεθρα,
Καρδαμύλην Ἐνόπην τε καὶ Ἱρὴν ποιήεσσαν
Φηράς τε ζαθέας ἠδ' Ἄνθειαν βαθύλειμον
καλήν τ' Αἴπειαν καὶ Πήδασον ἀμπελόεσσαν.
πᾶσαι δ' ἐγγὺς ἁλός, νέαται Πύλου ἠμαθόεντος·        295
ἐν δ' ἄνδρες ναίουσι πολύρρηνες πολυβοῦται,
οἵ κέ σε δωτίνῃσι θεὸν ὣς τιμήσουσι
καί τοι ὑπὸ σκήπτρῳ λιπαρὰς τελέουσι θέμιστας.
ταῦτά κέ τοι τελέσειε μεταλλήξαντι χόλοιο.
εἰ δέ τοι Ἀτρεΐδης μὲν ἀπήχθετο κηρόθι μᾶλλον,        300
αὐτὸς καὶ τοῦ δῶρα, σὺ δ' ἄλλους περ Παναχαιοὺς
τειρομένους ἐλέαιρε κατὰ στρατόν, οἵ σε θεὸν ὣς
τίσουσ'· ἦ γάρ κέ σφι μάλα μέγα κῦδος ἄροιο·

νῦν γάρ χ' Ἕκτορ' ἕλοις, ἐπεὶ ἂν μάλα τοι σχεδὸν ἔλθοι
λύσσαν ἔχων ὀλοήν, ἐπεὶ οὔ τινά φησιν ὁμοῖον            305
οἳ ἔμεναι Δαναῶν οὓς ἐνθάδε νῆες ἔνεικαν."
    Τὸν δ' ἀπαμειβόμενος προσέφη πόδας ὠκὺς Ἀχιλλεύς·
"διογενὲς Λαερτιάδη, πολυμήχαν' Ὀδυσσεῦ,
χρὴ μὲν δὴ τὸν μῦθον ἀπηλεγέως ἀποειπεῖν,
ᾗ περ δὴ φρονέω τε καὶ ὡς τετελεσμένον ἔσται,            310
ὡς μή μοι τρύζητε παρήμενοι ἄλλοθεν ἄλλος.
ἐχθρὸς γάρ μοι κεῖνος ὁμῶς Ἀΐδαο πύλῃσιν
ὅς χ' ἕτερον μὲν κεύθῃ ἐνὶ φρεσίν, ἄλλο δὲ εἴπῃ.
αὐτὰρ ἐγὼν ἐρέω ὥς μοι δοκεῖ εἶναι ἄριστα·
οὔτ' ἔμεγ' Ἀτρεΐδην Ἀγαμέμνονα πεισέμεν οἴω            315
οὔτ' ἄλλους Δαναούς, ἐπεὶ οὐκ ἄρα τις χάρις ἦεν
μάρνασθαι δηΐοισιν ἐπ' ἀνδράσι νωλεμὲς αἰεί.
ἴση μοῖρα μένοντι καὶ εἰ μάλα τις πολεμίζοι·
ἐν δὲ ἰῇ τιμῇ ἠμὲν κακὸς ἠδὲ καὶ ἐσθλός·
κάτθαν' ὁμῶς ὅ τ' ἀεργὸς ἀνὴρ ὅ τε πολλὰ ἐοργώς.       320
οὐδέ τί μοι περίκειται, ἐπεὶ πάθον ἄλγεα θυμῷ,
αἰεὶ ἐμὴν ψυχὴν παραβαλλόμενος πολεμίζειν.
ὡς δ' ὄρνις ἀπτῆσι νεοσσοῖσι προφέρῃσι
μάστακ', ἐπεί κε λάβῃσι, κακῶς δ' ἄρα οἱ πέλει αὐτῇ,
ὣς καὶ ἐγὼ πολλὰς μὲν ἀΰπνους νύκτας ἴαυον,            325
ἤματα δ' αἱματόεντα διέπρησσον πολεμίζων,
ἀνδράσι μαρνάμενος ὀάρων ἕνεκα σφετεράων.
δώδεκα δὴ σὺν νηυσὶ πόλεις ἀλάπαξ' ἀνθρώπων,
πεζὸς δ' ἕνδεκά φημι κατὰ Τροίην ἐρίβωλον·
τάων ἐκ πασέων κειμήλια πολλὰ καὶ ἐσθλὰ               330
ἐξελόμην, καὶ πάντα φέρων Ἀγαμέμνονι δόσκον
Ἀτρεΐδῃ· ὁ δ' ὄπισθε μένων παρὰ νηυσὶ θοῇσι
δεξάμενος διὰ παῦρα δασάσκετο, πολλὰ δ' ἔχεσκεν.
ἄλλα δ' ἀριστήεσσι δίδου γέρα καὶ βασιλεῦσι,
τοῖσι μὲν ἔμπεδα κεῖται, ἐμεῦ δ' ἀπὸ μούνου Ἀχαιῶν      335
εἵλετ', ἔχει δ' ἄλοχον θυμαρέα· τῇ παριαύων
τερπέσθω. τί δὲ δεῖ πολεμιζέμεναι Τρώεσσιν
Ἀργείους; τί δὲ λαὸν ἀνήγαγεν ἐνθάδ' ἀγείρας
Ἀτρεΐδης; ἦ οὐχ Ἑλένης ἕνεκ' ἠϋκόμοιο;
ἦ μοῦνοι φιλέουσ' ἀλόχους μερόπων ἀνθρώπων            340
Ἀτρεΐδαι; ἐπεὶ ὅς τις ἀνὴρ ἀγαθὸς καὶ ἐχέφρων

---

314 ὡς καὶ τετελεσμένον ἔσται **a**, cf. 310          320 line rejected C.19.
327 μαρναμένοις C.19.

63

τὴν αὐτοῦ φιλέει καὶ κήδεται, ὡς καὶ ἐγὼ τὴν
ἐκ θυμοῦ φίλεον, δουρικτητήν περ ἐοῦσαν.
νῦν δ' ἐπεὶ ἐκ χειρῶν γέρας εἵλετο καί μ' ἀπάτησε,
μή μευ πειράτω εὖ εἰδότος· οὐδέ με πείσει.                    345
ἀλλ', Ὀδυσεῦ, σὺν σοί τε καὶ ἄλλοισιν βασιλεῦσι
φραζέσθω νήεσσιν ἀλεξέμεναι δήϊον πῦρ.
ἦ μὲν δὴ μάλα πολλὰ πονήσατο νόσφιν ἐμεῖο,
καὶ δὴ τεῖχος ἔδειμε, καὶ ἤλασε τάφρον ἐπ' αὐτῷ
εὐρεῖαν μεγάλην, ἐν δὲ σκόλοπας κατέπηξεν·                    350
ἀλλ' οὐδ' ὣς δύναται σθένος Ἕκτορος ἀνδροφόνοιο
ἴσχειν· ὄφρα δ' ἐγὼ μετ' Ἀχαιοῖσιν πολέμιζον,
οὐκ ἐθέλεσκε μάχην ἀπὸ τείχεος ὀρνύμεν Ἕκτωρ,
ἀλλ' ὅσον ἐς Σκαιάς τε πύλας καὶ φηγὸν ἵκανεν·
ἔνθα ποτ' οἶον ἔμιμνε, μόγις δέ μευ ἔκφυγεν ὁρμήν.           355
νῦν δ' ἐπεὶ οὐκ ἐθέλω πολεμιζέμεν Ἕκτορι δίῳ,
αὔριον ἱρὰ Διὶ ῥέξας καὶ πᾶσι θεοῖσι,
νηήσας εὖ νῆας, ἐπὴν ἅλαδε προερύσσω,
ὄψεαι, αἴ κ' ἐθέλῃσθα καὶ αἴ κέν τοι τὰ μεμήλῃ,
ἦρι μάλ' Ἑλλήσποντον ἐπ' ἰχθυόεντα πλεούσας               360
νῆας ἐμάς, ἐν δ' ἄνδρας ἐρεσσέμεναι μεμαῶτας·
εἰ δέ κεν εὐπλοίην δώῃ κλυτὸς ἐννοσίγαιος
ἤματί κε τριτάτῳ Φθίην ἐρίβωλον ἱκοίμην.
ἔστι δέ μοι μάλα πολλά, τὰ κάλλιπον ἐνθάδε ἔρρων·
ἄλλον δ' ἐνθένδε χρυσὸν καὶ χαλκὸν ἐρυθρὸν                  365
ἠδὲ γυναῖκας ἐϋζώνους πολιόν τε σίδηρον
ἄξομαι, ἅσσ' ἔλαχόν γε· γέρας δέ μοι, ὅς περ ἔδωκεν,
αὖτις ἐφυβρίζων ἕλετο κρείων Ἀγαμέμνων
Ἀτρεΐδης· τῷ πάντ' ἀγορευέμεν ὡς ἐπιτέλλω
ἀμφαδόν, ὄφρα καὶ ἄλλοι ἐπισκύζωνται Ἀχαιοί,             370
εἴ τινά που Δαναῶν ἔτι ἔλπεται ἐξαπατήσειν
αἰὲν ἀναιδείην ἐπιειμένος· οὐδ' ἂν ἔμοιγε
τετλαίη κύνεός περ ἐὼν εἰς ὦπα ἰδέσθαι·
οὐδέ τί οἱ βουλὰς συμφράσσομαι, οὐδὲ μὲν ἔργον·
ἐκ γὰρ δή μ' ἀπάτησε καὶ ἤλιτεν· οὐδ' ἂν ἔτ' αὖτις         375
ἐξαπάφοιτ' ἐπέεσσιν· ἅλις δέ οἱ· ἀλλὰ ἕκηλος
ἐρρέτω· ἐκ γάρ εὖ φρένας εἵλετο μητίετα Ζεύς.
ἐχθρὰ δέ μοι τοῦ δῶρα, τίω δέ μιν ἐν καρὸς αἴσῃ.
οὐδ' εἴ μοι δεκάκις τε καὶ εἰκοσάκις τόσα δοίη
ὅσσά τέ οἱ νῦν ἔστι, καὶ εἴ ποθεν ἄλλα γένοιτο,           380
οὐδ' ὅσ' ἐς Ὀρχομενὸν ποτινίσεται, οὐδ' ὅσα Θήβας

Αἰγυπτίας, ὅθι πλεῖστα δόμοις ἐν κτήματα κεῖται,
αἵ θ' ἑκατόμπυλοί εἰσι, διηκόσιοι δ' ἀν' ἑκάστας
ἀνέρες ἐξοιχνεῦσι σὺν ἵπποισιν καὶ ὄχεσφιν·
οὐδ' εἴ μοι τόσα δοίη ὅσα ψάμαθός τε κόνις τε,                          385
οὐδέ κεν ὧς ἔτι θυμὸν ἐμὸν πείσει' Ἀγαμέμνων,
πρίν γ' ἀπὸ πᾶσαν ἐμοὶ δόμεναι θυμαλγέα λώβην.
κούρην δ' οὐ γαμέω Ἀγαμέμνονος Ἀτρεΐδαο,
οὐδ' εἰ χρυσείῃ Ἀφροδίτῃ κάλλος ἐρίζοι,
ἔργα δ' Ἀθηναίῃ γλαυκώπιδι ἰσοφαρίζοι·                                390
οὐδέ μιν ὧς γαμέω· ὁ δ' Ἀχαιῶν ἄλλον ἑλέσθω,
ὅς τις οἷ τ' ἐπέοικε καὶ ὃς βασιλεύτερός ἐστιν.
ἢν γὰρ δή με σαῶσι θεοὶ καὶ οἴκαδ' ἵκωμαι,
Πηλεύς θήν μοι ἔπειτα γυναῖκά γε μάσσεται αὐτός.
πολλαὶ Ἀχαιΐδες εἰσὶν ἀν' Ἑλλάδα τε Φθίην τε,                         395
κοῦραι ἀριστήων, οἵ τε πτολίεθρα ῥύονται·
τάων ἥν κ' ἐθέλωμι φίλην ποιήσομ' ἄκοιτιν.
ἔνθα δέ μοι μάλα πολλὸν ἐπέσσυτο θυμὸς ἀγήνωρ
γήμαντα μνηστὴν ἄλοχον, ἐϊκυῖαν ἄκοιτιν,
κτήμασι τέρπεσθαι τὰ γέρων ἐκτήσατο Πηλεύς·                          400
οὐ γὰρ ἐμοὶ ψυχῆς ἀντάξιον οὐδ' ὅσα φασὶν
Ἴλιον ἐκτῆσθαι εὖ ναιόμενον πτολίεθρον
τὸ πρὶν ἐπ' εἰρήνης, πρὶν ἐλθεῖν υἷας Ἀχαιῶν,
οὐδ' ὅσα λάϊνος οὐδὸς ἀφήτορος ἐντὸς ἐέργει,
Φοίβου Ἀπόλλωνος, Πυθοῖ ἔνι πετρηέσσῃ.                               405
ληϊστοὶ μὲν γάρ τε βόες καὶ ἴφια μῆλα,
κτητοὶ δὲ τρίποδές τε καὶ ἵππων ξανθὰ κάρηνα·
ἀνδρὸς δὲ ψυχὴ πάλιν ἐλθεῖν οὔτε λεϊστὴ
οὔθ' ἑλετή, ἐπεὶ ἄρ κεν ἀμείψεται ἕρκος ὀδόντων.
μήτηρ γάρ τέ μέ φησι θεὰ Θέτις ἀργυρόπεζα                            410
διχθαδίας κῆρας φερέμεν θανάτοιο τέλοσδε.
εἰ μέν κ' αὖθι μένων Τρώων πόλιν ἀμφιμάχωμαι,
ὤλετο μέν μοι νόστος, ἀτὰρ κλέος ἄφθιτον ἔσται·
εἰ δέ κεν οἴκαδ' ἵωμι φίλην ἐς πατρίδα γαῖαν,
ὤλετό μοι κλέος ἐσθλόν, ἐπὶ δηρὸν δέ μοι αἰὼν                        415
ἔσσεται, οὐδέ κέ μ' ὦκα τέλος θανάτοιο κιχείη.
καὶ δ' ἂν τοῖς ἄλλοισιν ἐγὼ παραμυθησαίμην
οἴκαδ' ἀποπλείειν, ἐπεὶ οὐκέτι δήετε τέκμωρ
Ἰλίου αἰπεινῆς· μάλα γάρ ἕθεν εὐρύοπα Ζεὺς

382; 383-4: lines rejected C.19.        394 γε μάσσεται Al; γαμέσσεται MSS
414 ἵωμι C.19; ἵκωμαι a.        416 line rejected Al.

χεῖρα ἑὴν ὑπερέσχε, τεθαρσήκασι δὲ λαοί.　420
ἀλλ' ὑμεῖς μὲν ἰόντες ἀριστήεσσιν Ἀχαιῶν
ἀγγελίην ἀπόφασθε—τὸ γὰρ γέρας ἐστὶ γερόντων—
ὄφρ' ἄλλην φράζωνται ἐνὶ φρεσὶ μῆτιν ἀμείνω,
ἥ κέ σφιν νῆάς τε σαῷ καὶ λαὸν Ἀχαιῶν
νηυσὶν ἔπι γλαφυρῇς, ἐπεὶ οὔ σφισιν ἥδε γ' ἑτοίμη,　425
ἣν νῦν ἐφράσσαντο ἐμεῦ ἀπομηνίσαντος·
Φοῖνιξ δ' αὖθι παρ' ἄμμι μένων κατακοιμηθήτω,
ὄφρα μοι ἐν νήεσσι φίλην ἐς πατρίδ' ἕπηται
αὔριον, ἢν ἐθέλησιν· ἀνάγκῃ δ' οὔ τί μιν ἄξω."
  Ὣς ἔφαθ', οἱ δ' ἄρα πάντες ἀκὴν ἐγένοντο σιωπῇ　430
μῦθον ἀγασσάμενοι· μάλα γὰρ κρατερῶς ἀπέειπεν·
ὀψὲ δὲ δὴ μετέειπε γέρων ἱππηλάτα Φοῖνιξ
δάκρυ' ἀναπρήσας· περὶ γὰρ δίε νηυσὶν Ἀχαιῶν·
"εἰ μὲν δὴ νόστόν γε μετὰ φρεσί, φαίδιμ' Ἀχιλλεῦ,
βάλλεαι, οὐδέ τι πάμπαν ἀμύνειν νηυσὶ θοῇσι　435
πῦρ ἐθέλεις ἀΐδηλον, ἐπεὶ χόλος ἔμπεσε θυμῷ,
πῶς ἂν ἔπειτ' ἀπὸ σεῖο, φίλον τέκος, αὖθι λιποίμην
οἶος; σοὶ δέ μ' ἔπεμπε γέρων ἱππηλάτα Πηλεὺς
ἤματι τῷ ὅτε σ' ἐκ Φθίης Ἀγαμέμνονι πέμπε
νήπιον, οὔ πω εἰδόθ' ὁμοιίου πολέμοιο,　440
οὐδ' ἀγορέων, ἵνα τ' ἄνδρες ἀριπρεπέες τελέθουσι.
τοὔνεκά με προέηκε διδασκέμεναι τάδε πάντα,
μύθων τε ῥητῆρ' ἔμεναι πρηκτῆρά τε ἔργων.
ὡς ἂν ἔπειτ' ἀπὸ σεῖο, φίλον τέκος, οὐκ ἐθέλοιμι
λείπεσθ', οὐδ' εἴ κέν μοι ὑποσταίη θεὸς αὐτὸς　445
γῆρας ἀποξύσας θήσειν νέον ἡβώοντα,
οἷον ὅτε πρῶτον λίπον Ἑλλάδα καλλιγύναικα
φεύγων νείκεα πατρὸς Ἀμύντορος Ὁρμενίδαο,
ὅς μοι παλλακίδος περιχώσατο καλλικόμοιο,
τὴν αὐτὸς φιλέεσκεν, ἀτιμάζεσκε δ' ἄκοιτιν,　450
μητέρ' ἐμήν· ἡ δ' αἰὲν ἐμὲ λισσέσκετο γούνων
παλλακίδι προμιγῆναι, ἵν' ἐχθήρειε γέροντα.
τῇ πιθόμην καὶ ἔρεξα· πατὴρ δ' ἐμὸς αὐτίκ' ὀϊσθεὶς
πολλὰ κατηρᾶτο, στυγερὰς δ' ἐπεκέκλετ' Ἐρινῦς,
μή ποτε γούνασιν οἷσιν ἐφέσσεσθαι φίλον υἱὸν　455
ἐξ ἐμέθεν γεγαῶτα· θεοὶ δ' ἐτέλειον ἐπαράς,
Ζεύς τε καταχθόνιος καὶ ἐπαινὴ Περσεφόνεια.　457

453 τῇ οὐ πιθόμην οὐδ' ἔρξα Al.

ἔνθ' ἐμοὶ οὐκέτι πάμπαν ἐρητύετ' ἐν φρεσὶ θυμὸς                            462
πατρὸς χωομένοιο κατὰ μέγαρα στρωφᾶσθαι.
ἦ μὲν πολλὰ ἔται καὶ ἀνεψιοὶ ἀμφὶς ἐόντες
αὐτοῦ λισσόμενοι κατερήτυον ἐν μεγάροισι,                                  465
πολλὰ δὲ ἴφια μῆλα καὶ εἰλίποδας ἕλικας βοῦς
ἔσφαζον, πολλοὶ δὲ σύες θαλέθοντες ἀλοιφῇ
εὑόμενοι τανύοντο διὰ φλογὸς Ἡφαίστοιο,
πολλὸν δ' ἐκ κεράμων μέθυ πίνετο τοῖο γέροντος.
εἰνάνυχες δέ μοι ἀμφ' αὐτῷ παρὰ νύκτας ἴαυον·                             470
οἱ μὲν ἀμειβόμενοι φυλακὰς ἔχον, οὐδέ ποτ' ἔσβη
πῦρ, ἕτερον μὲν ὑπ' αἰθούσῃ εὐερκέος αὐλῆς,
ἄλλο δ' ἐνὶ προδόμῳ, πρόσθεν θαλάμοιο θυράων.
ἀλλ' ὅτε δὴ δεκάτη μοι ἐπήλυθε νὺξ ἐρεβεννή,
καὶ τότ' ἐγὼ θαλάμοιο θύρας πυκινῶς ἀραρυίας                              475
ῥήξας ἐξῆλθον, καὶ ὑπέρθορον ἑρκίον αὐλῆς
ῥεῖα, λαθὼν φύλακάς τ' ἄνδρας δμῳάς τε γυναῖκας.
φεῦγον ἔπειτ' ἀπάνευθε δι' Ἑλλάδος εὐρυχόροιο,
Φθίην δ' ἐξικόμην ἐριβώλακα, μητέρα μήλων,
ἐς Πηλῆα ἄναχθ'· ὁ δέ με πρόφρων ὑπέδεκτο,                               480
καί μ' ἐφίλησ' ὡς εἴ τε πατὴρ ὃν παῖδα φιλήσῃ
μοῦνον τηλύγετον πολλοῖσιν ἐπὶ κτεάτεσσι,
καί μ' ἀφνειὸν ἔθηκε, πολὺν δέ μοι ὤπασε λαόν·
ναῖον δ' ἐσχατιὴν Φθίης, Δολόπεσσιν ἀνάσσων.
καί σε τοσοῦτον ἔθηκα, θεοῖς ἐπιείκελ' Ἀχιλλεῦ,                          485
ἐκ θυμοῦ φιλέων, ἐπεὶ οὐκ ἐθέλεσκες ἅμ' ἄλλῳ
οὔτ' ἐς δαῖτ' ἰέναι οὔτ' ἐν μεγάροισι πάσασθαι,
πρίν γ' ὅτε δή σ' ἐπ' ἐμοῖσιν ἐγὼ γούνεσσι καθίσσας
ὄψου τ' ἄσαιμι προταμὼν καὶ οἶνον ἐπισχών.
πολλάκι μοι κατέδευσας ἐπὶ στήθεσσι χιτῶνα                                490
οἴνου ἀποβλύζων ἐν νηπιέῃ ἀλεγεινῇ.
ὣς ἐπὶ σοὶ μάλα πολλ' ἔπαθον καὶ πόλλ' ἐμόγησα,
τὰ φρονέων, ὅ μοι οὔ τι θεοὶ γόνον ἐξετέλειον
ἐξ ἐμεῦ· ἀλλὰ σὲ παῖδα, θεοῖς ἐπιείκελ' Ἀχιλλεῦ,
ποιεύμην, ἵνα μοί ποτ' ἀεικέα λοιγὸν ἀμύνῃς.                             495
ἀλλ', Ἀχιλεῦ, δάμασον θυμὸν μέγαν· οὐδέ τί σε χρὴ
νηλεὲς ἦτορ ἔχειν· στρεπτοὶ δέ τε καὶ θεοὶ αὐτοί,
τῶν περ καὶ μείζων ἀρετὴ τιμή τε βίη τε.

458–61 τὸν μὲν ἐγὼ βούλευσα κατακτάμεν ὀξέι χαλκῷ, | ἀλλά τις ἀθανάτων παῦσεν
χόλον, ὅς ῥ' ἐνὶ θυμῷ | δήμου θῆκε φάτιν καὶ ὀνείδεα πόλλ' ἀνθρώπων, | ὡς μὴ πατροφόνος
μετ' Ἀχαιοῖσιν καλεοίμην b

καὶ μὲν τοὺς θυέεσσι καὶ εὐχωλῇς ἀγανῇσι
λοιβῇ τε κνίσῃ τε παρατρωπῶσ᾽ ἄνθρωποι     500
λισσόμενοι, ὅτε κέν τις ὑπερβήῃ καὶ ἁμάρτῃ.
καὶ γάρ τε Λιταί εἰσι Διὸς κοῦραι μεγάλοιο,
χωλαί τε ῥυσαί τε παραβλῶπές τ᾽ ὀφθαλμώ,
αἵ ῥά τε καὶ μετόπισθ᾽ Ἄτης ἀλέγουσι κιοῦσαι.
ἡ δ᾽ Ἄτη σθεναρή τε καὶ ἀρτίπος, οὕνεκα πάσας     505
πολλὸν ὑπεκπροθέει, φθάνει δέ τε πᾶσαν ἐπ᾽ αἶαν
βλάπτουσ᾽ ἀνθρώπους· αἱ δ᾽ ἐξακέονται ὀπίσσω.
ὃς μέν τ᾽ αἰδέσεται κούρας Διὸς ἆσσον ἰούσας,
τὸν δὲ μέγ᾽ ὤνησαν καί τ᾽ ἔκλυον εὐχομένοιο·
ὃς δέ κ᾽ ἀνήνηται καί τε στερεῶς ἀποείπῃ,     510
λίσσονται δ᾽ ἄρα ταί γε Δία Κρονίωνα κιοῦσαι
τῷ Ἄτην ἅμ᾽ ἕπεσθαι, ἵνα βλαφθεὶς ἀποτείσῃ.
ἀλλ᾽, Ἀχιλεῦ, πόρε καὶ σὺ Διὸς κούρῃσιν ἕπεσθαι
τιμήν, ἥ τ᾽ ἄλλων περ ἐπιγνάμπτει νόον ἐσθλῶν.
εἰ μὲν γὰρ μὴ δῶρα φέροι, τὰ δ᾽ ὄπισθ᾽ ὀνομάζοι     515
Ἀτρεΐδης, ἀλλ᾽ αἰὲν ἐπιζαφελῶς χαλεπαίνοι,
οὐκ ἂν ἔγωγέ σε μῆνιν ἀπορρίψαντα κελοίμην
Ἀργείοισιν ἀμυνέμεναι χατέουσί περ ἔμπης·
νῦν δ᾽ ἅμα τ᾽ αὐτίκα πολλὰ διδοῖ, τὰ δ᾽ ὄπισθεν ὑπέστη,
ἄνδρας δὲ λίσσεσθαι ἐπιπροέηκεν ἀρίστους     520
κρινάμενος κατὰ λαὸν Ἀχαιϊκόν, οἵ τε σοὶ αὐτῷ
φίλτατοι Ἀργείων· τῶν μὴ σύ γε μῦθον ἐλέγξῃς
μηδὲ πόδας· πρὶν δ᾽ οὔ τι νεμεσσητὸν κεχολῶσθαι.
οὕτω καὶ τῶν πρόσθεν ἐπευθόμεθα κλέα ἀνδρῶν
ἡρώων, ὅτε κέν τιν᾽ ἐπιζάφελος χόλος ἵκοι·     525
δωρητοί τε πέλοντο παράρρητοί τ᾽ ἐπέεσσι.
μέμνημαι τόδε ἔργον ἐγὼ πάλαι, οὔ τι νέον γε,
ὡς ἦν· ἐν δ᾽ ὑμῖν ἐρέω πάντεσσι φίλοισι.
Κουρῆτές τε μάχοντο καὶ Αἰτωλοὶ μενεχάρμαι
ἀμφὶ πόλιν Καλυδῶνα καὶ ἀλλήλους ἐνάριζον,     530
Αἰτωλοὶ μὲν ἀμυνόμενοι Καλυδῶνος ἐραννῆς,
Κουρῆτες δὲ διαπραθέειν μεμαῶτες Ἄρηϊ.
καὶ γὰρ τοῖσι κακὸν χρυσόθρονος Ἄρτεμις ὦρσε,
χωσαμένη ὅ οἱ οὔ τι θαλύσια γουνῷ ἀλωῆς
Οἰνεὺς ῥέξ᾽· ἄλλοι δὲ θεοὶ δαίνυνθ᾽ ἑκατόμβας,     535
οἴῃ δ᾽ οὐκ ἔρρεξε Διὸς κούρῃ μεγάλοιο.
ἢ λάθετ᾽ ἢ οὐκ ἐνόησεν· ἀάσατο δὲ μέγα θυμῷ.
ἡ δὲ χολωσαμένη δῖον γένος ἰοχέαιρα

ὦρσεν ἔπι χλούνην σῦν ἄγριον ἀργιόδοντα,
ὃς κακὰ πόλλ' ἔρδεσκεν ἔθων Οἰνῆος ἀλωήν·       540
πολλὰ δ' ὅ γε προθέλυμνα χαμαὶ βάλε δένδρεα μακρὰ
αὐτῆσιν ῥίζῃσι καὶ αὐτοῖς ἄνθεσι μήλων.
τὸν δ' υἱὸς Οἰνῆος ἀπέκτεινεν Μελέαγρος,
πολλέων ἐκ πολίων θηρήτορας ἄνδρας ἀγείρας
καὶ κύνας· οὐ μὲν γάρ κε δάμη παύροισι βροτοῖσι·      545
τόσσος ἔην, πολλοὺς δὲ πυρῆς ἐπέβησ' ἀλεγεινῆς.
ἡ δ' ἀμφ' αὐτῷ θῆκε πολὺν κέλαδον καὶ ἀϋτήν,
ἀμφὶ συὸς κεφαλῇ καὶ δέρματι λαχνήεντι,
Κουρήτων τε μεσηγὺ καὶ Αἰτωλῶν μεγαθύμων.
ὄφρα μὲν οὖν Μελέαγρος ἀρηίφιλος πολέμιζε,      550
τόφρα δὲ Κουρήτεσσι κακῶς ἦν, οὐδὲ δύναντο
τείχεος ἔκτοσθεν μίμνειν πολέες περ ἐόντες·
ἀλλ' ὅτε δὴ Μελέαγρον ἔδυ χόλος, ὅς τε καὶ ἄλλων
οἰδάνει ἐν στήθεσσι νόον πύκα περ φρονεόντων,
ἤτοι ὁ μητρὶ φίλῃ Ἀλθαίῃ χωόμενος κῆρ      555
κεῖτο παρὰ μνηστῇ ἀλόχῳ καλῇ Κλεοπάτρῃ,
κούρῃ Μαρπήσσης καλλισφύρου Εὐηνίνης
Ἴδεώ θ', ὃς κάρτιστος ἐπιχθονίων γένετ' ἀνδρῶν
τῶν τότε—καί ῥα ἄνακτος ἐναντίον εἵλετο τόξον
Φοίβου Ἀπόλλωνος καλλισφύρου εἵνεκα νύμφης·      560
τὴν δὲ τότ' ἐν μεγάροισι πατὴρ καὶ πότνια μήτηρ
Ἀλκυόνην καλέεσκον ἐπώνυμον, οὕνεκ' ἄρ' αὐτῆς
μήτηρ ἀλκυόνος πολυπενθέος οἶτον ἔχουσα
κλαῖεν ὅ μιν ἑκάεργος ἀνήρπασε Φοῖβος Ἀπόλλων—
τῇ ὅ γε παρκατέλεκτο χόλον θυμαλγέα πέσσων,      565
ἐξ ἀρέων μητρὸς κεχολωμένος, ἥ ῥα θεοῖσι
πόλλ' ἀχέουσ' ἠρᾶτο κασιγνήτοιο φόνοιο,
πολλὰ δὲ καὶ γαῖαν πολυφόρβην χερσὶν ἀλοία
κικλήσκουσ' Ἀΐδην καὶ ἐπαινὴν Περσεφόνειαν,
πρόχνυ καθεζομένη, δεύοντο δὲ δάκρυσι κόλποι,      570
παιδὶ δόμεν θάνατον· τῆς δ' ἠεροφοῖτις Ἐρινὺς
ἔκλυεν ἐξ Ἐρέβεσφιν, ἀμείλιχον ἦτορ ἔχουσα.
τῶν δὲ τάχ' ἀμφὶ πύλας ὅμαδος καὶ δοῦπος ὀρώρει
πύργων βαλλομένων· τὸν δὲ λίσσοντο γέροντες
Αἰτωλῶν, πέμπον δὲ θεῶν ἱερῆας ἀρίστους,      575
ἐξελθεῖν· καὶ ἀμῦναι, ὑποσχόμενοι μέγα δῶρον·

539–40 θρέψεν ἐπὶ χλούνην σῦν ἄγριον, οὐδὲ ἐῴκει | θηρί γε σιτοφάγῳ ἀλλὰ ῥίῳ
ὑλήεντι b, cf. Od. 9. 190f.     571 εἰαροπῶτις b

ὁππόθι πιότατον πεδίον Καλυδῶνος ἐραννῆς,
ἔνθα μιν ἤνωγον τέμενος περικαλλὲς ἑλέσθαι
πεντηκοντόγυον, τὸ μὲν ἥμισυ οἰνοπέδοιο,
ἥμισυ δὲ ψιλὴν ἄροσιν πεδίοιο ταμέσθαι.                      580
πολλὰ δέ μιν λιτάνευε γέρων ἱππηλάτα Οἰνεὺς
οὐδοῦ ἐπεμβεβαὼς ὑψηρεφέος θαλάμοιο,
σείων κολλητὰς σανίδας, γουνούμενος υἱόν·
πολλὰ δὲ τόν γε κασίγνηται καὶ πότνια μήτηρ
ἐλλίσσονθ’, ὁ δὲ μᾶλλον ἀναίνετο· πολλὰ δ’ ἑταῖροι,       585
οἵ οἱ κεδνότατοι καὶ φίλτατοι ἦσαν ἁπάντων·
ἀλλ’ οὐδ’ ὣς τοῦ θυμὸν ἐνὶ στήθεσσιν ἔπειθον,
πρίν γ’ ὅτε δὴ θάλαμος πύκ’ ἐβάλλετο, τοὶ δ’ ἐπὶ πύργων
βαῖνον Κουρῆτες καὶ ἐνέπρηθον μέγα ἄστυ.
καὶ τότε δὴ Μελέαγρον ἐΰζωνος παράκοιτις               590
λίσσετ’ ὀδυρομένη, καί οἱ κατέλεξεν ἅπαντα
κήδε’, ὅσ’ ἀνθρώποισι πέλει τῶν ἄστυ ἁλώῃ·
ἄνδρας μὲν κτείνουσι, πόλιν δέ τε πῦρ ἀμαθύνει,
τέκνα δέ τ’ ἄλλοι ἄγουσι βαθυζώνους τε γυναῖκας.
τοῦ δ’ ὠρίνετο θυμὸς ἀκούοντος κακὰ ἔργα,              595
βῆ δ’ ἰέναι, χροῒ δ’ ἔντε’ ἐδύσετο παμφανόωντα.
ὣς ὁ μὲν Αἰτωλοῖσιν ἀπήμυνεν κακὸν ἦμαρ
εἴξας ᾧ θυμῷ· τῷ δ’ οὐκέτι δῶρ’ ἐτέλεσσαν
πολλά τε καὶ χαρίεντα, κακὸν δ’ ἤμυνε καὶ αὔτως.
ἀλλὰ σὺ μή μοι ταῦτα νόει φρεσί, μηδέ σε δαίμων           600
ἐνταῦθα τρέψειε, φίλος· κάκιον δέ κεν εἴη
νηυσὶν καιομένῃσιν ἀμυνέμεν· ἀλλ’ ἐπὶ δώροις
ἔρχεο· ἶσον γάρ σε θεῷ τείσουσιν Ἀχαιοί.
εἰ δέ κ’ ἄτερ δώρων πόλεμον φθισήνορα δύῃς,
οὐκέθ’ ὁμῶς τιμῆς ἔσεαι πόλεμόν περ ἀλαλκών.”          605
   Τὸν δ’ ἀπαμειβόμενος προσέφη πόδας ὠκὺς Ἀχιλλεύς·
“Φοῖνιξ, ἄττα γεραιέ, διοτρεφές, οὔ τί με ταύτης
χρεὼ τιμῆς· φρονέω δὲ τετιμῆσθαι Διὸς αἴσῃ,
ἥ μ’ ἕξει παρὰ νηυσὶ κορωνίσιν εἰς ὅ κ’ ἀϋτμὴ
ἐν στήθεσσι μένῃ καί μοι φίλα γούνατ’ ὀρώρῃ.           610
ἄλλο δέ τοι ἐρέω, σὺ δ’ ἐνὶ φρεσὶ βάλλεο σῇσι·
μή μοι σύγχει θυμὸν ὀδυρόμενος καὶ ἀχεύων,
Ἀτρεΐδῃ ἥρωϊ φέρων χάριν· οὐδέ τί σε χρὴ
τὸν φιλέειν, ἵνα μή μοι ἀπέχθηαι φιλέοντι.
καλόν τοι σὺν ἐμοὶ τὸν κήδειν ὅς κ’ ἐμὲ κήδῃ·          615

602 δώρων a

70

ἶσον ἐμοὶ βασίλευε καὶ ἥμισυ μείρεο τιμῆς.
οὗτοι δ᾽ ἀγγελέουσι, σὺ δ᾽ αὐτόθι λέξεο μίμνων
εὐνῇ ἔνι μαλακῇ· ἅμα δ᾽ ἠοῖ φαινομένηφι
φρασσόμεθ᾽ ἤ κε νεώμεθ᾽ ἐφ᾽ ἡμέτερ᾽ ἦ κε μένωμεν.''
Ἦ, καὶ Πατρόκλῳ ὅ γ᾽ ἐπ᾽ ὀφρύσι νεῦσε σιωπῇ            620
Φοίνικι στορέσαι πυκινὸν λέχος, ὄφρα τάχιστα
ἐκ κλισίης νόστοιο μεδοίατο· τοῖσι δ᾽ ἄρ᾽ Αἴας
ἀντίθεος Τελαμωνιάδης μετὰ μῦθον ἔειπε·
''διογενὲς Λαερτιάδη, πολυμήχαν᾽ Ὀδυσσεῦ,
ἴομεν· οὐ γάρ μοι δοκέει μύθοιο τελευτὴ            625
τῇδέ γ᾽ ὁδῷ κρανέεσθαι· ἀπαγγεῖλαι δὲ τάχιστα
χρὴ μῦθον Δαναοῖσι καὶ οὐκ ἀγαθόν περ ἐόντα,
οἵ που νῦν ἕαται ποτιδέγμενοι. αὐτὰρ Ἀχιλλεὺς
ἄγριον ἐν στήθεσσι θέτο μεγαλήτορα θυμόν,
σχέτλιος, οὐδὲ μετατρέπεται φιλότητος ἑταίρων,            630
τῆς ᾗ μιν παρὰ νηυσὶν ἐτίομεν ἔξοχον ἄλλων,
νηλής· καὶ μέν τίς τε κασιγνήτοιο φονῆος
ποινὴν ἢ οὗ παιδὸς ἐδέξατο τεθνηῶτος·
καί ῥ᾽ ὁ μὲν ἐν δήμῳ μένει αὐτοῦ πόλλ᾽ ἀποτείσας,
τοῦ δέ τ᾽ ἐρητύεται κραδίη καὶ θυμὸς ἀγήνωρ            635
ποινὴν δεξαμένῳ· σοὶ δ᾽ ἄλληκτόν τε κακόν τε
θυμὸν ἐνὶ στήθεσσι θεοὶ θέσαν εἵνεκα κούρης
οἴης· νῦν δέ τοι ἑπτὰ παρίσχομεν ἔξοχ᾽ ἀρίστας,
ἄλλα τε πόλλ᾽ ἐπὶ τῇσι· σὺ δ᾽ ἵλαον ἔνθεο θυμόν,
αἴδεσσαι δὲ μέλαθρον· ὑπωρόφιοι δέ τοί εἰμεν            640
πληθύος ἐκ Δαναῶν, μέμαμεν δέ τοι ἔξοχον ἄλλων
κήδιστοί τ᾽ ἔμεναι καὶ φίλτατοι, ὅσσοι Ἀχαιοί.''
Τὸν δ᾽ ἀπαμειβόμενος προσέφη πόδας ὠκὺς Ἀχιλλεύς·
''Αἶαν διογενὲς Τελαμώνιε, κοίρανε λαῶν,
πάντα τί μοι κατὰ θυμὸν ἐείσαο μυθήσασθαι·            645
ἀλλά μοι οἰδάνεται κραδίη χόλῳ, ὁππότε κείνων
μνήσομαι, ὥς μ᾽ ἀσύφηλον ἐν Ἀργείοισιν ἔρεξεν
Ἀτρεΐδης, ὡς εἴ τιν᾽ ἀτίμητον μετανάστην.
ἀλλ᾽ ὑμεῖς ἔρχεσθε καὶ ἀγγελίην ἀπόφασθε·
οὐ γὰρ πρὶν πολέμοιο μεδήσομαι αἱματόεντος,            650
πρίν γ᾽ υἱὸν Πριάμοιο δαΐφρονος, Ἕκτορα δῖον,
Μυρμιδόνων ἐπί τε κλισίας καὶ νῆας ἱκέσθαι
κτείνοντ᾽ Ἀργείους, κατά τε σμῦξαι πυρὶ νῆας.

616  line rejected C.19.

ἀμφὶ δέ τοι τῇ ἐμῇ κλισίῃ καὶ νηΐ μελαίνῃ
Ἕκτορα καὶ μεμαῶτα μάχης σχήσεσθαι ὀΐω."          655
  Ὣς ἔφαθ', οἱ δὲ ἕκαστος ἑλὼν δέπας ἀμφικύπελλον
σπείσαντες παρὰ νῆας ἴσαν πάλιν· ἦρχε δ' Ὀδυσσεύς.
Πάτροκλος δ' ἑτάροισιν ἰδὲ δμωῇσι κέλευσε
Φοίνικι στορέσαι πυκινὸν λέχος ὅττι τάχιστα.
αἱ δ' ἐπιπειθόμεναι στόρεσαν λέχος ὡς ἐκέλευσε,          660
κῶεά τε ῥῆγός τε λίνοιό τε λεπτὸν ἄωτον.
ἔνθ' ὁ γέρων κατέλεκτο καὶ Ἠῶ δῖαν ἔμιμνεν.
αὐτὰρ Ἀχιλλεὺς εὗδε μυχῷ κλισίης ἐυπήκτου·
τῷ δ' ἄρα παρκατέλεκτο γυνή, τὴν Λεσβόθεν ἦγε,
Φόρβαντος θυγάτηρ, Διομήδη καλλιπάρῃος.          665
Πάτροκλος δ' ἑτέρωθεν ἐλέξατο· πὰρ δ' ἄρα καὶ τῷ
Ἶφις ἐΰζωνος, τήν οἱ πόρε δῖος Ἀχιλλεὺς
Σκῦρον ἑλὼν αἰπεῖαν, Ἐνυῆος πτολίεθρον.
  Οἱ δ' ὅτε δὴ κλισίῃσιν ἐν Ἀτρεΐδαο γένοντο,
τοὺς μὲν ἄρα χρυσέοισι κυπέλλοις υἷες Ἀχαιῶν          670
δειδέχατ' ἄλλοθεν ἄλλος ἀνασταδόν, ἔκ τ' ἐρέοντο·
πρῶτος δ' ἐξερέεινεν ἄναξ ἀνδρῶν Ἀγαμέμνων·
"εἴπ' ἄγε μ', ὦ πολύαιν' Ὀδυσεῦ, μέγα κῦδος Ἀχαιῶν,
ἤ ῥ' ἐθέλει νήεσσιν ἀλεξέμεναι δήιον πῦρ,
ἦ ἀπέειπε, χόλος δ' ἔτ' ἔχει μεγαλήτορα θυμόν;"          675
  Τὸν δ' αὖτε προσέειπε πολύτλας δῖος Ὀδυσσεύς·
"Ἀτρεΐδη κύδιστε, ἄναξ ἀνδρῶν Ἀγάμεμνον,
κεῖνός γ' οὐκ ἐθέλει σβέσσαι χόλον, ἀλλ' ἔτι μᾶλλον
πιμπλάνεται μένεος, σὲ δ' ἀναίνεται ἠδὲ σὰ δῶρα.
αὐτόν σε φράζεσθαι ἐν Ἀργείοισιν ἄνωγεν          680
ὅππως κεν νῆάς τε σαῷς καὶ λαὸν Ἀχαιῶν·
αὐτὸς δ' ἠπείλησεν ἅμ' ἠοῖ φαινομένηφι
νῆας ἐϋσσέλμους ἅλαδ' ἑλκέμεν ἀμφιελίσσας.
καὶ δ' ἂν τοῖς ἄλλοισιν ἔφη παραμυθήσασθαι
οἴκαδ' ἀποπλείειν, ἐπεὶ οὐκέτι δήετε τέκμωρ          685
Ἰλίου αἰπεινῆς· μάλα γάρ ἑθεν εὐρύοπα Ζεὺς
χεῖρα ἑὴν ὑπερέσχε, τεθαρσήκασι δὲ λαοί.
ὣς ἔφατ'· εἰσὶ καὶ οἵδε τάδ' εἰπέμεν, οἵ μοι ἕποντο,
Αἴας καὶ κήρυκε δύω, πεπνυμένω ἄμφω.
Φοῖνιξ δ' αὖθ' ὁ γέρων κατελέξατο, ὣς γὰρ ἀνώγει,          690
ὄφρα οἱ ἐν νήεσσι φίλην ἐς πατρίδ' ἕπηται
αὔριον, ἢν ἐθέλῃσιν· ἀνάγκῃ δ' οὔ τί μιν ἄξει."
  Ὣς ἔφαθ', οἱ δ' ἄρα πάντες ἀκὴν ἐγένοντο σιωπῇ

μῦθον ἀγασσάμενοι· μάλα γὰρ κρατερῶς ἀγόρευσε.
δὴν δ᾽ ἄνεῳ ἦσαν τετιηότες υἷες Ἀχαιῶν·            695
ὀψὲ δὲ δὴ μετέειπε βοὴν ἀγαθὸς Διομήδης·
"Ἀτρεΐδη κύδιστε, ἄναξ ἀνδρῶν Ἀγάμεμνον,
μὴ ὄφελες λίσσεσθαι ἀμύμονα Πηλεΐωνα,
μυρία δῶρα διδούς· ὁ δ᾽ ἀγήνωρ ἐστὶ καὶ ἄλλως·
νῦν αὖ μιν πολὺ μᾶλλον ἀγηνορίῃσιν ἐνῆκας.        700
ἀλλ᾽ ἤτοι κεῖνον μὲν ἐάσομεν, ἤ κεν ἴῃσιν,
ἦ κε μένῃ· τότε δ᾽ αὖτε μαχήσεται, ὁππότε κέν μιν
θυμὸς ἐνὶ στήθεσσιν ἀνώγῃ καὶ θεὸς ὄρσῃ.
ἀλλ᾽ ἄγεθ᾽, ὡς ἂν ἐγὼ εἴπω, πειθώμεθα πάντες·
νῦν μὲν κοιμήσασθε τεταρπόμενοι φίλον ἦτορ         705
σίτου καὶ οἴνοιο· τὸ γὰρ μένος ἐστὶ καὶ ἀλκή·
αὐτὰρ ἐπεί κε φανῇ καλὴ ῥοδοδάκτυλος Ἠώς,
καρπαλίμως πρὸ νεῶν ἐχέμεν λαόν τε καὶ ἵππους
ὀτρύνων, καὶ δ᾽ αὐτὸς ἐνὶ πρώτοισι μάχεσθαι."
Ὣς ἔφαθ᾽, οἳ δ᾽ ἄρα πάντες ἐπήνησαν βασιλῆες,      710
μῦθον ἀγασσάμενοι Διομήδεος ἱπποδάμοιο.
καὶ τότε δὴ σπείσαντες ἔβαν κλισίηνδε ἕκαστος,
ἔνθα δὲ κοιμήσαντο καὶ ὕπνου δῶρον ἕλοντο.

694 line rejected Al.

73

# COMMENTARY

**1-89.** *The Achaean Assembly.* Book 9 opens with an Achaean assembly, a counterpart to the Trojan council of war at 8. 485-565: cf. Introduction pp. 16ff. Achaean defeatism contrasts with Trojan self-confidence, and Hector's unquestioned dominance with the feebleness of Agamemnon, whose subordinates criticize him and take control of events.

**1 φυλακὰς.** Acc. plural of φυλακή, 'watch'.

**2 Φύζα.** Φύζα and Φόβον (Panic and Rout), personified, like Ἔρις, etc.: cf. 4. 440f., Athena assisted in urging on the Achaeans by Δειμός, Φόβος, and Ἔρις, 'sister and companion of Ares'. On φύζα cf. P. Chantraine, *Études sur le vocabulaire grec* (Paris, 1950), 23.

**3 βεβολήατο.** 3rd person plural (from -ηντο: in the Ionic dialect original ν in the 3rd person endings -νται, -ντο, may appear as α) of βολέω, cf. 9 βεβολημένος. βολέω stands to βάλλω as βρομέω to βρέμω, θροέω to θρέομαι, πολέω to πέλω, φορέω to φέρω, etc.: they have a more intense meaning than the simple verbs (Schwyzer, *Gr. Gramm.* i. 719f.).

**4-8** This stormy simile, reflecting the chaotic mood and shattered morale of the Achaeans, contrasts with the serene simile (starry sky) which reflected the self-confidence of the Trojans, 8. 555-61. Note the crisp alliteration, κῦμα κελαινὸν κορθύεται, πολλὸν παρὲξ φῦκος.

**5 Βορέης.** The regular Homeric form, offered here too by the manuscripts. As the line is thus metrically deficient, like 23. 195, some scholars have wanted to read βορρῆς or βορρᾶς, the latter the Attic form. The ancients believed Homer's text contained 'headless' verses which began with a short syllable, thus three times διὰ μὲν ἀσπίδος ἦλθε φαεινῆς ὄβριμον ἔγχος (Schulze, *Quaest. Epicae,* 399); but such lines occur to allow expressions into the text which naturally open the verse, but which do not scan there. That does not cover this line (Wackernagel, *Sprachl. Untersuchungen,*

75

151f.). 9. 5 and 23. 195 remain puzzling. It may be that the singer's pronunciation helped the lines to sound metrical (as *Βορρέας*). Boreas and Zephyrus are described as both blowing from Thrace. Some scholars have tried to use this as an indication of the home of the poet, placing him in the north-west of Asia Minor; others point out that the indication suits Troy itself and so perhaps cannot be pressed for information about the author. The vividness of this simile, and its truth to the stormy Aegean, were praised by Robert Wood in 1769 (*Essay on the Original Genius and Writings of Homer*, 20ff.); cf. also 4. 275-80, 422-7; 7. 63-5; 11. 305-9.

**7 παρὲξ.** All along the shore.

**9** Agamemnon is depicted with some consistency as a man who passes from one extreme mood to the opposite. At times overconfident, as when he insults Achilles in 1 and other subordinates in 4. 339ff., 370ff., or implicitly trusts the misleading Dream sent by Zeus (2. 55ff., with the dry comment of wise Nestor, 2. 80f.: 'If anybody else had told us such a dream, we should not believe a word of it'), he collapses in moments of difficulty—at 14. 65ff. he again proposes immediate flight; cf. also 2. 185ff.

**11 κλήδην.** To prevent the Trojans from hearing what they are doing, the men are to be assembled by individual summons. This has often been thought more appropriate for the summoning of a council of chiefs, rather than a mass assembly; but the audience has no difficulty in imagining how this could be done. The contrast is with the enormous din made by the Achaeans as they gathered—in more confident times—for the assembly in Book 2. 86-100. But the address, line 17, does suggest a meeting of commanders: see note.

**13 τετιηότες.** The verb from which this form comes appears only in the perfect: *τετίημαι* and, as here, the active perfect participle. Both active and passive forms have the same meaning, 'in distress'. The original sense of the perfect active tense was intransitive and present, conveying a state: so *ὄλωλα*, 'be in a state of ruin', *ὄδωδα*, 'have a smell', etc.; so too 573 *ὀρώρειν*, pluperfect, 'was in the air'. Later the perfect was increasingly assimilated to the other active tenses, as expressing a relation of time.

**14-16** This simile is repeated at 16. 3-5, where Patroclus weeps for the sufferings of the Achaeans. It is unusual but not

76

unparalleled for a simile to recur, and in Book 16 the typically Homeric comparison with a natural feature is heavily emphasized by the contrast, when it is immediately followed by Achilles brutally comparing Patroclus to a little girl in tears round her mother's skirts. That passage recalls this one: the grief which Achilles here has caused his enemy, reaches his friend in Book 16, as a result of his refusal to be swayed in Book 9; and it will reach Achilles when it causes Patroclus' death. Tears: early Greeks wept without shame, and there was a proverb 'Good men are always prone to tears', αἰεὶ δ' ἀριδάκρυες ἀνέρες ἐσθλοί.

**17-27** This speech is made up, with minute variations, of lines which Agamemnon spoke, 2. 110 ff., in what was there a deliberately misleading proposal to abandon the expedition and return home. There he intended the troops to reject the defeatist scheme; here it is put forward seriously. It is inept to argue that the repetition is in some way 'ironical': it is just a repetition—the singer felt no need to try to improve on the lines. It is typical of Agamemnon's lack of real leadership that in both cases his audience react in the way opposite to that which he intends (de Jong, *Narrators and Focalizers*, 190). At 14. 74 ff. Agamemnon will again propose flight; in Book 2 it was Odysseus who contradicted him, here it is Diomedes, and in Book 14 both Odysseus and Diomedes. The scenes form a structured crescendo (Janko, *Commentary* on 14. 65-81).

**17** This address suggests that Agamemnon is talking to the chiefs, not to the mass of the army. It is the more puzzling that in 2. 110 we read ὦ φίλοι ἥρωες Δαναοί, θεράποντες Ἄρηος—a line which is appropriate to a mass assembly. Conversely, at the end of Book 9 the envoys report back to the chiefs, who are waiting up in Agamemnon's tent (669 f.), yet Odysseus' gloomy report produces a silence described in exactly the same way: the 'sons of the Achaeans' were dismayed—as if all the army were present. We detect a lack of exact focus on the facts.

**19-20** When was the promise made to Agamemnon? 20 = 2. 113 = 2. 288 = 5. 716, ascribing the promise variously to Zeus, the Achaeans, and the goddesses Hera and Athena (see Hainsworth ad loc.). All knew that Troy was doomed, even the Trojans (6. 447 ff.); therefore it must have been predicted—sometime.

**22 δυσκλέα.** More correctly, or more anciently, δυσκλεέ(α).

**23-5** These lines are not as appropriate here, where Agamemnon is talking of abandoning the attempt on Troy, as they were at 2. 116-18, where he was trying to suggest that, despite his surface despondency, in reality Troy could still be taken. The Alexandrian scholars Aristophanes and Aristarchus deleted them. We face an insoluble question: how far was the poet content to repeat, amid generally relevant lines, some which were less so?

**24 πολίων κατέλυσε κάρηνα.** 'has brought down the heads of many cities'. A related image, *Il.* 16. 100, cf. *Od.* 13. 388, Τροίης ἱερὰ κρήδεμνα λύωμεν, 'unfasten the girdle' of Troy, with the nuance of violation.

**26** The first person πειθώμεθα is a politeness to the audience; the speaker includes himself among those whom he asks to obey him, to soften the peremptoriness of his command. Cf. e.g. 704.

**28 οὐ . . . ἔτι.** As often, this does not correspond exactly to the English 'no longer', but to 'from now, not'. Cf. e.g. 8. 356 ὁ δὲ μαίνεται οὐκέτ' ἀνεκτῶς: not that Hector used to rage acceptably, but 'his present raging is unendurable'. Cf. 164, 418.

**29, 30** These lines are repeated at 693, 694. Some readers will think that this repetition is meant to be noticed, and that it contributes to the effect and shape of the Book as a whole. In both cases it is the high-spirited Diomedes who breaks the gloomy silence.

**31-49** This speech of Diomedes is a good morale-raiser, but it makes no positive proposal; that is the meaning of Nestor's criticism, 56—'You have not reached the τέλος.' The wise elder makes the positive suggestion.

**32 ἀφραδέοντι.** An invention for metrical convenience (last two feet of the line) from ἀφραδέες; cf. δυσμενέες, δυσμενέοντες; ὑπερμενέες, ὑπερμενέοντες.

**33** This reminds us of the disastrous quarrel which arose from criticism of Agamemnon in Book 1, cf. 1. 76 ff. Diomedes, more tactful than Achilles (1. 85-91), tries to prevent that happening again.

**34 ff.** 'You insulted my courage.' Diomedes refers to Agamemnon's insulting rebuke to him at 4. 370-5, 399-400, 'You are not the fighter your father was!'—a very clear example of a reference across many hundreds of lines. Diomedes declined to resent it in the press of preparing for battle (4. 412-18), but now the opportunity has presented itself for paying Agamemnon out. It is important that Diomedes is not prepared to be slighted without reply, but he is prepared to wait for satisfaction. He thus offers a counter model of heroism to that of Achilles. If Achilles had been like Diomedes, he could still have been heroic; but there would have been no tragic *Iliad*. Diomedes again rebukes Agamemnon for a defeatist speech at 14. 109ff; cf. note on 57.

**36 ἠμὲν νέοι ἠδὲ γέροντες.** Cf. *Od.* 1. 396 νέοι ἠδὲ παλαιοί. A 'polar expression' where a word suggests its opposite. This is an example of 'pleonasm', verbal fullness strictly unnecessary but popular with Greek writers at all periods. Cf. ad 124 and 477; and e.g. *Od.* 4. 141, 23. 66; E. Kemmer, *Die polare Ausdrucksweise in der griechischen Literatur* (Würzburg, 1903).

**37 Κρόνου πάις ἀγκυλομήτεω.** Not an ancient formula, as it contains both genitive singular in -ου (and in a position where, metrically, it cannot have replaced an older -οο), and the Ionic form ἀγκυλομήτεω (for older *ἀγκυλομήταο). The epithet—'of twisty plans'—presumably relates to Cronus' ambush and castration of his father Uranus, see Hesiod, *Theogony* 164ff.; a story deriving from the East (M. L. West, *Commentary on Hesiod, Theogony*, (Oxford, 1966) pp. 19ff.).

**38f.** This criticism of Agamemnon is essentially that made by Achilles, 1. 225ff. (Agamemnon 'has the heart of a deer' and never goes into battle) and 9. 320-34 (Agamemnon stays behind while others are fighting, and he keeps most of the booty). Diomedes makes it much less offensively. It is at the heart of the plot of the *Iliad*: the greatest king is not the greatest warrior— hence the friction.

On Agamemnon's sceptre, cf. 2. 100-9: it comes from Zeus and is inherited by Agamemnon, πολλῇσιν νήσοισι καὶ Ἄργεϊ παντὶ ἀνάσσειν, 'to be king over many islands and all Argos'. It is the visible mark of being a king (σκηπτοῦχος βασιλεύς)—compare the 'king' who stands happily watching his farm-workers, σκῆπτρον ἔχων, holding a sceptre, on the Shield of Achilles (18. 556-8).

**40 δαιμόνιε:** cf. 1. 561 δαιμονίη. The meaning seems to be that the person addressed is behaving unaccountably, perhaps under the influence of some δαίμων; roughly, 'You strange creature!'

**42 ὥς τε νέεσθαι.** Only here in *Il.*, and once in *Od.* (17. 21), is ὥστε constructed with the infinitive. This is a common usage in classical Greek, here beginning to appear; cf. notes on 103, 320, 337, 374.

**44** Aristarchus condemned this feeble line, which has no purpose but to introduce the unnecessary verb ἑστᾶσι. In an ordinary written text we should have no hesitation in deleting it, but in a poem with an oral background it is impossible to be sure that the original poet may not have been the one who (perhaps only occasionally) introduced it.

**46 εἰ δὲ . . . φευγόντων.** Cf. 262 εἰ δέ σὺ μέν μευ ἄκουσον. εἰ here seems to retain the original sense, not 'if' but something like 'so be it', 'well and good!' *Let* them run away; we will stay.

**47–9** Sthenelus is Diomedes' second in command. Diomede is the son of Tydeus, Sthenelus of Capaneus, two of the Seven against Thebes; both met grisly ends there. The sons were among the Epigonoi, the less interesting next generation, who succeeded in capturing the city, cf. 4. 403 ff. Diomedes has entered the Trojan cycle from his original place in the Theban one, a striking instance of the potential fluidity of heroic legend. Achilles expresses a rather similar thought to Patroclus, but characteristically with greater passion and exaggeration, 16. 97–100: 'Would that every Trojan and every Argive might perish, and you and I survive, that we alone might take Troy.' Achilles is an exaggerated Diomedes. Behind these passages perhaps lies the story of the early sack of Troy by Heracles and Telamon alone (J. T. Kakridis in *Gymn.* 78 (1971), 509); cf. also parallel passages where a hero expresses his dauntless will by saying he will fight on, if necessary, alone (5. 473, Hector, cf. 8. 527; 3. 290, Menelaus). Cf. Ø. Andersen, *Diomedes*, 120. One version of the story said that Peleus sacked Iolcus 'alone, without an army'; Pindar, *Nem.* 3. 34, cf. [Hesiod], *frag.* 211.

**τέκμωρ.** Cf. 417, 7. 30 'the goal of (taking) Troy.'

**49 σὺν γὰρ θεῷ.** Cf. 6. 171 θεῶν ὑπ' ἀπήμονι πομπῇ. It is vitally important for the *Iliad* that at bottom, beneath all the apparent indifference or amorality of heaven, the cause of the Achaeans is just: cf. 4. 160 ff., 235; 7. 349 ff., 401–3. For the rhythm and confident statement cf. 5. 256 τρεῖν μ' οὐκ ἐᾷ Παλλὰς Ἀθήνη (and 1. 175, 3. 440).

εἰλήλουθμεν. Older form of Attic: ἐληλύθαμεν.

**50** Diomedes succeeds in restoring morale; cf. 7. 403 (the identical line), 9. 710, 14. 133.

**52–78** Nestor makes thinly veiled criticism of Agamemnon and proposes a dinner for the leaders.

**52 ἱππότα Νέστωρ:** sometimes (mysteriously) Γερήνιος ἱππότα Νέστωρ. Cf. note on 162.

Nestor is the great expert on chariot-warfare: 4. 303–9, 'This is how men of old did it', and 11. 743 ff.—the two most convincing pieces of chariot-fighting in the *Iliad* (Finsler, *Homer*, 1. 144; Kirk in *CAH*³ ii. 2. 839–40); he also is full of advice on chariot-racing (23. 306–48). Other men called ἱππηλάτα are also of the older generation: Phoenix, Tydeus (4. 387), Oeneus (577), Peleus (438). The two-syllable names, also characteristic of the generation before that of the Homeric heroes (Atreus, Peleus, Theseus), support the idea that this is conscious on the poet's part—chariot warfare was a speciality of the age just before his own subject-matter.

**53 πέρι.** With καρτερός: exceedingly. Cf. *Il.* 18. 549 τὸ δὴ πέρι θαῦμα τέτυκτο, an exceeding marvel. μέν is followed not by δέ but by καί, as often.

**54–5** There are two areas in which a hero can win glory: battle (μάχη κυδιάνειρα), and counsel (ἀγορὴ κυδιάνειρα). A man desires to be a 'speaker of words and a doer of deeds' (9. 443). In addition to that general point, it is relevant that Agamemnon, insulting Diomedes in the passage to which the hero referred at 34 f., said he was 'inferior to his father in battle, but better in talking' (4. 399). The tactful Nestor makes the point that Diomedes is excellent at both. Achilles eventually must realize that while he himself is unequalled in battle, others are better in planning (18. 105). Other possible dualities are intelligence (φρένες) versus good looks, *Od.* 8. 167 ff.; or looks versus prowess, *Od.* 18. 1–4, cf. *Il.* 2. 671–5; 3. 44 f.—or, of course, royal position versus prowess, 9. 38 f.

**56 πάλιν ἐρέει:** 'speak in opposition'. Cf. 4. 357 πάλιν δ' ὅ γε λάζετο μῦθον, 'he spoke in the opposite sense'.

**57** Nestor tells Diomedes again that he is his junior, 10. 76: Diomedes gives a reply only later, 14. 110–12—'I shall produce a plan, and let nobody grudge me', οὕνεκα δὴ γενεῆφι νεώτατός εἰμι μεθ' ὑμῖν, 'because I am the youngest among you' .

These Diomedes passages link Books 4, 9, 10, 14, in a way which seems deliberate and meant to be noticed—one of the threads which hold the *Iliad* together. And the contrast between Diomedes and Achilles, the possible and the impossible hero, is part of the architecture of the poem. It must be part of the conception of the last poet ('Homer'); as has been pointed out (Codino, *Introduzione a Omero*, 49) Diomedes is prominent, apart from these linking scenes and other links in 7, 8, and 14 *init.*, only in 5, 7, 10, and 23; in ten books of the *Iliad* he is not named at all. Originally at home in the Theban cycle, he is a late-comer to the Trojan one. A second contrast, equally meant to be noticed, is that between youth and age—the youngest and oldest of the Achaean heroes, with their appropriate qualities.

**58 γενεῆφιν:** 'by birth'. -φι, originally an instrumental or locative case-ending, is in epic available for forming metrically useful datives like this one (= γενεῇ), or even genitives: as ἀπ' ἐσχαρόφιν, *Od.* 7. 169; 19. 389. Cf. notes on 168, 384; and Chantraine, *GH* i. 234–6.

**59** A feeble line, not ejected by the ancient scholars, but perhaps to be deleted (Heyne); it is repetitive, and πεπνυμένα βάζεις, 'you speak with prudence', is weakened by the addition of the second accusative ('you address the kings with prudence').

**60 εὔχομαι εἶναι.** A common Homeric periphrasis for 'I am'. εὔχομαι seems to have as its original meaning 'assert loudly'; thence 'boast' and 'vow'; cf. A. W. H. Adkins in *CQ* 19 (1969).

**62 ἀτιμήσει:** future with κε, K–G i. 209; *Il.* 9. 262, 1. 523, 4. 176, etc.

**63** 'Without brotherhood, without law, without hearth-fire is the man who is in love with hateful civil strife.' That is, he resembles an uncivilized, isolated, cannibal Cyclops: *Od.* 9. 112–15, 273–6—τοῖσιν δ' οὔτ' ἀγοραὶ βουληφόροι οὔτε θέμιστες (*Od.* 9. 112). The relevance of this generalization is clear, and it is made unambiguous by the positioning immediately before it of the name of Agamemnon. He it is who has stirred up strife within the community—'not at all with our approval', as Nestor will tell him at 108. The general form Nestor gives it is for politeness' sake, especially as he is speaking in the presence of the army; he will be franker when the chiefs are alone (96ff.). This is a damning judgement, which tells against the view that only the competitive virtues, not the co-operative ones, are really valued by Homer: thus 'The competitive system of values, then, must always in the last resort override the cooperative in Homer' (A. W. H. Adkins, *Merit and Responsibility* (Oxford, 1960), 40; cf. Introduction, p. 15 f., 24 ff.). War is, among other things, splendid; but anyone who likes quarrelling within his own community is hateful, cf. 1. 176 f., 5. 890 f. ἀφρήτωρ and ἀνέστιος never recur in Homer; ἀθέμιστος is used especially of the Cyclops.

**ἀφρήτωρ.** The ancient IE word *bhrater, 'brother', is in Greek specialized to refer not to blood kin but to membership of a 'phratry', a self-recruiting group of men for cult purposes—like the Arval Brethren at Rome. In classical Athens every male citizen must belong to a phratry. For blood kin, Greek used the invented term ἀδελφός, 'from one womb'. Phratries are mentioned in Homer only here and (again Nestor) at 2. 362; apparently an element of later social life has effected a couple of entries into the text. Cf. A. Andrewes, 'Phratries in Homer', *Hermes*, 89 (1961).

Three negative epithets: Richardson on *Hymn Cer.* 200; 24. 157 οὔτε γάρ ἐστ᾽ ἄφρων οὔτ᾽ ἄσκοπος οὔτ᾽ ἀλιτήμων. Vedic poetry offers parallels to the pairing of epithets with the same fore-element, like ἀγήραον ἀθάνατόν τε (*Il.* 2. 447): West in *JHS* 108 (1988), 156, M. Durante, *Sulla preistoria della tradizione poetica greca*, ii (Rome, 1976), 151 f. Three are still more emphatic. 'Unhousel'd, disappointed, unaneled' (Shakespeare); 'Unrespited, unpitied, unreprieved' (Milton).

The generalizing use of ἐκεῖνος: cf. 312; *Od.* 6. 158; 8. 209, 14. 158.

**64 ἐπιδημίου ὀκρυόεντος.** The exclusively poetical word ὀκρυόεις arose from misdivision of phrases involving κρυόεις 'chilly'; the original formula here must have been ἐπιδημίοο κρυόεντος. The genitive ending -οο (in addition to -οιο and -ου) soon fell out of use, and formulae which depended upon it became unmetrical; hence redivision as ἐπιδημίου ὀκρυόεντος, the -ου being shortened by correption. So too 6. 344. That gave the language a new word: ὀκρυόεις, imagined as meaning 'horrible' or something similar. Leumann, *HW* 49 f.; Palmer, *Greek Language*, 95. i; note on 440; Janko, *Commentary* on 4. 15; *HHH* 87–94. Strife outside the community group is by no means as bad: cf. 24. 262, where Priam insults his sons as ἀρνῶν ἠδ᾽ ἐρίφων ἐπιδήμιοι ἁρπακτῆρες, 'robbers of lambs and goats in the community'—they don't go abroad to do their rustling.

**66 ἐφοπλισόμεσθα.** A short-vowel aorist subjunctive, cf. 165.

**ἕκαστοι:** 'each detachment'.

**67 λεξάσθων.** From λέχομαι: 'let them bivouac outside the wall'. This passage seems to look forward to Book 10, in which the sentries are found as described here. The defensive wall was built in Achilles' absence, 7. 33 ff., 436 ff. It will be breached by the Trojans in Book 12. There is a space between it and the defensive ditch (τάφρος): cf. also 87.

**69 βασιλεύτατος.** Cf. 169, 392 βασιλεύτερος, comparative and superlative forms of a noun, 'more of a king', irregularly: cf. 8. 483 κύντερον 'more of a dog', so 'more shameless'. βασιλεύτερον used as an adjective, agreeing with γένος, at Od. 15. 533. The word is perhaps motivated in part by attempts in the Dark Age to understand the position of Agamemnon, as in some forgotten sense supreme. Cf. note on 97 f.

**70** Feasting is of high importance in Homer, as a mark of status and also a source of obligation. Agamemnon reproaches chieftains who seem to be holding back from battle, saying 'You are the first to be invited by me, when the Achaeans make a feast for the chieftains: there you enjoy the roast meat and the goblets of sweet wine', but now you look idly on instead of fighting (4. 343–8). Cf. also the celebrated speech of Sarpedon on the theme of *noblesse oblige* (12. 310 ff.). Hospitality is a duty of rank and also a vital means of winning and keeping supporters (ἑταῖροι, ἔται): cf. O. Murray, 'The Greek Symposion in History', in: E. Gabba (ed.), *Tria Corda: Scritti in onore di A. Momigliano* (Como, 1983) 259 f. In this case, too, Nestor means to speak to Agamemnon with a frankness which he reserves for a setting at which the common soldiers will not be present to hear.

**71** Homer is very careful to exclude the motif of drunkenness from the *Iliad*, but there is plenty of wine. Apart from this Thracian wine, cf. 7. 467 f., wine from Lemnos.

**72 ἠμάτιαι:** 'every day'.

**εὐρέα πόντον.** The true accusative masculine of εὐρύς is εὐρύν. The phrase εὐρέα πόντον is created by the wish to extend to the accusative case the dative formula εὐρέι πόντῳ (6 occurrences in *Il.* and *Od.*).

73 'All hospitality is yours; you are the chief.' In later Greek this δέ would normally be an explanatory γάρ: cf. note on 496–7.

74 πολλῶν δ' ἀγρομένων τῷ πείσεαι. 'When many are gathered together (genitive absolute; aorist middle participle of ἀγείρω), you will be guided by the man who . . .'

75 βουλὴν βουλεύσῃ. Example of the 'internal' accusative, in which the meaning of an intransitive verb is given more elaborate expression by the addition of a cognate noun in the accusative case. Thus *Il.* 2. 121 ἄπρηκτον πόλεμον πολεμίζειν; 4. 27 ἱδρῶ ὃν ἵδρωσα, 'the sweat which I sweated', etc. It is common in Greek, and familiar also in Latin (*servitutem servire*, etc.).

χρεώ: used as a verb, cf. 21. 322.

77 τίς ἂν τάδε γηθήσειεν; For the extension of meaning which makes γηθέω transitive, cf. 8. 378, and conversely 13. 352, ἤχθετο γάρ ῥα | Τρωσὶν δαμναμένους ('he was distressed at their being beaten by the Trojans').

78 Seems meant as an answer to 8. 541 'this day will bring ruin to the Achaeans'. Nestor has of course not heard that line uttered by Hector: see note on 372.

79–88 The sentries are posted. Seven second-rank heroes command them. These men will reappear in Book 10, showing that the apparently isolated *Doloneia* is more firmly anchored in the poem than is sometimes thought: 10. 57f., 97f., 180ff., 255ff. They also mirror on the Achaean side the precautions of Hector, described at 8. 517f. It was pointed out by D. H. F. Gray, *JHS* 78 (1958), 47, that these names contain a high proportion which are known to be Mycenaean: such names 'are most common in family histories and passages which may be called feudal; and this is an indication of the subject-matter of the Mycenaean poetry which was the ancestor of our epics'. Three of these men are killed later in the poem: 13. 518, 13. 541, 13. 576; their deaths come so closely together as to suggest that the poet at that point, or the poet of that passage, has this passage in mind.

Do the seven guardians mean that the wall had seven gates? So, suggestively, H. W. Singer, *Hermes*, 120 (1992), 402f., pointing to the ancient reading ἕπτ' (for εὖ) at 7. 339, and to the 'seven gates' of Thebes, themselves ultimately deriving from Eastern conceptions rather than actual facts (Thebes seems never to have had seven gates): cf. W. Burkert, *Die orientalisierende Epoche* . . . (SB Heidelberg, 1984), 99 ff.

**85** *Seven times one hundred sentries*: evidently 'heroic exaggeration' (Willcock) rather than anything like realism.

**89 γέροντας.** Compare 2. 404 ff. (Agamemnon) κίκλησκεν δὲ γέροντας ἀριστῆας Παναχαιῶν, listing Nestor, Idomeneus, the two Ajaxes, Diomedes, Odysseus, and Menelaus. This is the high command; cf. 422. The word does not of course—except in the peculiar case of Nestor—imply great age, but high position; cf. the Roman *senatus* (assembly of *senes*, elders) and the Spartan γερουσία. Cf. 574 γέροντες Αἰτωλῶν, the leading Aetolians. In Troy, however, cf. 6. 113f. ὄφρ' ἂν ἐγὼ βήω προτὶ Ἴλιον, ἠδὲ γέρουσιν | εἴπω βουλεύτῃσι . . . and 3. 146ff. (the δημογέροντες), we find a group of men who are past fighting and good only for counsel; an overseas expedition like that of Agamemnon is no place for such people, and Nestor needs to be specially explained.

**91–181** *The Leaders Dine.* Agamemnon, criticized by Nestor, promises gifts to reconcile Achilles.

**91–2** Formulaic lines for a meal, 11 times in Homer. It is observable that the poet prefers to elide the actual eating and does not describe the menu: the food is 'sustaining', it is 'ready', and the heroes satisfy their (abstractly expressed) desire of drinking and eating. Food in Homer is generally moral and symbolic in treatment rather than culinary. Heroes are not shown eating anything less heroic than roast beef.

**92–5** = 7. 323–4; but at 7. 327 Nestor opened with the line Ἀτρείδη τε καὶ ἄλλοι ἀριστῆες Παναχαιῶν. Here, more ominously, he addresses Agamemnon alone from the beginning.

**96 ff.** Nestor opens the speech which will criticize Agamemnon's disastrous folly in the most flattering way he can: ἐν σοὶ μὲν λήξω, etc. Cf. Hesiod, *Theog.* 34, the Muses shall be sung of πρῶτόν τε καὶ ὕστατον; ibid. 48 (Zeus); and Gow's note on Theocritus 17. 1, ἐκ Διὸς ἀρχώμεσθα καὶ ἐς Δία λήγετε Μοῖσαι. The expression is in form appropriate to a hymn, here mollifyingly applied to Agamemnon. Cf. also 11. 761.

**97 f. πολλῶν λαῶν ἔσσι ἄναξ.** In some way Agamemnon is a greater king than the others. Nestor says he is φέρτερος . . . ἐπεὶ πλεόνεσσιν ἀνάσσει (1. 281); his god-given sceptre marks him as ruler of 'many islands and all Argos' (9. 108). The poet no longer has a clear picture of the way in which such a king might have functioned, as doubtless in his world there was no such 'great' ruler, only a memory that once upon a time, in Mycenae rich in gold, there used to be one; the scribal record-system, for instance, of Mycenae and Pylos in 'Mycenaean' times has been forgotten, and Homer's world is illiterate. That produced an ambiguity about the relationship of Agamemnon and Achilles which is important for the *Iliad*: in some sense Achilles is inferior, but he is not strictly a subordinate, and if he decides to go home there is nothing that can be done (1. 169ff., 618f., 682ff.). Cf. O. Taplin, 'Agamemnon's Role in the *Iliad*', in: C. B. R. Pelling (ed.), *Characterisation and Individuality in Greek Literature* (Oxford, 1990), 60–82.

**99** On the σκῆπτρον cf. note on 38f. θέμιστες, with the sceptre, given by Zeus to kings: 2. 206; 9. 298. θέμις, of which this is the unexplained plural form, comes from the root of τίθημι, 'establish': 'established' procedures (in the absence of formalised laws) are the 'right', 'legal', procedures. Kings whose θέμιστες are crooked, σκολιαί, cause general disaster, 16. 387.

**βουλεύῃσθα.** Verbs in historic sequence can be followed by subordinate verbs in the subjunctive, not the optative, when the effect is one which continues into present time; e.g. 9. 495, and 1. 158, 6. 357–8.

**101 κρηῆναι.** Aorist infinitive of κραιαίνω, epic form of κραίνω, 'bring to pass'; cf. E. Benveniste, *Le Vocabulaire des institutions indo-européennes* (Paris, 1969), ii. 37.

**102 σέο δ' ἕξεται.** 'He will depend on you, whatever he starts.' With ἔχω in this sense cf. *Od.* 6. 197, 11. 346 (van Leeuwen).

**103 δοκεῖ.** The contracted form of (normal Homeric) δοκέει; the word, if not necessarily the whole line (Hoekstra, *Homeric Modifications*, 144), must be a very late element. Cf. note on 42.

**105 νοέω.** In English, a perfect tense: 'I have been thinking'. In Greek, as in most European languages, normally a present tense.

**106 Βρισηΐδα κούρην.** The name systems: Briseis, daughter of Briseus, of Brisa (on Lesbos, 9. 128–32), and Chryseis, daughter of Chryses, of Chryse (in the Troad), are unique in Homer. Briseis is called κούρη Βρισῆος, 'daughter of Briseus' (1. 392, 9. 132), and also κούρη Βρισηΐς, as here and 19. 261; so that when she is called simply 'Briseis', as at 1. 184, it is not clear whether that is a name, in the full sense, or a patronymic. Some later scholars were sufficiently unhappy about this oddity to give her a 'real' name, Hippodameia (ΣA in 1. 392). We are approaching the classical practice of calling slaves simply after their place of origin— Κίλισσα, Σύρος, Ἀνδρία, etc. At 128f., 270f., it is said that she was captured on Lesbos, but at 2. 690 it was from Lyrnessus in the Troad; she had no real setting, and clearly she is not a real mythical figure with a story—and children—of her own.

**107 ἔβης κλισίηθεν ἀπούρας.** One of a number of phrases which suggest a different version of events from that narrated in Book 1: that Agamemnon did not send two heralds to fetch Briseis (1. 320ff.) but took her himself. So 1. 184 ἐγὼ δέ κ' ἄγω Βρισηΐδα καλλιπάρηον | αὐτὸς ἰὼν κλισίηνδε, 1. 356 = 1. 507, αὐτὸς ἀπούρας. Perhaps the story was sometimes sung in that form. One might guess that Homer preferred the version which did not bring Agamemnon and Achilles into a confrontation so likely to become deadly; Achilles treated the heralds with distinguished courtesy (1. 329ff.). See also A. Teffeteller in *CQ* 40 (1990), 16-20. When the scene of her abduction appears in art, after 480 BC (Friis Johansen, *The Iliad in Early Greek Art* (Copenhagen, 1967), 155f.), it is sometimes the two heralds who take her, sometimes the king himself.

**108-9** Nestor refers to his speech at 1. 254-84.

**109f. σῷ μεγαλήτορι θυμῷ εἴξας.** A hero should be 'greathearted', μεγαλήτωρ, μεγάθυμος; the words occur more than 100 times in the *Iliad*, and they are words of praise. But 'yielding to one's great heart' means recklessness and folly: so Meleager, 9. 598 εἴξας ᾧ θυμῷ, lost the reward he could have had. Cf. *Od.* 9. 492ff., where Odysseus' men urge him not to speak to the Cyclops, ἀλλ' οὐ πεῖθον ἐμὸν μεγαλήτορα θυμόν—so he reveals his name, and allows his enemy to impose a deadly curse on him. The paradox of heroism, that a hero must be high-spirited, proud, and capable of anger, but that anger and touchiness may make him a disaster and not a blessing to his people, is at the heart of the *Iliad*: cf. 11. 763f., 16. 30-5, 18. 97-105. Agamemnon yields to his anger; so does Achilles, who is vainly urged to 'restrain his μεγαλήτορα θυμόν' (9. 255) and 'subdue his great θυμόν' (9. 496), and who in the end curses his anger (18. 107–11). Ancient writers often take the *Iliad* as a text on the evils caused by the passions, as in the splendid second *Epistle* of Horace's first book. Cf. Introduction p. 15 f, 24 ff.

110 In Book 1, Agamemnon boasted that *he* was the man whom Zeus honoured, 1. 174 f. Events have shown his error, as he must admit at 9. 116–17.

113 δώροισιν . . . ἔπεσσί τε. Men and gods alike expect soft words and more substantial compensation, cf. 1. 97–100, 9. 497–501. Phoenix says the heroes of old, when offended, δωρητοί τε πέλοντο παραρρητοί τ' ἐπέεσσι, 9. 526. The ancients were not much interested in mere change of mind or apology, without compensation; forgiveness is a characteristically Christian virtue. But to withstand prayer was hateful: a celebrated fragment of Aeschylus (fr. 161R) says that of all the gods only Thanatos does not care for gifts and is shunned by Peitho (Persuasion). Agamemnon produces the gifts but no softening words: that is left for Phoenix.

115 οὔ τι ψεῦδος. Accusative in apposition to ἄτας: 'in telling of my blunder you did not tell a falsehood'. Cf. *Od.* 7. 297. Agamemnon will unpack the notion of ἄτη more fully in his self-exculpatory speech, 19. 90 ff.

116 ἀασάμην. This middle form presumably has passive force, cf. A. Schmitt, *Selbständigkeit und Abhängigkeit* (1990), 260 n. 280; cf. 9. 537, 11. 340 ἀάσατο δὲ μέγα θυμῷ. On ἄτη here and in Agamemnon's apology in 19. 76 ff., cf. H. Erbse, *Untersuchungen zur Funktion der Götter im hom. Epos* (Berlin, 1986), 10 ff., who however regards ἀασάμην as middle: 'I deceived myself'. On ἄτη see generally W. F. Wyatt in *AJP* 103 (1982), 247–76. The word is normally used retrospectively, in the attempt to understand or to palliate past conduct: 'something must have come over me!'

117 ὅν τε. 'Epic' τε, common with relative pronouns: cf. Chantraine, *GH* ii. 239 f. The nuance here is of regularity.

118 τοῦτον. Agamemnon avoids uttering his enemy's name, cf. 129, 131, 142, in contrast with Achilles' repeated dwelling on the name of 'Atreus' son' (332, 339, 341, 369) to fan his own anger. Compare Achilles' address to Agamemnon, 19. 56, with Agamemnon's embarrassed opening in reply, 19. 78 ff.; and contrast Achilles' chivalrous speech at 23. 890–7 with

Agamemnon's silence in reply. The characterization of both is consistent.

ἔτεισε. A reminder of Thetis' emphatic prayer to Zeus, 1. 505–10: τίμησόν μοι υἱόν . . . Ἀγαμέμνων . . . ἠτίμησεν . . . τεῖσον . . . τείσωσιν . . . τιμῇ. Achilles insists (9. 608–9) that τιμή from Zeus, not from Agamemnon, is what he cares about. Honour is what the hero takes seriously.

**119** After 119 an ancient quotation gives the line ἢ οἴνῳ μεθύων ἢ μ᾿ ἔβλαψαν θεοὶ αὐτοί: 'Either I was drunk or the gods made me fall.' Such an utterance is out of keeping with Homer, who is at pains to exclude or play down the motif of drunkenness: Achilles indeed calls Agamemnon οἰνοβαρές, 1. 225, but the hint is nowhere followed up.

**121-30** The compensating gifts are well discussed by Hainsworth ad loc., who makes the point that they are meant to be overwhelmingly lavish.

**122-56** Repeated at 264-98, word for word except for a few slight changes involved with the change of subject ('I shall' to 'he will'). This is of course the Homeric way with messengers: but it does raise a difficulty for any theory that the poems were exclusively the product of improvising. In passages like this either the singer aimed at exact repetition, or the subsequent tradition has ironed out any irregularities or innovations and produced exact repetition (so A. B. Lord, *Companion to Homer*, 195).

**122** Tripods were used for cooking, but also apparently as treasures in themselves. Some survivors are handsomely decorated. Tripods were often dedicated to gods; they feature among the prizes at Patroclus' funeral games, 23. 259, as also do λέβητες, cauldrons to be heated on them.

τάλαντα. A talent of gold in the classical period is an enormous sum. The Homeric 'talent', the value of which we do not know, must be much smaller.

**124** ἀθλοφόρους, οἳ ἀέθλια ποσσὶν ἄροντο. This form of enlargement by repetition is not uncommon; cf. 3. 15 f., 24. 488 περιναιέται ἀμφὶς ἐόντες, and Macleod's Commentary; Od. 1. 299 f. πατροφονῆα | Αἴγισθον δολόμητιν, ὅς οἱ πατέρα κλυτὸν ἔκτα. More examples, K-G 2. 582⸱8. πηγούς puzzled ancient scholars who can only guess at its meaning—'some say "white", others "black"', says the lexicographer Hesychius.

125 ἀλήϊος. More probably 'without booty' than 'without crops', with ἀκτήμων: as their opposites are used together at 5. 613 πολυκτήμων πολυλήϊος.

128 ἀμύμονα ἔργα ἰδυίας. Homer, 'in point of purity a most blameless writer' (William Cowper, letter to Rev. J. Newton, 3 Dec. 1785), plays down any hint that these women might serve a sexual purpose: cf. the women who are offered as prizes in the games, 23. 262 (ἀμύμονα ἔργα ἰδυῖαν) and 23. 704 (πολλὰ δ' ἐπίστατο ἔργα). The ἔργα are housewifely skills, above all weaving. But they come from Lesbos, where women were famous for their beauty, and where beauty-contests were held (Alcaeus fr. G 2, 33 f. LP), home of Briseis too (131); so they are good lookers. Agamemnon, like Ajax (636-8), cannot understand why seven girls are not seven times as good as one; but for Achilles the point is that he *loved* Briseis (342-3).

On Achilles' raids in the Troad and on neighbouring islands, cf. O. Taplin in *Chios*, ed. J. Boardman and C. E. Vaphopoulou-Richardson (Oxford, 1986), 15-20.

133 τῆς εὐνῆς. 'Her bed', not 'that bed', cf. *Od.* 2. 206 εἵνεκα τῆς ἀρετῆς ἐριδαίνομεν, 'we are competing for her excellence' (of Penelope). This oath is demanded by Odysseus, 19. 175, and publicly sworn by Agamemnon, 19. 257-65; passages which clearly recall this one. Cf. ad 276.

134 θέμις. 'The regular way', cf. note on 99. θέμις, as opposed to δίκη (relations between households or communities), was originally 'l'ordre de la maison et de la famille': Benveniste, *Vocabulaire . . . I-E*, ii. 104 f. So, in Agamemnon's view, even if he *had* done it, he would still not be in the wrong.

137 νῆα . . . νηησάσθω: with effective echo-effect, 'let him heap up for himself gold and silver' (νηέω: partitive genitive).

139 αὐτὸς ἑλέσθω. That is, enjoying the prerogative of the commander-in-chief; cf. 9. 130 ἐξελόμην, 9. 332-3. The virtuous Nestor makes it clear that enjoyment of the captured women was a great motive for the besiegers, 2. 354-6.

141 Ἄργος . . . Ἀχαιϊκόν. The Peloponnese; more generally, 'home'.

οὖθαρ ἀρούρης. οὖθαρ is akin to Eng. *udder*, Latin ˈuber (whence Eng. *exuberance*, originally 'fertility'). The metaphor, only found at

141 = 183, means 'the most fertile of land'; cf. the Biblical 'land flowing with milk and honey'.

143 τηλύγετος. Epic epithet of unknown origin, used of specially loved offspring; of a daughter, 3. 175.

θαλίη. 'Amid great abundance.'

144f. As Agamemnon's daughters the Attic tragedians make us familiar with Electra and Iphigeneia, who was sacrificed to Artemis at Aulis on the way to Troy. Other early poets had other versions. Homer never mentions Iphigeneia, though some have taken 1. 106 as a covert allusion to her; human sacrifice is not to the taste of the Homeric epic (at 18. 337 = 23. 23 we read that the motive for killing Trojan youths at Patroclus' funeral was vengeance, not any kind of sacrifice); rather as the epic does not tell us that Orestes killed his mother (Od. 3. 310 shows that it knows about her death), or that Oedipus and his mother had children together (Od. 11. 274). Tragedy relishes just those aspects of the myth which epic eschews. Cf. J. Griffin in JHS 97 (1977). The three daughters listed here, of whom Iphianassa clearly rules out the possibility of a daughter called Iphigeneia, have names which sum up the virtues of a king: Golden Right, People's Justice, Mighty Rule. (Χρυσόθεμις was 'originally an allusion to feudal dues paid in gold', acc. Webster, From Mycenae to Homer (London, 1958), 121.)

146 φίλην. 'To be attached to him', common meaning of φίλος in Homer (despite D. B. Robinson, 'Homeric φίλος', Owls to Athens ed. E. Craik = Festschrift for K. J. Dover, (Oxford, 1990), 97–108).

ἀνάεδνον. Normally Homer talks in terms of 'bride-price' rather than 'dowry': the bridegroom must pay the bride's father, e.g. the touching account of Iphidamas, 11. 241–7. The word is ἔδνα, also ἔεδνα (cf. Chantraine, GH i. 182), originally Ϝέδνα: ἀνάεδνον, 'without paying bride-price', which could be considerable. At other times the poems seem to envisage the reverse, dowry, system: that too can be called ἔεδνα; Od. 1. 277 = 2. 196. Cf. Janko on 13. 365–7 and refs.; A. M. Snodgrass, JHS 74 (1974), 114–25. Sometimes no doubt both things happened, or both families contributed to set up the new couple.

147 πρὸς οἶκον Πηλῆος. Originally Ϝοῖκος, cf. Latin vicus. It is assumed that Achilles after marriage will live in his father's house. That is true of the large family of Priam (6. 243–50) and

apparently also of Nestor (*Od.* 3. 396 with the note of S. R. West). It is not clear whether it is a historic memory.

μείλια. Connected with μειλίσσω, 'soften'. Not a regular word for 'gifts'; apparently used here because the situation is irregular. In English, 'goodwill offerings'.

**149–53** These seven towns are surprisingly far south-west, not near Mycenae but in southern Messenia, 'on the edge of sandy Pylos'; that is, in or near the kingdom not of Agamemnon but of Nestor. The poet has no clear conception of the constitutional position of Agamemnon (notes on 69, 97), and the implication here may be that he is supreme over the whole Peloponnese. Menelaus was prepared to sweep away a πόλις and build a new one for Odysseus (*Od.* 3. 174ff.). These towns perhaps are to be thought of as constituting a separate unit, between the kingdoms of Nestor and Menelaus.

The implication seems to be that Achilles is to leave his home and become a minor prince dependent on Agamemnon.

**150** Homer constantly makes the third element, in a line which lists three, longer than the other two: e.g. 1. 145 ἢ Αἴας ἢ Ἰδομενεὺς ἢ δῖος Ὀδυσσεύς; 1. 400 Ἥρη τ' ἠδὲ Ποσειδάων καὶ Παλλὰς Ἀθήνη; 2. 478 Σχοῖνόν τε Σκῶλόν τε καὶ εὐρύχορον Μυκαλησσόν; 6. 48 χαλκός τε χρυσός τε πολύκμητός τε σίδηρος, 5. 403 σχέτλιος, ὀβριμοεργός, ὃς οὐκ ὄθετ' αἴσυλα ῥέζων; 9. 187 καλῇ δαιδαλέῃ, ἐπὶ δ' ἀργύρεον ζυγὸν ἦεν. That is an ancient device of Indo-European rhetoric, and it helps to explain why nouns and names which come late in the line regularly have 'ornamental' epithets. Cf. Behaghel, 'Das Gesetz der wachsenden Glieder', *IF* 35 (1909) 111; M. L. West in *JHS* 108 (1988), 155.

**154** πολύρρηνες πολυβοῦται. Two similar adjectives in asyndeton, cf. 5. 613 πολυκτήμων πολυλήιος, 1. 99 ἀπριάτην ἀνάποινον, *Od.* 15. 406 εὔβοτος εὔμηλος; and 9. 63 ἀφρήτωρ ἀθέμιστος ἀνέστιος. Cf. Ø. Andersen in *Glotta*, 60 (1982), 7–13.

**155** θεὸν ὣς τιμήσουσι. Sc. by punctiliously paying their dues. Cf. the related phrases θεὸς δ' ὣς τίετο δήμῳ (×6), θεὸν (θεοὺς) ὣς εἰσορόωσιν (×3), θεῷ ὣς εὐχετόωντο (×3). See note on 211. ὣς lengthens the preceding vowel, because it is from Ϝως, from IE *suō.

**156** τελέουσι. Future, 'they will fulfil ordinances of prosperity'.

ΣAD on the unique use of λιπαράς: ὅσα δεῖ βασιλέα λαμβάνειν
παρὰ τῶν ὑπηκόων, εὐκόλως δώσουσιν· τουτέστι, καὶ ὑποταγέντες
αὐτῷ κατὰ τὸ δίκαιον λαμπροὺς φόρους τελέσουσιν, 'What a king
should get from his subjects, they will give cheerfully; that is, as
his subordinates they will pay shining tribute'. It may be relevant
that the special stones which serve as a king's seat of judgement
are said to be 'glistening with oil', *Od.* 3. 406ff.: cf. S. R. West ad
loc. for refs. to the anointing of holy stones. The glistening appear-
ance of health contrasts with the evaporation caused by misery:
*Od.* 5. 160; 18. 204; 19. 204ff.; 5. 151 οὐδέ ποτ' ὄσσε | δακρυόφιν
τέρσοντο, κατείβετο δὲ γλυκὺς αἰών. The Erinyes suck the liquid
from the bodies of their victims, Aesch. *Eum.* 264-7; 302; ἀλίβας,
'corpse', was thought by the ancients to mean 'dried up'.

**157 μεταλλήξαντι.** Conditional, 'if he abandons his anger'. The
spelling of -λήξαντι with double λλ represents the common occur-
rence in Homer of a 'liquid' consonant (λ, μ, ν, ρ) lengthening the
preceding vowel in pronunciation.

**158-61** Odysseus, who repeats Agamemnon's offer word for
word, has the tact not to quote these blustering lines to Achilles,
cf. note on 299. Agamemnon makes a transparent attempt to
regain some of the 'face' he has lost—but his tone is still mild
when compared with 1. 180-7.

**158 δμηθήτω.** Third person imperative of the aorist passive of
δάμνημι. Cf. 496 ἀλλ', Ἀχιλεῦ, δάμασον θυμὸν μέγαν; 18. 113 θυμὸν
δαμάσαντες ἀνάγκῃ. Between δμηθήτω and ὑποστήτω comes a
parenthesis, in the Homeric manner: Chantraine, *GH* ii. 353. Cf.
e.g. 6. 429, 16. 126-8.

**159** Cf. the line quoted as proverbial by Plato, *Rep.* 390e δῶρα
θεοὺς πείθει, δῶρ' αἰδοίους βασιλῆας. Such a verse could naturally
wear a cynical look.

**160 ὑποστήτω.** 'Let him take his place below me.' Far from
expressing regret, Agamemnon is determined to rub in his
superiority.

**βασιλεύτερος.** See note on 69.

**161** Greater age gives a right to respect in Homer; the first-born
'knows more', 'has seen more', 19. 219, etc.; the Erinyes, aveng-
ing spirits, 'always side with the elder', 15. 204.

162 Γερήνιος. The ancients were baffled by this epithet.

ἱππότα: this word, like μητίετα, is perhaps an original vocative form, retained for metrical convenience in the nominative. Characters with two-syllable names—Nestor, Oeneus, Peleus, Phoenix, Phyleus, Tydeus—receive it at line-end. Such characters tend to be of a previous generation (so Antilochus is son of Nestor, Agamemnon of Atreus, Diomedes of Tydeus, Achilles of Peleus; and note Theseus among the heroes of Nestor's youth, 1. 240), and in fact names of this kind occur on the Linear B tablets as those of ordinary people—so Cretheus, Neleus, even Nestor (T. B. L. Webster, *From Mycenae to Homer* (London, 1958), 119). Perhaps they came with time to be felt as archaic in form, and the word ἱππότα and the related phrase γέρων ἱππηλάτα - - | to be archaic too, and so especially appropriate. See note on 52.

164 δῶρα μέν . . . Nestor seems to imply that Agamemnon's offer is satisfactory so far as the gifts go, but that it fails to produce the 'softening words' which at 113 he said should accompany them (Taplin, *Soundings*, 70).

οὐκέτ'. 'Now not', rather than 'no longer': cf. note on 28.

διδοῖς. Cf. 261 ἄξια δῶρα δίδωσι μεταλλήξαντι χόλοιο, 519. In English these present tenses of δίδωμι mean 'offer'; cf. *Od.* 16. 432, of a suitor who has been trying to kill Odysseus' son Telemachus, παῖδά τ' ἀποκτείνεις. The present tense need not imply the successful completion of the action. With the form (regular: δίδως) cf. 519 διδοῖ, 5. 880 ἀνιεῖς, 6. 523 μεθιεῖς, 13. 732 τιθεῖ: Chantraine, *GH* i. 298f.

165 κλητοὺς ὀτρύνομεν. κλητούς, 'picked men'; ὀτρύνομεν, aorist subjunctive with short vowel, a courteous first person ('let us send . . .'), to avoid giving a direct command.

167 τούς = (Attic) οὕς.

οἱ δὲ πιθέσθων. Superfluous δέ, the longer construction being lost to sight, and the utterance beginning afresh; cf. for instance 9. 300-1, 2. 716-17 οἳ δ' ἄρα Μηθώνην καὶ Θαυμακίην ἐνέμοντο . . . τῶν δὲ Φιλοκτήτης ἦρχεν. Common in Homer; not uncommon in Herodotus and other authors. Chantraine, *GH* ii. 356f.; B. E. Perry, 'The Early Greek Capacity for Viewing Things Separately', *TAPA* 68 (1937), 411. For the construction of future indicative with ἄν, cf. Chantraine, *GH* ii. 223.

168 Φοῖνιξ . . . ἡγησάσθω. This is the first we hear of Phoenix, a

character whom it is not easy to imagine as figuring largely in the tradition before the *Iliad*; generally Achilles' tutor was thought to be Chiron, the righteous Centaur. Homer knows that story, but in keeping with his usual dislike of the monstrous and non-human he keeps it in the background (*Il.* 4. 219, 11. 830-2, 16. 143, 19. 390), giving the hero a fully human tutor in Phoenix. Here we are not told anything about him; that comes where it is relevant, at the start of his appeal to Achilles, vv. 430-95. The point about him is his especially close and emotional relationship with Achilles. Nestor himself does not go, the old man Phoenix serving as his unexpected replacement; but he will have a scene of his own, powerful in procuring Achilles' return, in 11. 618 ff.

Ever since antiquity there has been intense discussion of the number of the envoys to Achilles: were there two, or three? Is Phoenix one of them? Cf. the Appendix. The dual verb forms which follow (note on 182) imply two; and there are other oddities about the position of Phoenix. He is exclusively Achilles' friend, yet he seems to come with the others from Agamemnon (implied by Achilles' words at 427 and 615-19, apparently a plea to Phoenix to spend the night in Achilles' hut, cf. note on 615). Two is the usual number for an embassy in Homer. Some have argued that Phoenix is to act not as an envoy but as a guide, or to prepare the way (Σ in 168): the problem with such explanations is that he apparently neither guides nor prepares for the arrival of Odysseus and Ajax, which comes as a surprise (186 ff., esp. 193 ταφὼν δ᾽ ἀνόρουσεν Ἀχιλλεύς). Moreover, the poet says (192) ἡγεῖτο δὲ δῖος Ὀδυσσεύς—Odysseus it was who led the way. It is not possible to dispose entirely of this difficulty; note on 182. The unexplained oddity of Phoenix being with Agamemnon resembles others: the fact that Chryseis was captured at the sack of Thebe, while her own city of Chryse is still intact (Σ on 1. 366 attempt an explanation: she was there on a visit); the surprising presence in Phthia, when Achilles and Patroclus leave for Troy, of Patroclus' father Menoetius, 11. 765. They have in common a certain high-handed reluctance to be bothered with peripheral questions of detail; cf. notes on 223-4, 676.

**170** A lady does not appear unattended (οὐκ οἴη, ἅμα τῇ γε καὶ ἀμφίπολοι δύ᾽ ἕποντο, 6 times), and great chiefs do not go on a mission alone. Eurybates serves as a herald at 1. 320. The names, presumably felt as 'Road Man' and 'Far Walker', are appropriate to envoys. For such 'speaking names' of minor, functional characters, cf. *Il.* 5. 59, *Τέκτων Ἀρμονίδης*, the father of a craftsman; 17. 323 *Περίφας Ἠπυτίδης* ('Great Voice, son of Caller'), the herald; *Od.* 22. 330, the singer *Φήμιος Τερπιάδης* ('Vocal, son of Delight'); the rather comical Phaeacians with their nautical names, *Od.* 8. 111ff.; Von Kamptz, *Homerische Personennamen* (1982), 25f.; Edwards, *Commentary* (Vol. 5 of G. S. Kirk's Comm. on the *Iliad*) on *Il.* 17. 322–6.

**171 φέρτε.** Archaic form without thematic linking vowel: cf. *κλῦτε, ἔστε, στῆτε.* Cf. J. Wackernagel, *Kleine Schriften*, 1260; R. Schmitt, *Indogermanische Dichtung und Dichtersprache* (1967), 263f. Such imperative forms are normally aorist, not (as here) present, except from verbs in -*μι*. This unique present form has parallels in Vedic formulae.

**173 ἐαδότα.** Perfect participle of *ἁνδάνω*: 'pleasing', 'acceptable', agreeing with *μῦθον*.

**174–7** These formulaic lines recur at *Od.* 3. 338–40, *Od.* 21. 270–3; mixing wine for a group libation is a typical scene, e.g. *Od.* 21. 263ff.; Arend 70–7, Mark W. Edwards, *TAPA* 105 (1975), 56.

**178, 179 ὡρμῶντο, ἐπέτελλε.** As they got into motion, the garrulous Nestor still had advice to give (imperfect). Cf. his long harangue of advice to Antilochus before the chariot race, which the recipient entirely disregards, 23. 306–48. The poet likes Nestor and is amused by him. Presumably the reason why Nestor is not himself one of the envoys is because of Phoenix: we do not want another old man in the episode. He will work on Achilles indirectly, through Patroclus, at 11. 656ff., cf. 804ff. and the opening of Book 16.

**180 ἕκαστον, μάλιστα.** Both of these words more naturally imply three than two listeners, i.e. Phoenix as well as Odysseus and Ajax; *ἑκάτερον* and *μᾶλλον* would be expected for two. Ancient scholars argued this point both ways: *ΣA* in 9. 180; *ΣbT* in 3. 1.

**182** The sea, constantly *πολύφλοισβος* as it was when old Chryses walked beside it alone to pray to his god (1. 34), contrasts the unchanging face of nature with human emotions.

**183 γαιηόχῳ ἐννοσιγαίῳ.** Beside the sea they naturally pray to

97

Poseidon, who is 'holder of the earth' (imagined as surrounded by water, the stream of Ocean) and 'earth-shaker' (as god of earth-quakes).

**184 Αἰακίδαο.** 'Grandson of Aeacus', the father of Peleus.

**186 ff.** *Arrival and Reception of Visitors.* A typical scene, well analysed by Arend (28–35). Regular elements: the new arrival stands [in the doorway], is seen, a host gets up and hurries to greet him, [takes him by the hand], leads him in, seats him on a chair, offers hospitality, they begin to talk. Mark W. Edwards, *TAPA* 105 (1975), 63 f., points out that the motif of 'leading in' is here a little displaced, as the arrivals seem already to be in the building. The poet has avoided introducing a subordinate figure to greet and bring in the heroes: Achilles does it himself.

At 2. 771–9 we heard that Achilles among his ships κεῖτ' ἀπομηνίσας Ἀγαμέμνονι, while his men amused themselves with discus throwing, javelins, and archery; it is a surprise that we find him engaged in music. The detail is important for our perception of Achilles, who is not merely the most formidable warrior but also has a depth of feeling (revealed in this Book) and of insight (revealed in Book 24, especially 24. 518–51) unsurpassed in the poem. He also utters more—and more striking—similes than any other character (Moulton, *Similes* 100). Agamemnon, we feel, would have no music in his nature. But his theme is glorious deeds, and his instrument is a spoil of conquest—from the sack of the city where he killed the father and brothers of Andromache, 6. 414 ff. Heroic song, like heroism itself, is inseparable from human tragedy. The thought is suggested that Achilles, who has aspired to win κλέος ἄφθιτον by a heroic life and death, himself is aware of the poetic tradition, and of himself as a part of it; as Helen, who thinks of herself as a figure of future song (6. 357), weaves into her handiwork the struggles fought over her (3. 125). One of the typical Homeric scenes is the tableau described as a newcomer finds the person whom he seeks busy with some occupation (Arend, *Typische Szenen*, i. 3; Taplin, *Homeric Soundings*, 74–82); as in this case, they may set an emotional background to the scene which follows (de Jong 109 f.).

**186 εὗρον.** A plural form, immediately following the dual ἱκέσθην; so too 195 φῶτας. Such combination, or confusion, is not un-common: K-G i. 73; Burkert in *Wiener Studien*, 10 (1976), 8 n.

12 lists examples. The dual was no longer alive for the Ionian singers, who sometimes seem to regard its forms as simply alternative plurals which might serve a metrical function.

**187** See note on 150. The ζυγόν is the cross-piece between two 'horns' of the lyre: the lyre, like Homer's heroic song itself, is a rich work of art.

**189 κλέα.** Here and at 524 the older form is κλέε', from κλέϝος.

**190** Patroclus: the envoys do not mention him or appeal to his influence with Achilles in their speeches, and he remains silent and unobtrusive in Book 9. His time to intervene will come: 11. 596ff., 16 init.

**191 δέγμενος.** Like some other verbs in Homer, δέχομαι preserves traces of athematic conjugation (without linking vowel between stem and termination), thus 1. 23 δέχθαι, 2. 420 δέκτο, here δέγμενος: Chantraine, GH 1. 296. 'Waiting for Achilles, when he should stop singing.' So Od. 9. 174 τῶν δ' ἀνδρῶν πειρήσομαι, οἵ τινες εἰσιν; Il. 5. 85 Τυδείδην δ' οὐκ ἂν γνοίης ποτέροισι μετείη: instead of saying 'Let me try what sort of men these are', 'You could not tell which side Diomedes was on.'

**192-3 τὼ δὲ βάτην . . . στάν.** On these duals, see note on 182. The scene reminds us of the arrival of the two κήρυκες to take away Briseis, 1. 327-32; they too stood before Achilles in silence (332).

**194 αὐτῇ σὺν φόρμιγγι.** This use of αὐτός means 'complete with', 'still holding the lyre'; cf. 541; 14. 498, of a beheading: ἀπήραξεν δὲ χαμᾶζε | αὐτῇ σὺν πήληκι κάρη, the head still in the helmet.

**θάασσεν.** Imperfect; in English, pluperfect: 'the seat where he had been sitting'.

**197 ἦ τι μάλα χρεώ.** 'There must be some urgent occasion', cf. 10. 85. Achilles emphasizes that he regards them as his friends, cf. 204 φίλτατοι ἄνδρες, not as mere envoys of his enemy. With him all is spontaneous and emotional.

**200 εἷσεν.** Aorist of ἵζω, 'he seated them', in contrast with the imperfect ἄγε: 'taking them in' was a process, seating them a single act. Only in the sixth century did the Oriental habit come in of reclining at meals.

**ἐν κλισμοῖσι τάπησί τε.** The crimson rugs were spread on the seats, cf. *Od.* 10. 352f. Thetis sent a supply of them when her son sailed: 16. 221–4.

**203 ζωρότερον δὲ κέραιε.** 'Mix it stronger'. Greeks at all times drank their wine diluted with water. An extreme instance: dilution at the rate of twenty to one was needed for the specially intoxicating wine which fuddled the Cyclops (*Od.* 9. 209). A vessel tablet in Linear B lists a *ka-ra-te-ra*, (crater, mixing bowl), which shows that the practice goes back to Mycenaean times (MY Ue 611, cf. Ventris and Chadwick, *Documents*,² 331; 495). Only hardened boozers drank ἄκρατος (Latin, *merum*). Even gods are imagined as 'mixing' their nectar: *Od.* 5. 93. Here Achilles surely orders a stronger mix, to greet his visitors. Cf. Catullus 27. 2 *inger mi calices amariores* (with less water), though the word ζωρός is obscure, and Empedocles seems to have taken it to mean the opposite: 31 B35. 15 DK.

**204 οἱ γὰρ.** Not, as in later Greek, the definite article with φίλτατοι, but a demonstrative: 'these are my dearest friends . . .'

'Under my roof': Ajax will appeal to this fact as one which ought to have weight: 640.

**206 κρεῖον.** 'Meat tray' for carving the roast meat.

**κάββαλεν,** aorist of καταβάλλω.

**207 ἐν δ' ἄρα νῶτον ἔθηκε.** In Homeric Greek the prepositions and verbs have still not yet united indissolubly to form compound verbs. This appears to be an archaism: already on the Linear B tablets the compound verbs are indivisible. A remarkable example of the tenacity of the oral epic style. Cf. Introduction p. 29. In Attic Greek the elements cannot be separated in this way, and one must say ἐνέθηκε δέ; but this sort of division is a regular feature of Homeric style.

The back was the cut of honour, cf. 7. 321 νώτοισιν δ' Αἴαντα διηνεκέεσσι γέραιρεν. Achilles is courteous in his hospitality, a trait which helps to prepare us for his entertainment of Priam in 24.

**209 τῷ.** Automedon held the meat for Achilles to carve. In 16 he is Patroclus' charioteer, but again in 24 (474, 574, 625) he serves at table. Homeric men are not specialists: Automedon has an *aristeia* as a warrior, 17. 426–542.

**210ff.** There is a similar but fuller description of barbecueing meat, 1. 459ff.

211 **Μενοιτιάδης.** Patroclus.

**ἰσόθεος φώς.** the phrase comes 14 times in Homer, always at the end of the line. See note on 155 for other formulae of divine honour paid to mortals; but despite these courtesies an unbridgeable gap remained, cf. 1. 573f., 5. 438-42, 16. 705-11, 21. 451-7.

212 An ancient variant existed to this line, not found in any manuscript but quoted by later writers (cf. 23. 228) αὐτὰρ ἐπεὶ πυρὸς ἄνθος ἀπέπτατο, παύσατο δὲ φλόξ. We hear of the πυρὸς ἄνθος at [Aeschylus] *PV* 7, and of *flammai flos* at Lucretius 1. 900; the variant seems to have been well known, but in the text of the *Iliad* the reading of the manuscripts is to be preferred. The variant may have originated in some lost epic poem and been erroneously attached to this place. Cf. 23. 228 τῆμος πυρκαϊὴ ἐμαραίνετο, παύσατο δὲ φλόξ.

214 **πάσσε δ' ἁλός.** Partitive genitive, 'sprinkled some salt'. θείοιο, perhaps because—like gold—salt does not corrupt.

215 **ἐλεοῖσιν.** 'Serving tables.'

217 The meal resembles one of kebabs and pitta bread. Homer never mentions vegetables, no doubt for stylistic reasons: roast meat is heroic, salads are not.

219 **τοίχου τοῦ ἑτέροιο.** 'Against the opposite wall', genitive of place; cf. Macleod on *Il.* 24. 598.

221-2 = 91-2. Odysseus and Ajax have already dined once this evening, as Odysseus points out, 225f. Homeric etiquette compels them to eat again, before coming to serious business, and it is inept to object to line 222 on the ground that the heroes were now not really hungry (ΣA in 222), or to emend the text. ('It would have been better if he had said ἂψ ἐπάσαντο', said Aristarchus—who, it is important to observe, did not put his reading into the text, 'from excess of caution, finding the other reading in many manuscripts'. That illustrates his scholarly method). This rule is raised to an extraordinary power when Achilles obliges Priam to eat with him, despite his mourning, in token of human fellowship (24. 601ff.), an example of the way in which Homer achieves his most striking effects by reworking and deepening his usual repertoire of motifs, not by abandoning it.

223-4 Ajax nods to Phoenix, and Odysseus begins to speak. This is very unlike Homeric good manners, which tend to be rather formal; and it is not explained why Odysseus cuts in. It was implied at 168 that Phoenix was to go first and be in the lead, and Ajax's gesture seems to be in line with that. Scholars ancient and modern have supplied psychological inventions. An ancient guess was that 'Odysseus wanted Achilles to exhaust his anger on him and then yield to affection to someone closer to him, namely Phoenix' (ΣA); van Leeuwen alleged that 'Ajax and Odysseus had decided this on the way'. Some ancient commentators argued that Ajax did not signal Phoenix to start, but to ask if it was time to start (ΣbT; so Motzkus 106–10). Willcock finds 'a typical Homeric feat of character-drawing . . . We observe ponderous Aias, the unassertive Phoinix, and Odysseus quick off the mark.' Such speculations are without real foundation. It is vital for the scene as a whole that the first speech should convey Agamemnon's formal offer of satisfaction, and the eloquent Odysseus (3. 221 ff.) was a good mouthpiece; only after that offer has been made and rejected can we have the quite different and much more emotional appeal of Phoenix (note on 432). That is to say, in the full version of the scene which we have in Book 9 it must be so. The story could be told in other ways, shorter and differently arranged, and doubtless it was; as at other notable points (notes on 182 and 676 ff.), the poet responsible for 9 shows himself unconcerned about smoothing the details of the narrative and more interested in the characters and their speeches.

**224 πλησάμενος δ᾽ οἴνοιο.** Late form which disregards the digamma (Ϝοίνοιο, cf. Latin *vinum*, *wine*).

**δείδεκτ᾽:** cf. 4. 4 *al.* δειδέχατ᾽ ἀλλήλους: 'pledged', 'drank to', Achilles; reduplicated forms with present sense, related to δειδίσκομαι (δέπαϊ χρυσέῳ δειδίσκετο, 18. 121) and ultimately to δείκνυμαι (196) 'greet'.

**225–306 The Speech of Odysseus.** Odysseus lives up to the praise given to him as an orator by the Trojan Antenor (3. 204–24). He opens with a 7-line introduction (225–31): the situation is grave. That is then spelt out in detail, three 4-line sentences setting out the Trojan successes and threats, and an 8-line summary urging immediate intervention (232–5, 236–9, 240–3, 244–51). The first section of his speech thus has an elegant shape. The second section (252–61) reminds Achilles of his father's parting words and warning against indulgence in anger; it closes with a deft transition ('Cease your anger, and Agamemnon will reward you') to reporting Agamemnon's offers (262-99), repeated in the same words with minimal changes (note on 134). Naturally Odysseus has the tact to replace Agamemnon's blustering conclusion (158-61), 'Let him acknowledge my superiority', with a 7-line one of his own—the counterpart in length of his opening (300-6)—in two parts, an appeal and an enticement: 'Even if you are implacable to Agamemnon, save the rest of us': and also, 'Now you can catch Hector!' Odysseus avoids presenting himself as the envoy of Agamemnon, and speaks not of the king's sufferings but of the Achaeans' as a whole, and of Achilles' opportunities to win honour and reward. It is an able performance, but the vehemence and personal passion of Achilles' reply make it look, by comparison, thin and impersonal, the speech of a mouthpiece. Odysseus makes no comment of his own on events, and he expresses no sympathy, either with Agamemnon or with Achilles. Hainsworth (*Commentary* ad loc.) gives a useful analysis of the speech in technical rhetorical terms (Odysseus' speech is 'the best organized of the four speakers').

**225 οὐκ ἐπιδευεῖς.** Sc. ἐσμέν, cf. Schwyzer, *Gr. Gramm.* ii. 623.

**δαιτὸς ἐΐσης:** 'evenly shared' is a standard epithet of meals in Homer, placing the emphasis on a moral and human, rather than a gastronomic, quality. On his wanderings Odysseus must take care that all his men get their fair share, *Od.* 9. 42 = 549, δασσάμεθ', ὡς μή τίς μοι ἀτεμβόμενος κίοι ἴσης.

**227 πάρα:** (so accented) = πάρεστι.

**228-31** The emphatic repetition δαίνυσθ' . . . οὐ δαιτός is further echoed by the deltas of διοτρεφές, δοιῇ δέ, δύσεαι. 'We are not concerned with the delights of the table but . . .'

**230 σαωσέμεν.** A transitive verb (aorist infinitive of σαόω, by-form of σῴζω), while ἀπολέσθαι is intransitive; the combination is awkward. Bekker plausibly conjectured σόας ἔμεν, 'whether the ships are saved or lost'.

**231 δύσεαι ἀλκήν.** From 'putting on' armour the verb is extended to a metaphor, 'putting on' fighting spirit; a determined warrior can be 'clothed in it', ἐπιειμένος ἀλκήν (7. 164); an impudent person can be 'clothed in shamelessness', 372. Conversely, it can

enter into the warrior, using the same verb, δύνω: 239 κρατερὴ δέ
ἑ λύσσα δέδυκεν, cf. 17. 210 δῦ μιν Ἄρης; 19. 16 μιν ἔδυ χόλος. We
are not far here from such mythical ideas as that of the aegis,
which when worn terrifies opponents (15. 229), or the Gorgon's
head on Athena's shield (5. 741 f.) or Agamemnon's (11. 36), or
even the κεστὸς ἱμάς, the magical talisman which makes a goddess
who wears it sexually irresistible (14. 214 f.), or the helmet of
Hades, which makes the wearer invisible (5. 844 f.).

**232-43** See note on 225-306 on structure. Odysseus gives
Achilles a compressed account of the events of Book 8 and the
position at 8. 487 ff.

**232-5** 'The Trojans are menacing the ships.'

**234 πυρὰ πολλά.** These are the fires ordered by Hector at 8. 509
and described at 8. 554 ff. Of course, Odysseus cannot really know
what the Trojans and Hector are saying: we have heard it, and
Odysseus is allowed to share our knowledge (other examples of
this technique: Taplin, *Homeric Soundings*, 150 n. 4).

**235** = 12. 107, 126; 17. 639. Here it means that 'they (the
Trojans) will not be held back but will fall upon the ships'; but at
12. 126 it must mean that 'the Achaeans would not resist but be
killed by the ships'. A striking example of misunderstanding which
gives a new sense to a formulaic expression.

**236-9** 'Zeus is on the side of Hector.'

**236 ἐνδέξια σήματα φαίνων.** Two of these favourable omens are
recorded in 8: 8. 133, thunder, and a bolt of lightning in front
of Diomedes' chariot; 8. 170, three claps of thunder from Mount
Ida. Zeus is lord of the sky and its phenomena, ἐρίγδουπος ('loud
thunderer') and ἀργικέραυνος ('of the bright lightning'), and his
name (originally something like *d(i)ieus) is from the same IE root
as Latin *dies*, 'day', Sanskrit *dyáuh*, 'god of the sky', 'day'. Hence
such expressions as Διὸς ὄμβρος, 'the rain that comes from Zeus',
5. 91; 'Zeus the cloudgatherer', νεφεληγερέτα; Zeus also grants
clear sky, 17. 646. Cf. A. B. Cook, *Zeus.* i: 'Zeus God of the Bright
Sky' (Cambridge, 1914).

**237 σθένεϊ βλεμεαίνων.** This formula is used of Hector by the poet
himself, 8. 337: 'exulting in his prowess'.

**239 λύσσα.** The behaviour of a mad dog, κύνα λυσσητῆρα, as
Hector is called by Teucer at 8. 299; probably connected with the

word λύκος, 'wolf'. λύσσα δέδυκεν, see note on 231; the meaning is the same as that of the superficially opposite expression, λύσσαν ἔχων, 305. Homer is familiar with ecstatic, Berserker fighting, cf. the description of Hector, thrust on by Zeus, 'raging' (μαίνεται) like Ares, and foaming at the mouth: ἀφλοισμὸς δὲ περὶ στόμα γίγνετο, τὼ δέ οἱ ὄσσε | λαμπέσθην βλοσυροῖσιν ὑπ' ὀφρύσιν . . ., 15. 605-8. Achilles too has λύσσα, but the poet gives it no such inhuman features: 21. 542-3. Cf. B. Lincoln, 'Homeric Lussa', IF 80 (1975), 98-105.

**240-3** 'Hector plans our complete destruction.'

**240 ἠῶ δῖαν.** Originally, and more metrically, ἠόα. This refers to Hector's words, 8. 530-41.

**241 στεῦται.** With στεῦτο, the only occurring forms of an ancient verb, originally meaning 'vow'. Leumann, Homerische Wörter, 21.

**242 πυρός.** The genitive, where the dative might have been expected, is an extension of the usage with verbs of filling and sharing; it reappears with ἐμπιμπράναι at 16. 81; cf, 2. 415, 6. 331; Od. 17. 23. Hector will in the event succeed in half-burning one ship: 16. 122-4, 16. 293-4.

**242-3** Echo Hector's words, 8. 182-3.

**245 ἐκτελέσωσι . . . εἴη.** The fear is that Hector's threats may be fulfilled; in that case, the consequence would be that 'we should perish'. The further, second, fear is added on, optative to subjunctive, as a separate and more remote apprehension. Cf. Od. 22. 77; Chantraine, GH ii. 299.

**246 φθίσθαι.** Like ἔφθιτο, φθίμενος, and some other forms, ancient athematic aorists from φθίνω: Chantraine, GH i. 381.

**247 ἀλλ' ἄνα.** ἀλλά often introduces commands, a usage in which it is not well rendered in English with 'but'. ἄνα seems to be equivalent to ἀνάστηθι: roughly = English 'Come on!'

**249-50 μῆχος.** Always recurs in this position and in the phrase οὐδέ τι μῆχος (×4). Here almost a doublet with ἄκος ('and there is no remedy to find a cure for the evil, once done'); and ῥεχθέντος is unique in Homer, the aorist passive of ῥέζω occurring only in the proverbial phrase ῥεχθὲν δέ τε νήπιος ἔγνω (17. 32; 20. 198). The poet can perhaps be seen going out of his way to get in the jingle ἄχος/ἄκος, in the same position in the line.

**251 φράζευ.** 'Take thought.' Achilles sarcastically echoes this word, 347: φραζέσθω,'let Agamemnon take thought'.

**ἦμαρ.** κακὸν ἦμαρ = 'suffering disaster', as δούλιον ἦμαρ = 'condition of slavery', ἐλεύθερον ἦμαρ = 'condition of freedom', ἦμαρ ὀρφανικόν (22. 490) 'being an orphan'. In this sense ἦμαρ means 'the condition in which one finds oneself'; cf. *Od.* 18. 137f. τοῖος γὰρ νόος ἐστὶν ἐπιχθονίων ἀνθρώπων, | οἷον ἐπ' ἦμαρ ἄγῃσι πατὴρ ἀνδρῶν τε θεῶν τε: 'a man's mood, state of mind, depends on the condition in which Zeus puts him at the time'; as it changes, so he is ἐφήμερος, 'in the power, at the mercy, of the "day"' — mortals change in response to changing conditions, as gods do not. Cf. Pindar, *Pyth.* 8. 95ff., H. Fränkel, *Wege und Formen frühgriechischen Denkens* (Munich, 1960), 23–39.

**252–9** Odysseus reminds Achilles of his father's parting words: he was present (11. 764–6). So, but more tactfully, and with more success, Nestor reminds Patroclus of the same scene, and of the parting words of his father: 11. 765ff. Phoenix, too, will appeal to Peleus' farewell: 252 = 439 = 11. 766. Nestor reports Peleus' words to Achilles differently, to suit his different purpose, 11. 784, as αἰὲν ἀριστεύειν καὶ ὑπείροχον ἔμμεναι ἄλλων; here the emphasis is not on competition but on co-operation. The parting scene is referred to also at 7. 124ff. and 18. 324ff.

**252 ὦ πέπον.** Odysseus strikes a note of intimacy with this fresh address.

**254 Ἀθηναίη τε καὶ Ἥρη.** The two goddesses constantly active on the Achaean side. Athena is the companion and patron of heroes in their heroic activities: she tells of her constant support for Heracles, 8. 362ff., she was the companion of Tydeus (4. 390, 5. 124–6) and of his son Diomedes (5. 124–6, 246 τρεῖν μ' οὐ ἐᾷ Παλλὰς Ἀθήνη, etc.) as she is of Odysseus and of his son Telemachus. That is connected with her Mycenaean role as personal goddess of the king; note that in Athens her temple and the king's house are the same building, *Od.* 7. 80–1. Cf. Burkert, *Greek Religion* (1985), 139–43. A spectacular instance of Athena magnifying Achilles: 18. 202ff. Hera intervenes in Achilles' favour: 1. 55, 208; 18. 168; 21. 328. Less intimate speakers content themselves with saying that 'the gods' or '(a) god' made Achilles so strong: 1. 178, 290.

**255 μεγαλήτορα θυμόν.** See on 109.

**256 ἴσχειν.** The use of the infinitive to convey a command is ancient and common: Chantraine, *GH* ii. 316.

**φιλοφροσύνη γὰρ ἀμείνων.** This has a proverbial ring, cf. Hesiod, *Erga* 365 = Homeric *Hymn to Hermes* 36, οἴκοι βέλτερον εἶναι, ἐπεὶ βλαβερὸν τὸ θύρηφιν; I. 274 ἀλλὰ πίθεσθε καὶ ὔμμες, ἐπεὶ πείθεσθαι ἄμεινον; 12. 412 ἀλλ᾽ ἐφομαρτεῖτε· πλεόνων δέ τοι ἔργον ἄμεινον; *Od.* 22. 104, 374. But the word φιλοφροσύνη comes only here in Homer, and the sentiment ('good fellowship is best') may be, within the heroic tradition, rather late. The sentiment is important to the *Iliad*, see on 109. φιλοφροσύνη: cf. φίλα φρονέων, *Il.* 4. 219 etc., and its opposite, κακὰ φρονέων.

**257 ἔρις.** Repeatedly denounced in the *Iliad*: 1. 177, 5. 891. Achilles, after the event, curses it: 18. 107. A central point of the poem.

**258 = 11.** 790 (Nestor to Patroclus).

**260 χόλον θυμαλγέα.** Also ascribed to Achilles at 4. 513. χόλος pains the angry man's own heart; though it is also 'as sweet as honey' to experience (18. 108-9). Anyone who has ever sulked will admit the truth of both statements.

**261 μεταλλήξαντι.** See on 157.

**262 εἰ δέ.** See on 46.

**264ff.** = 122ff.

**269** This line has had to be changed from 127 to eliminate the first person. The decorative epithet μώνυχες is dropped, to make room for Agamemnon's name.

**272** Grammatical change from 130 has led to the introduction of the stop-gap τότε. Allusions to division of booty: 1. 124ff., 166ff.; 2. 227; 11. 696; 16. 56; *Od.* 14. 232.

**276** At 134 the line had the form ἢ θέμις ἀνθρώπων πέλει, ἀνδρῶν ἠδὲ γυναικῶν. This is the only change not forced by grammar: Odysseus could have repeated 134. The alteration must be a psychologically motivated one—at this most sensitive point Odysseus thinks it well to throw in an extra 'my lord'. M. D. Reeve argued (*CQ* 22 (1972), 1-2) that this line was composed before 134, and 269 before 127, so that the poet 'started with Odysseus' speech and made only the necessary alterations of· person' when he subsequently came to compose Agamemnon's. That would be a surprising procedure, and the argument seems to me to fail on line 272, where the word τότε has had to be brought in to make 130 scan in the first person.

**300** Odysseus replaces Agamemnon's blustering conclusion (158-61) with a much more tactful one: Achilles should not sacrifice his friends, however much he may hate Agamemnon. The appeal is put more emotionally by Ajax, 630-2, 641-2.

**301** περ. Emphasizes the word it follows: 'the others, at any rate'.
δέ: see on 167.

**302** This promise of honour is repeated by Phoenix, 603 ἶσον γάρ σε θεῷ τείσουσιν Ἀχαιοί.

**303** The thought of Achilles winning honour leads to a particular application: he could get the glory of killing Hector!
σφι. 'Among them', 'with them'; for the dative cf. 4. 95 πᾶσι δέ κε Τρώεσσι χάριν καὶ κῦδος ἔλοιο.

**304f.** Cf. 352-4: in the old days Hector was too careful.
λύσσαν: see on 239.

**306** Compare Hector's over-confident words about Diomedes, 8. 532-8, and about Achilles, 18. 305-8.

**307-429** *Achilles' reply to Odysseus' speech*. It falls into four main parts, after a short introduction.

Introduction: 308-14   Let me be absolutely frank:
1: 315-45   My grievance against Agamemnon
   316-20 There has been no gratitude for merit         A
   321-2 I am no better off for my exertions and risks    B
   323-4 like a self-sacrificing mother bird            C
   325-9 I have lived an existence of exertion       B
   330-3 while Agamemnon has done nothing and grabbed
      the spoils                             A
   334-7 My prize alone he has taken away—the wife
      whom I loved                         A
   337-43 and yet we are making war over the theft of
      a wife!                               B
   344-5 he has taken her and cheated me; never again!   A
2*a*: 346-63   Agamemnon's situation without me: let him
      think about it
   346-50 Without me, he has built a fine wall

351-5 but it won't keep out Hector—who was not so brave, when I was fighting

356-63 but now I won't fight him; and tomorrow I shall sail home

2*b*: 364-77   My position without Agamemnon

364-7 I have plenty, at home and here

367-9 except what Agamemnon took back;

369-77 give him my refusal publicly: I won't have any more to do with him; he's cheated me once—to hell with him!

3: 378-426   Agamemnon's gifts in their true light

378-87 I won't touch his gifts, however enormous

388-97 I won't marry his daughter—I'll find a wife at home

298-408 and live in comfort: no prize is worth a man's life

410-16 and my life, if glorious, will be short.

4: 417-26   Advice to the Achaeans: abandon the expedition!

427-9 Phoenix can stay here and sail home in the morning.

This is the most splendid speech in Homer, in range and power. The envoys expected Achilles to accept Agamemnon's offer. Nestor called them δῶρα . . . οὐκέτ' ὀνοστά (164); Phoenix begs Achilles to accept what is, in the eyes of one who loves him, adequate compensation (515-23); Ajax is frankly baffled by his refusal (636-9). It is at this point that the plot of the *Iliad* changes its direction and its nature. From a simple story of an aggrieved hero forcing his king to reward and honour him (1. 213 καί ποτέ τοι τρὶς τόσσα παρέσσεται ἀγλαὰ δῶρα | ὕβριος εἴνεκα τῆσδε, Athena's promise; 1. 505-10 'Honour my son!'—Thetis' prayer to Zeus), a familiar story line as we see from 524-6—Achilles' refusal to accept the compensation, or to suggest terms which he would accept, turns events into a baffling position, in which neither Agamemnon nor Achilles knows what to do next. The compromise resolution is the substitution of Patroclus, which leads to tragedy for Achilles; his success in the plan of Book 1 is now meaningless, as he admits in Book 18: μῆτερ ἐμή, τὰ μὲν ἄρ μοι Ὀλύμπιος ἐξετέλεσσεν· | ἀλλὰ τί μοι τῶν ἦδος, ἐπεὶ φίλος ὤλεθ' ἑταῖρος | Πάτροκλος; . . . τὸν ἀπώλεσα . . . (18. 79-81). His refusal here is thus the hinge of the whole plot, and it is vital for the poem that it should be powerful and convincing.

Achilles' speech is an explosion of hoarded anger, which floods out with pathos, irony, bitterness, and the passionate rejection of the life and death of a hero, if it must be lived on terms without χάρις, gratitude and honour due to a man who accepts the heroic destiny and performs it. Brooding on his treatment, Achilles has begun to ask why he should fight and die. When his prizes, his share of the spoils, were tokens of honour, they were precious; now that he has been dishonoured he sees them, and the concrete compensation now offered by Agamemnon, as mere objects of cash value—and no quantity of objects of that sort can be worth a man's life. Cf. D. B. Claus in *TAPA* 105 (1975), 21 ff. (p. 23, Agamemnon has . . . 'transformed the gifts (γέρα) from their proper status as a mere symbol of Achilles' *arete* into a practical measure of it'). Heroism is a cheat, if Agamemnon can break his bargain by refusing to treat a hero as he deserves (ἀπάτησε, 344; ἐκ . . . ἀπάτησε, 375). It is important that the prize of which he is robbed is not a gold cup or some similar possession but a woman, whom he claims to love; the wound is deeper and evokes a different kind of sympathy. The style shows extraordinary range: massive single-line generalizations, rhetorical questions, pathetic comparisons, and a skilful use of short and chopped utterances beside long sentences which build up to a crushing climax. Achilles found no χάρις in Odysseus' careful speech. R. P. Martin, *Language of Heroes*, 167–70, sets out this speech, underlining the formulaic expressions in it. Achilles can be seen to use devices familiar in formal rhetoric, but 'only to transcend them or put them to daring and startling new uses' (R. B. Rutherford, edn. of *Odyssey* 19 and 20 (Cambridge, 1992), 61): rhetorical questions (337–41), the enumeration of his own achievements (325–32), and the deriding of Agamemnon's (348–50); the repeated negatives at the climax (379–91). This intensity is specific to Achilles' way of speaking, and he is given by the poet a special vocabulary, emotional and vivid, including αἱματόεις (of days), ἀναιδείην ἐπιειμένος, εἰκοσάκις, ἐπισκύζομαι, ἐφυβρίζω, θυμαλγής, κύνεος, λεϊστή, τρύζομαι (cf. 1. 148–71 and J. Griffin, 'Homeric Words and Speakers', *JHS* 106 (1986).

**308-13** Plato makes the sophist Hippias comment on these lines: 'In these verses he makes clear the character (τρόπος) of each of the two men: that Achilles is veracious and straightforward, while Odysseus is versatile and mendacious—he shows us Achilles saying this to Odysseus' (*Hippias Minor* 364e–7).

309 ἀπηλεγέως ἀποειπεῖν. The adverb ἀπηλεγέως occurs in Homer only in this phrase (also *Od.* 1. 373); the repeated απ caught the singer's ear. ἀποειπεῖν here must mean 'declare', 'state', not 'deny' (as at 510, 675), cf. 23. 361 ἀληθείην ἀποείποι. ἀπηλεγέως comes, or was thought to come, from ἀλέγω: 'without caring for anything or anybody', 'bluntly'. The effect of this announcement is to make Odysseus' polished oration look rather shallow.

311 τρύζητε. A vigorous word: strictly 'coo', like doves (τρυγόνες); here 'murmur'. The sole appearance of the verb in Homer.

ἄλλοθεν ἄλλος. More vigorous alliteration, cf. 309, helping the cruelly sharp image.

312 ἐχθρὸς γάρ μοι κεῖνος. The thought is expressed in general terms. Strictly, its first application is to Achilles himself: 'I speak frankly—any other way would be hateful to me.' But it carries also a disobliging second meaning, in its implied contrast with what has just been said. Motzkus (11) thinks the second meaning of κεῖνος is not Odysseus but Agamemnon. Plato refers it to Odysseus, *Hippias Minor* 365a. Taplin (*Homeric Soundings*, 69 f.) sees in these lines a glance by Achilles at Odysseus' failure to express any real emotion on Agamemnon's part: his words don't come from his heart.

312–13 Achilles' emphasis on sincerity looks forward to his repeated charge that Agamemnon has deceived him, 344, 375. Odysseus, famous for his κακοὶ δόλοι (4. 339), and in the *Odyssey* a world-class liar (cf. Athena's words, *Od.* 13. 287–99, 330–2), is in later Greek thought constantly contrasted with the bluff, straightforward Ajax, the hero who should have won the armour of Achilles if Odysseus had not cheated him: Pindar, *Nem.* 7. 20 ff., *Isth.* 3–4. 53 ff.; Sophocles, *Ajax*; *Carmina Convivialia* 15 and 16P; Plato, *Hippias Minor*, *init.* These are the two possible modes of heroism, and Greeks insisted that Achilles' was the better.

We know, but Achilles does not, that *he* has just been compared with Hades by Agamemnon (158 f.), a passage tactfully omitted by Odysseus; for us, then, there is an ironical echo, among the rest of the resonance of this passage (A. Thornton in *Glotta*, 56 (1978), 4).

315 The phrasing recalls and enlarges on Agamemnon's self-

confident words, 1. 287–9 and Achilles' reply, 1. 295–6 (Martin, *Language of Heroes*, 207).

**316–17 ἐπεὶ . . . νωλεμὲς αἰεί.** = 17. 147f. The repetition suggests that the lines are not to be treated as unHomeric and unique in their thought, as is sometimes argued. Achilles' point is that he has acted like a hero but has not been treated like one—not only by Agamemnon but by the other Achaeans, too (316, οὔτ' ἄλλους Δαναούς, replying to 301f.).

**οὐκ ἄρα . . . ἦεν.** A common Greek idiom, where English uses the present tense: 'after all, there was (all the time) no χάρις'. Cf. Hesiod, *Erga* 11 οὐκ ἄρα μοῦνον ἔην Ἐρίδων γένος—'after all, there are two kinds of competitiveness'; *Il.* 8. 163 γυναικὸς ἄρ' ἀντὶ τέτυξο 'after all, you are no better than a woman'. χάρις: cf. Hoekstra on *Od.* 15. 139; Taplin, *Homeric Soundings*, 59. χάρις is, or should be, reciprocal: χάρις χάριν γάρ ἐστιν ἡ τίκτουσ' ἀεί, Soph. *Ajax* 522.

**318–20** Three single-line expressions of proverbial type; 318–19 are generalized accounts of Achilles' treatment on this expedition, but 320 is universally true of all men. Many scholars have ejected it from the text (Bekker, Leaf, etc.). On the other hand, it does foreshadow the theme of death, and of Achilles' own death, so important from 401ff., and the 'universal' meaning can also be felt to be present in the word μοῖρα in 318: not only 'Agamemnon doesn't give fair shares', but also 'all men's lot is death'. The next two lines bring out both senses successively (D. B. Claus, *TAPA* 105 (1975), 18 n. 7). Achilles expressed resentment at the unfair distribution of prizes already at 1. 161ff.

**319 κακός.** 'The coward', cf. e.g. 6. 443, 11. 408; ἐσθλός, 'the brave man'.

**320 κάτθαν'.** For κατέθανε, gnomic or timeless aorist.

**ὅ τ' ἀεργὸς ἀνὴρ ὅ τε πολλὰ ἐοργώς.** This use of ὁ ἡ τό to classify a type, regular in later Greek, is rare in Homer and doubtless late; cf. 13. 278 ἔνθ' ὅ τε δειλὸς ἀνήρ, ὅς τ' ἄλκιμος, ἐξεφαάνθη. Note that in 319 κακός and ἐσθλός would have the definite article in later Greek. ἐοργώς was originally ϝεϝοργώς, from ϝεργ-, the root of English 'work'.

**321 περίκειται.** Like περίεστι, περισσός: 'there is nothing extra for me.'

**322 ἐμὴν ψυχὴν παραβαλλόμενος.** 'Staking, risking, my own life.' This looks forward to 401 ff.

**323 ἀπτῆσι.** Dative plural of ἀπτήν, 'unfledged'.

**323–4** Similes uttered by the characters may have a more openly emotional colouring than those uttered by the poet: compare 16. 3–4 with 16. 7–11, also spoken by Achilles, who produces another memorably emotional comparison at 21. 282f. Similes spoken by the characters tend to be more intense; they are never as lengthy and elaborate as some of those in the narrative. I do not find this one 'petulant' (Hainsworth ad loc.).

**324 κακῶς δ' ἄρα οἱ πέλει αὐτῇ.** A separate sentence, not grammatically subordinate as it would naturally be in later formal Greek; cf. 6. 509f., a striking example; 21. 94.

**326 ἤματα δ' αἱματόεντα.** The jingle has helped to distort the expected word-order (πολλὰ δὲ ἤματα), in favour of one which is rhetorically powerful ('many sleepless nights—and the days I spent were bloody').

**327 ὀάρων.** 'Fighting men for their wives.' Achilles' thoughts are on booty and its unfair distribution, but this bitter line leads to questioning the whole rationale of the expedition. The men he kills are defending their families, cf. 24. 541–2 'Here I sit at Troy, far from home, bringing grief on you and your children', a perspective which makes the war repulsive. There is the further absurdity, that the justification for the war in the first place was the abduction of a wife, the thought which will be powerfully developed at 337ff. ὄαρ is a rare word of unknown etymology.

**328–9 δώδεκα δὴ σὺν νηυσὶ . . . πεζὸς δ' ἔνδεκα.** Chiastic word-order (ABBA).

**Τροίην.** The dependent area of Troy and its towns. Briseis and Chryseis were captured on such a raid—a regular feature of life in the Homeric age; e.g. *Od.* 3. 71–4, 14. 220–34, 17. 470–2. Cf. the conventional epithet of heroes, πτολίπορθος (used four times of Achilles in *Il.*).

After this point there is a noticeable change of rhythm. Hitherto most lines have been end-stopped, the movement stately; now the pace quickens, with many run-ons between lines, as Achilles turns from generalizations to narrative.

**330ff.** π̲α̲σ̲έων κ̲ε̲ι̲μήλια π̲ολλὰ κ̲αὶ . . . π̲άντα φ̲έρων Ἀγαμέμνονι

113

Ἀτρείδη . . . δεξάμενος διὰ παῦρα δασάσκετο πολλὰ δ' ἔχεσκεν. Sound-patterns reinforce Achilles' rising anger. Also the echo, at the same point in the line, φέρων | μένων: I did the bringing, he did the sitting.

διὰ . . . δασάσκετο. Frequentative imperfect of διαδατέομαι.

In this emotional style the device of enjambment ('run-on') appears constantly: 335-43 is very unusual in the number of lines which are grammatically incomplete, the fullest form of enjambment. It is here not simply a device for generating line from line, but a sophisticated effect, conveying the overflowing anger of Achilles, not to be kept within moral or metrical bounds.

**331-2 δόσκον . . . δασάσκετο . . . ἔχεσκεν.** Frequentative imperfects, which never take an augment. This was Agamemnon's invariable behaviour. Cf. 1. 225-30.

**332 Ἀτρείδη.** Achilles in his anger repeats this hated name, see on 118, emphasized by its 'run-on' position, cf. 339, 341, 369.

**334** 'Other things he gave as booty . . .'

**336** Not, of course, (as van Leeuwen), 'He has a wife at home—let him sleep with her!' but 'He has taken, and he has got, my wife whom I love.' Achilles applies to his captive concubine the phrase which will be used when Odysseus after twenty years embraces the devoted wife Penelope: κλαῖε δ' ἔχων ἄλοχον θυμαρέα (Od. 23. 232). That is exaggeration, which Achilles defends at 342-3—she is no ordinary captive girl. Later on we hear that Briseis had hopes of marrying Achilles (19. 297-9), but that is not the point here, where she must be an ἄλοχος to enable Achilles to make the connection with Helen.

**336-7 θυμαρέα . . . τῆ . . . τερπέσθω. τί . . . Τρώεσσιν:** alliteration.

**τερπέσθω.** So much for Agamemnon's oath of restraint (274-5)!

**δεῖ.** The only appearance in Homer of this extremely common word. A bit of ordinary speech has got into this doubtless comparatively late composition. Cf. note on 42.

**339, 341 Ἀτρείδης.** As at 332, 369, this name is placed first in the line and followed by a heavy pause. The effect is to emphasize it; see on 118. Achilles is obsessed with his enemy.

Enjambment is a typical device of the oral poet (Introduction,

p. 38), but this concentration of pauses after Ἀτρείδης is not the product of simple oral composition. Ἀτρείδης occurs 66 times in the *Iliad*, but in 29 cases it is not the first word in the line. We can take it that we have a deliberate effect here.

**μερόπων.** μέροψ is a poetry word of unknown meaning, used only of people; cf. P. Vivante in *Glotta*, 58 (1980).

**341 ἀγαθὸς καὶ ἐχέφρων.** The word ἀγαθός usually (and no doubt traditionally) means 'brave fighter' in Homer. Here it means 'good man' in a very different sense, closer to that which it will be given by Plato and the philosophers: a man who accepts his responsibilities, a family man. In Iliadic terms, Hector rather than Paris, cf. 6. 350–3: Hector is ἀμείνων, the comparative of ἀγαθός. The poet helps the meaning by adding ἐχέφρων, 'thoughtful', the only appearance of the epithet in the *Iliad*; in the *Odyssey* it is used eight times of Penelope, once (13. 332) of Odysseus. It looks as though a word normally thought more appropriate to praise a woman has, in two exceptional passages, been used to praise a man, for qualities rather different from those of straightforward heroism. It is natural to think that behind the *Iliad* and *Odyssey* lay harder, more simply macho heroic songs.

**342 τὴν αὐτοῦ (ἄλοχον).** This usage of the definite article with possessive pronoun is unique in Homer.

**343 ἐκ θυμοῦ φίλεον.** This striking phrase recurs only at 486, see note. The past tense·is rather chilling. Later Achilles will say, 'I wish she had died before causing such a quarrel', cf. 19. 59–60. He is not to be thought of as a romantic lover.

**δουρικτητήν.** Cf. 16. 57 δουρὶ δ᾽ ἐμῷ κτεάτισσα.

**344 ἐκ χειρῶν.** Cf. 16. 59 τὴν ἄψ ἐκ χειρῶν ἕλετο κρείων Ἀγαμέμνων | Ἀτρείδης = 18. 444.

**ἀπάτησεν.** Achilles reverts to this accusation at 371 ἐξαπατήσειν, 375 ἐκ . . . ἀπάτησε. He means that Agamemnon has not kept the implicit promise that he will be treated like a hero. Achilles makes a contrast with his own straightforwardness (308–14).

**345f.** Assonance: μή μεν πείρατω . . . με πείσει, and νηήσας εὖ νῆας.

**347 φραζέσθω.** As if in answer to what Odysseus said to him, 251: φράζευ ὅπως Δαναοῖσιν ἀλεξήσεις κακὸν ἦμαρ. It is for

Agamemnon, not Achilles, to take counsel; and with 'the other kings', for Achilles himself will take no further part in his βουλαί (374). Odysseus reports this line: 680.

**348-50** Achilles ironically admires the wonderful things which Agamemnon has done without him (note the singular verbs and repeated δή)—a fine wall!

The building of the wall: 7. 337ff., 436ff. τάφρον, a moat round the wall; σκόλοπας, pointed stakes: 7. 440-1. The point is that while Achilles would fight they had no need of such things. καὶ δὴ ... καὶ ... ἐν δὲ σκόλοπας ...: the defences are enumerated in a way that builds them up; 'but even so he can't manage Hector'— and the build-up is sabotaged. The perverse argument of Page, *History and the Homeric Iliad*, 319f., that the wall was not mentioned in the poem until after the time of Thucydides, was refuted by M. L. West, *CR* 19 (1969), 256-60 and O. Tsagarakis, *Hermes*, 97 (1969), 129-35.

**351 σθένος Ἕκτορος.** Like such expressions as βίη Ἡρακληείη, ἱερὸν μένος Ἀλκινόοιο, ἱερὴ ἲς Τηλεμάχοιο, an elevated periphrasis for 'the mighty Hector'.

**351-6** We recall that at 8. 532ff. Hector was promising to kill Diomedes.

The name of Hector turns out to be a transition to the theme 'I shall go home tomorrow'—an elegant piece of construction. That previously the Trojans did not dare to leave the shelter of their walls to fight is repeated by Poseidon, 13. 105ff., and Hera, 5. 788ff., and effectively admitted by Hector, 15. 718-25; he, however, blames the timidity of the Trojan γέροντες, who would not let him follow his inclination and fight by the ships (cf. Ø. Andersen, *HSCP* 93 (1990), 33f.: 'The reason why different grounds are given for the same state of affairs is that both Hektor and Achilles make up the past as it suits them.').

**354 ὅσον ἐς Σκαιάς.** 'Only as far as the Scaean Gates'. Cf. 6. 237 Ἕκτωρ δ᾽ ὡς Σκαιάς τε πύλας καὶ φηγόν ἵκανεν. The oak tree, often mentioned (7. 22, 60; 11. 70; 21. 549), was very close to the Scaean ('left-hand') Gate of the city, in front of which the great single combats took place: wounded Trojans could be treated under the oak (5. 693); Trojans in retreat could feel safe there (11. 170). From that gate the Trojan elders watched Paris fight

Menelaus; both Hector (22. 6) and Achilles (22. 360) were killed before it.

**355 οἶον.** 'Me alone', adjective, not (unparalleled) adverb. We are not told this story in detail. Cf. the time when Achilles came upon Lycaon and captured him (21. 35ff.), and the time he pursued Aeneas (20. 187ff.): other stories on the fringe of the main events of the *Iliad*. I cannot follow the elaborate consequences read into the phrase by Martin, *Language of Heroes*, 176.

**356** Note the elegant turn: the Achaean Wall suggests Hector; Achilles used to fight with him, but not now, and, with a contemptuous glance at the bait offered by Odysseus at the end of his appeal, 304 νῦν γάρ χ᾽ Ἕκτορ᾽ ἕλοις—but now 'As I do not want to fight Hector', Achilles declares that he will go home.

**357–63** This splendid sentence expands and dwells upon and makes vivid what in Book 1 was settled in half a line—νῦν δ᾽ εἶμι Φθίηνδε (1. 169). Achilles has thought out all the details of his going, and rubs them in to his hearers.

**πᾶσι θεοῖσι.** There was apparently a cult of 'all the gods' in Mycenaean times: cf. M. Gérard-Rousseau, *Les mentions religieuses dans les tablettes mycéniennes* (1968), 170ff.

**359** The grammar breaks off: not a first-person verb, to agree with the participles νηήσας and ῥέξας, but a formulaic line (= 4. 353) is used with extraordinary effect, to make two good psychological points: Achilles' departure will not be a furtive business but done, according to his nature, openly; and—with cruel irony—just possibly Odysseus may be sufficiently interested in the scene to get up and watch the ships sail past. Compare the ironic Zeus to Hera, 8. 470f.: 'In the morning, if you are interested, you will see the son of Cronus behaving still more high-handedly . . .'

**360** We contemplate the picture: the sea, rich in fish, and the well-manned ships sailing over it. An effective line, very much in Achilles' manner; cf. the sudden vision of the mountains and sea between Phthia and Troy, ἐπεὶ ἦ μάλα πολλὰ μεταξὺ | οὔρεά τε σκιόεντα θάλασσά τε ἠχήεσσα (1. 156f.). and his taunt over Iphition: 'You lie dead, far from your home', Ὕλλῳ ἐπ᾽ ἰχθυόεντι καὶ Ἕρμῳ δινήεντι (20. 392). Achilles suddenly opens up wide vistas: cf. J. Griffin in *JHS* 86 (1986) 53f.

**363** The pace and mood of the speech have slowed down to

serenity, before Achilles' anger finds a second wind at 367ff. The speech has a shape; it is not a mere outburst of rage. This line was put by Plato into the mouth of Socrates, predicting his own death: *Crito* 44b2. The distance from the Troad to Phthia is something over 200 miles.

**364 ἐνθάδε ἔρρων.** ἔρρω, most commonly in the imperative ἔρρε, ἐρρέτω (377) 'Go to hell!', has the nuance 'Go (to one's cost)'; this alliterative phrase recurs at 8. 239. κάλλιπον = κατέλιπον.

**364 ff.** '(I shall go home); at home I have all I want, both old possessions and new spoils—but *one* prize Agamemnon has taken back—'. The thought of what he has reminds Achilles of what he has no longer. The connection of thought is eminently natural, and Achilles' anger naturally flares up again.

**367-77** The utterance is extraordinarily abrupt, chopped into short units with sharp transitions which never complete a sentence: ἐμφαντικώτεροι γίνονται οἱ λόγοι θᾶττον διακοπτόμενοι, observe the ancient commentators: 'the utterances are the more emphatic for being more abruptly cut off.' Achilles speaks in a rather similar manner at 16. 65-79 (cf. the discussion of parallels in D. Lohmann, *Die Komposition der Reden in der Ilias*, 274), and again at 19. 147-52. It is not easy to find examples of comparable energy on the lips of any other speaker.

**366 ἐϋζώνους.** The epithet is only used of women; cf. the description of Calypso dressing: περὶ δὲ ζώνην βάλετ' ἰξυῖ | καλὴν χρυσείην, *Od.* 5. 231. The ζώνη is an important item of women's dress.

**367 ἄσσ' ἔλαχόν γε.** 'All I have been allotted, which isn't much' (γε); but '*the* prize' (the one I care about) . . .

**ὅς περ ἔδωκεν.** According to what he is arguing, Achilles says that Briseis was given to him either by Agamemnon, as here (cf. 331), or by all the Achaeans collectively (as 1. 162, 276, 299, 392).

**369 Ἀτρεΐδης.** See on 339. The recurrence of this name marks Achilles' turn to fresh anger.

**370 ἀμφαδόν.** Achilles wants what Nestor tactfully tried to avoid (70-2, 94ff.): a public humiliation for Agamemnon.

**371 ἐξαπατήσειν.** See on 344.

**372 ἀναιδείην ἐπιειμένος.** The phrase comes elsewhere only in

Achilles' denunciation of Agamemnon, 1. 149; it is a striking phrase, and looks more like an allusion to that specific passage than a regular formula. Cf. Martin, *Language of Heroes*, 173f.

**373-4** The thought of Agamemnon's effrontery leads the speaker into an aside on it—'shameless though he is, he couldn't look me in the face'. Dogs do openly and without embarrassment what humans do not, or should not; and so they embody shamelessness. The echo of 1. 149 in 372 suggests that κύνεος . . . εἰς ὦπα here echoes 1. 159, κυνῶπα. It is to over-interpret this passage to suppose that Achilles only refuses because Agamemnon did not come in person, as some commentators on 11. 608-11 have done.

**374** συμφράσσομαι. Picks up 345-6, 'let him plan with the other kings, not with me'.

οὐδὲ μὲν ἔργον. As ϝέργον originally had a digamma, so that this phrase would be unmetrical, doubtless it is a late development for οὐδέ τι ἔργον (*Od.* 19. 323, 20. 378).

**374-8** An extraordinary sequence of very short staccato utterances: Achilles speaks rather in this style at 19. 148-50.

**375** ἐκ . . . ἀπάτησε. i.e. ἐξηπάτησε: see on 344.

ἤλιτεν: from ἀλιταίνω, 'wronged me'.

**376** ἅλις δέ οἱ. 'He should be content with that'; cf. the indignant question οὐχ ἅλις . . .; 'isn't it (bad) enough . . . ?', 5. 349, 17. 450, 23. 670. The extreme brevity of this phrase, interrupting the course of the sentence, is highly unusual for Homer. Original form: ϝάλις δέ ϝοι.

**376-7** ἔκηλος ἐρρέτω. 'He can go to Hell (ἐρρέτω) with no interference from me (ἔκηλος)'. We must here be close to colloquial Ionic Greek; cf. Archilochus' poem on the loss of his shield: τί μοι μέλει ἀσπὶς ἐκείνη; | ἐρρέτω· ἐξαῦτις κτήσομαι οὐ κακίω (fr. 5 West)—'What do I care about that shield? Let it go—I'll get another just as good.'

**377** In Attic ἐξείλετο γὰρ αὐτοῦ ὁ Ζεὺς τὰς φρένας; cf. 6. 234. Agamemnon must confess the truth of this. 19. 137: ἀλλ' ἐπεὶ ἀασάμην καί μευ φρένας ἐξέλετο Ζεύς. μητίετα, originally vocative; like κυανοχαῖτα, νεφεληγερέτα, etc., this archaic form came to be used as a nominative.

**378-97** Achilles now turns to the gifts offered by Agamemnon

(262–99). From a man so hated, nothing can be acceptable; to make it clear that the point is not to elicit larger offers, Achilles indulges the hyperbole natural to a speech of angry rejection. The sentence builds up into a crushing threefold rejection; echoed at a high point of the *Odyssey*, 22. 61ff. The negatives are effective: οὐδὲ . . . οὐδ' ὅσα . . . οὐδ' εἰ . . . οὐδέ κεν ὥς.

**378 ἐν καρὸς αἴσῃ.** The ancients were puzzled by the exact meaning of this expression of scorn. It seems to mean 'to the extent that I honour a scrap, a clipping' (akin to κείρω, 'clip'). Perhaps we hear an echo of Agamemnon's words at line 142 τείσω δέ μιν ἶσον Ὀρέστῃ (Martin 196).

**379–88** in effective contrast with the abrupt style of 367–77, a long climactic sentence, in which suspense accumulates through the elaborate account of Egyptian Thebes to a crushing conclusion.

**379** Achilles alone, in the *Iliad*, talks like this: *cf.* 22. 349, refusing burial to Hector, (the only other occurrence of 'ten times' and 'twenty times') οὐδ' εἴ κεν δεκάκις τε καὶ εἰκοσινήριτ' ἄποινα . . . οὐδ' εἴ κεν . . . οὐδ' ὥς . . . The vigour of the language suits the fiery nature of the hero. But he will be reconciled with Agamemnon, and he will allow Hector's body to be ransomed.

**380 =** *Od.* 22. 62: the *Odyssey* passage looks derivative from this one, and comparison is interesting, as an example of the milder nature of the other epic: Odysseus' threats to the Suitors are notably less powerful than Achilles' speech here.

**381** Orchomenos (see 2. 511–6) and Thebes (4. 374–400) were the great cities of Boeotia in the Mycenaean period and in myth. Orchomenos was associated with the Minyae (Ὀρχομενὸν Μινύειον, 2. 511) a people who in the classical period had disappeared; Minyas, its eponym, was son of Chryses ('gold man')—evidence of its wealth. A king of the thirteenth century BC was buried there in an impressive tholos-tomb, as big as the 'Treasury of Atreus' at Mycenae. Thebes was famous for its seven (legendary) gates, (Hesiod, *Erga* 162 f), attacked by the Seven against Thebes.

**382–4** These lines make the only reference to Egypt in *Il.*, (in *Od.* there are many, and 382 = *Od.* 4. 127); the audience imagined that Thebes in 381 was the Boeotian city, and suddenly finds that it is its Egyptian homonym. The passage looks like an addition (382 del. Verrall, 383–4 del. Heyne); but the effect it achieves, of suspense, is effective. Can the lines be dated? Some scholars have thought of the glories of the 18th Dynasty and a date about 1400 BC; W. Burkert, *WS* 10 (1976), 5-21, makes a good case for allusion to the 25th Dynasty, (after 715 BC), the destruction of the city by the Assyrian Assurbanipal in 663 BC being fresh in the minds of the audience; but 'there is no reason why Egyptian Thebes cannot be a Mycenaean reminiscence', argues R. Janko (*Commentary*, iv. p. 14 n. 21). We cannot, and need not, decide.

**384 σὺν ἵπποισιν καὶ ὄχεσφιν.** -φι, originally an ending of the Indo-European instrumental case, survived in epic and was used on a number of dative and genitive forms. The present phrase is a formulaic and repeated one. -φι doubtless gave a ring of antiquity to the line, and metrically it was very useful. Cf. notes on 58 and 618.

**387** Achilles demands payment of a very different kind, 'till he repay me in full his heart-grieving insult'. What is he demanding? At 1. 241-3 he envisages the slaughter of Achaeans by Hector, at 1. 409-12 their massacre by the ships, at 16. 98-100 their annihilation; at 9. 373 he seems to be complaining that Agamemnon has not come in person to grovel. The poem as a whole perhaps suggests a wounding contrast between the cool and vicarious atonement offered here by Agamemnon and the heart-broken figure of Priam at Achilles' feet, 24. 473 ff: Priam really does suffer (Taplin 269 f). The audience can supply any of these goals, or feel that Achilles himself is not clear about his meaning. The important thing is that Agamemnon faces an enigmatic demand which he cannot meet.

**θυμαλγέα.** Elsewhere in *Il.* used only of χόλον, either the anger of Achilles (4. 513, 9. 260) or an anger compared to it (565). Achilles seems to retort that his provocation, too, was grievous.

**388** Achilles turns to the next part of Agamemnon's offers (283-90).

**οὐ γαμέω Ἀγαμέμνονος.** Some see a pun here: 'The daughter I will not marry of No-Marriage' (Martin, *The Language of Heroes*, 221). I hear a jingle.

**389 f. κάλλος . . . ἔργα.** Accusatives of respect ('rival Aphrodite in respect of beauty', 'in beauty'): K-G. i. 316. The ἀρετή of a woman consists of δέμας and φυή, (beauty and stature), φρένες and ἔργα, (fidelity and housewifely skills): cf. 1. 115, οὐ δέμας οὐδὲ φυήν, οὔτ᾽ ἄρ φρένας οὐδέ τι ἔργα, a line on which an ancient commentator observes 'in a single verse he has summed up the whole ἀρετή of a woman.'

The rhyme, ἐρίζοι—ἰσοφαρίζοι, perhaps makes the lines into a unit, crushingly succeeded by the words 'not even then . . .' while the concluding οὐδέ μιν ὥς γαμέω ends with an echo of the middle of 388.

**392 βασιλεύτερος.** At 160 Agamemnon demanded that Achilles yield, ὅσσον βασιλεύτερός εἰμι. That line was not repeated to Achilles by the prudent Odysseus (300ff.), but Achilles reacts as if he had heard it; on this technique cf. Taplin, *Soundings*, 150 n. 4; and note on 78. In Book 1 Agamemnon did claim to be φέρτερος (1. 186, cf. 1. 281), and the claim is at the heart of the great quarrel; βασιλεύτερος and βασιλεύτατος are confined, in *Il.*, to Book 9, and the appearance of βασιλεύτερος here seems to go with that 'local' preference. Achilles is heavily ironical: 'I'm not good enough for him!'

**394** The manuscripts read γαμέσσεται, alleged to be future middle of γαμέω and to mean 'he will arrange a marriage for me'. This meaning of the verb is unparalleled; and the rhythm is also rare, word-division after the fourth trochee being avoided ('about once in 550 lines', M. L. West, *Greek Metre*, (Oxford, 1982), 38 n. 18). It was doubtless for these reasons that Aristarchus conjectured γυναῖκά γε μάσσεται, 'will seek a wife for me'. This future form of μαίομαι does not occur, but ἐπιμάσσεται is found from ἐπιμαίομαι. Aristarchus seems to be right; cf. Chantraine, *GH* i. 450. γε 'as far as a wife goes': αὐτός, with no officious help from Agamemnon. So Menelaus found a husband for his daughter and a bride for his son: *Od.* 4. 3–12.

**395 Ἀχαιΐδες.** 'Achaean women'. ἀν᾽ Ἑλλάδα 'Hellas' still means, not all Greece, but an area in Thessaly; cf. 2. 683. Like 'Hellas', 'Hellenes' was subsequently extended from a tribal to a national sense.

**397 τάων ἥν κ᾽ ἐθέλωμι:** sardonic echo of Agamemnon's offer of the pick of his daughters, 288 τάων ἥν κ᾽ ἐθέλησθα. ἐθέλωμι: see note on 414. 397 shows clearly the process by which such first person forms were created: the singer wanted a form of the same metrical shape as ἐθέλησθα.

**398–416** The name of Agamemnon ceases to be spoken, and Achilles turns to less angry and more reflective thoughts and tone. He could marry and live in peace; what can possibly recompense him for the loss of his life? Treasures and possessions, the rewards of honour, in this perspective lose their value, and Achilles rejects heroism itself—at least on the terms he associates with Agamemnon.

**399 γήμαντα.** Even when the main clause has a dative, a dependent infinitive clause regularly takes a subject in the accusative: Chantraine, *GH* ii. 313.

**μνηστὴν ἄλοχον:** 'a (regularly) courted wife'.

**ἐϊκυῖαν:** cf. 392 ὅστις οἷ τ' ἐπέοικε: 'a well-matched' partner. Both ἄλοχος and ἄκοιτις (masc. ἀκοίτης) originally mean 'bedfellow', the prefix a- (to λέχος, κοίτη) being the same as that in ἀδελφός (from δελφύς, 'womb': 'born of the same womb', 'brother'/'sister'); but here we are talking of a wedded wife. It is inept to argue, as M. I. Finley does in *The World of Odysseus*, 147, that 'in this man's world . . . the Greek does not say "wives", it says "bedmates"', and to draw inferences from that about the low position of women. In English 'wife' originally meant simply 'woman', before becoming specialized of married ones. A Frenchman still says 'ma femme'; that does not mean that marriage does not exist in France.

**401–3** Troy had been fabulously opulent, before the Achaeans came:

πρὶν μὲν γὰρ Πριάμοιο πόλιν μέροπες ἄνθρωποι
πάντες μυθέσκοντο πολύχρυσον πολύχαλκον·
νῦν δὲ δὴ ἐξαπόλωλε δόμων κειμήλια καλά,   (18. 288–90; cf. 24. 543–8)

403 = 22. 156, in a context of high pathos.

υἷας Ἀχαιῶν ×21, υἷες Ἀχαιῶν ×29, κοῦροι Ἀχαιῶν ×7, in *Il*.: all at the end of the hexameter. The locution sounded exotic to later Greeks; Herodotus makes Croesus refer to the Λυδῶν παῖδας (1. 27. 3), cf. Αἰθιόπων παισί (3. 21. 3), Ἰώνων παῖδας (5. 49. 2), παῖδες Ἀθηναίων (5. 77. 4); at the Battle of Salamis the cry was ὦ παῖδες Ἑλλήνων, A. *Pers.* 402, cf. Eur. *Hec.* 930: a trace of an ancient grand manner. Line 402 appears to be a variant of the twice occurring line Ἴλιον ἐκπέρσαι εὖ ναιόμενον πτολίεθρον (2. 133, 13. 380).

**404–5** Pytho: an ancient name of Delphi (which never occurs in

Homer), mentioned twice each in *Il.* and *Od.* The 'stone threshold' of Pytho is mentioned again, *Od.* 8. 80, where we hear of the oracle, the basis of Delphi's wealth. Scholars disagree on the question whether Delphi was a cult centre in the Mycenaean period, and whether there was unbroken continuity through the Dark Age: Kirk gives a cautious affirmative (*Commentary* on 2. 519), Burkert a decided negative (*Greek Religion*, 49: bibliography on the question, p. 366 nn. 22 and 23). The reference here is likely to be not earlier than 700 BC, cf. C. Morgan, *Athletes and Oracles* (Cambridge, 1990) 10; Taplin, *Homeric Soundings*, 33f., who observes 'Delphi's wealth could hardly have been "legendary" before 700 BC.'

**406–7** an elegant chiasmus (ABA): 'They can be carried off, cattle and sheep; they can be acquired peacefully, tripods and horses: but the life of a man is neither to be carried off nor taken', the verbal adjectives ringing the subjects. Martin (*The Language of Heroes*, 219) sees a polemic echo of ἀλήϊος and ἀκτήμων in Agamemnon's speech, 9. 125–7 in Achilles' use of ληϊστοί and κτητοί. The ψυχή is the 'breath' of life which leaves at death.

**407 ἵππων ξανθὰ κάρηνα:** periphrasis for ξανθοὶ ἵπποι. 'Heads' is so used of men: 11. 499f. τῇ ῥα μάλιστα | ἀνδρῶν πῖπτε κάρηνα, 'where men were falling thickest'; of oxen, 23. 260. The dead are νεκύων ἀμενηνὰ κάρηνα, *Od.* 10. 521; an expression already hard to understand in the fifth century BC, as we know from a fragment of Aristophanes (*PCG* iii. 2. 233). In tragedy both men and women can be addressed as 'head': e.g. Soph. *Antigone* 1 ὦ κοινὸν αὐτάδελφον Ἰσμήνης κάρα—'O my own sister Ismene'.

**409 ἀμείψεται.** Subjunctive: 'pass the fence of the teeth', a formulaic expression.

**410–16** Elsewhere Achilles is promised a short life (1. 352, 416; 18. 59), apparently without a choice; his first words to his mother are an acceptance of it—μῆτερ, ἐπεί μ' ἔτεκές γε μινυνθάδιόν περ ἐόντα: 1. 352. The motif of a choice of destinies is not unparalleled, cf. 13. 665–70: a prophet's son, forewarned that his destiny was either to die of disease or to fall at Troy. Both times the effect is to emphasize the death at Troy. Prophetic utterances are especially liable to be mentioned at one moment and ignored or denied at another: cf. 16. 36–9, 49–51, but 18. 8–11. Achilles is not shown actually taking this decision, like Orestes in

Aeschylus' *Choephoroe* (894 ff.) or other characters in Tragedy; epic is not like that.

**411** κήρ, like μοῖρα, is in Homer not predetermination of the events of a life but the fixing of the time of death.

**412-13** Celebrated lines. The hero must embrace early death, like the Irish hero Cuchúlainn (*The Táin* p. 85): 'If I achieve fame I am content, though I had only one day on earth.' In his disillusion Achilles thinks of rejecting it; and when he does fight on and accept it, that is without pleasure or gusto for him.

κλέος ἄφθιτον. It was seen in the nineteenth century that this phrase is identical with the Sanskrit *srávas áksitam*. Twentieth-century scholars have seen in it a survival from very ancient Indo-European epic poetry, concerned like the *Iliad* with glory and death: R. Schmitt, *Dichtung und Dichtersprache in Indogermanischer Zeit* (1967), 61 ff., 'Der Ruhm als Zentralbegriff indogermanischer Heldendichtung'; Nagy, *The Best of the Achaeans*, 141 ff.; id., *Pindar's Homer* (Johns Hopkins, 1990), 244 n. 126; Martin, *The Language of Heroes*, 182 f. It is objected (M. Finkelberg, *CQ* 36 (1986), 1–5) that the formulaic expression in Homer is (ὅου) κλέος οὔποτ' ὀλεῖται cf. 2. 235, 7. 91; cf. also *Od.* 4. 584 ἵν' ἄσβεστον κλέος εἴη) and κλέος ἄφθιτον ἔσται a specially invented variant; the objection is acute and worth pondering. Cf. also P. Floyd in *Glotta*, 58 (1980), 133–57. There are no fewer than 24 personal names compounded with κλέος in Homer, from Ἀγακλέης to Φέρεκλος (listed: Ebeling, *Lexicon Homericum*, 816). Other Homeric words, too, from this area of thought find parallels in poetry of other Indo-European peoples: cf. M. L. West in *JHS* 108 (1988), 154-5. G. Nagy argues that the passage alludes to immortality as conferred by the epic itself (*Greek Mythology and Poetics*, 122 ff. (p. 136)): Achilles 'is in effect saying that he will be immortalized by his own epic tradition . . . the theme of a hero's immortalization has been shifted from the realm of cult to the realm of epic itself . . . (138) The epic perspective has the logical sequence reversed: by placing epic above cult, Homeric poetry allows the hero, *even before he dies*, to have the kind of *timē* that befits a cult hero. What he still has to earn by dying is κλέος itself . . .'. The reader must decide whether so self-conscious and modern a self-reference is really to be seen in the line. Do we really believe that Achilles, at such a moment, is presented as talking about himself as a figure in literature?

**413 ὤλετο.** The aorist in the apodosis of a future conditional marks the result as fixed: '(In that case) it is lost indeed'. Cf. 4. 160ff., K–G i. 165.

**414 ἴωμι.** The manuscripts offer the unmetrical form ἵκωμαι. ἵκωμι is an implausible conjecture: ἱκνέομαι does not elsewhere have active forms, while ἱκ- has a long ι. More likely ἴωμι, from εἶμι, conjectured by August Nauck. This form of subjunctive is an artificial creation, not an inherited form; the singers coined first persons in -ωμι to match true 3rd persons in -ησι and optatives in -οιμι. Cf. 397 ἐθέλωμι, 24. 717 ἀγάγωμι, 18. 63 ἴδωμι; Chantraine, *GH* i. 461f.; and note on 397.

**415 ἐπὶ δηρόν.** δηρόν originally had a digamma, δϝ-; the lengthened ι is a memory of that.

**416** A feeble line, ejected by the ancient critics. Though composed in a regular Homeric manner, a run-on verb filled out with formulaic material (cf. *Od.* 17. 476), it has the look of an invention to provide a verb for the second half of 415.

**417 καὶ δέ.** Only in Homeric verse do these particles come directly together, without words between: 'the former particle denoting that something is added, the latter that what is added is distinct from what precedes' (Denniston, *Greek Particles*[2], 199). 'And another thing . . .'.

**418 οὐκέτι δήετε τέκμωρ.** οὐκέτι 'Now you will not,' see note on 28. δήετε: δήω exists only in present forms with future sense, 'will find', cf. εἶμι; νέομαι 'I shall return': Schwyzer, *Gr. Gramm.* ii. 265. τέκμωρ: see note on 47.

**420 χεῖρα ἑήν.** Cf. 4. 251 ὄφρα ἴδητ' αἴ κ' ὕμμιν ὑπέρσχῃ χεῖρα Κρονίων. The hand of Zeus becomes almost visible: 15. 695, he thrusts Hector on χειρὶ μάλα μεγάλῃ.

**422 γερόντων.** See note on 89. γέρας . . . γερόντων. Ancient scholars guessed that these words, which here jingle suggestively, were related etymologically; not so, cf. Benveniste, *Le vocabulaire des institutions I–E*, ii. 48–9.

**424 σάῳ.** Subjunctive of σαόω = σῴζω, from *σαόῃ.

**425–6** The tone is ironical: 'this plan, which they have thought up in my absence, won't work—.'

**427–9** Achilles ends his speech with a turn to make it clear that the discussion is at an end; but with it the poet deftly directs our attention to Phoenix, who will speak next. Phoenix 'belongs' with Achilles, not Agamemnon, and it is never explained why he has not been with him. These lines delicately skirt that question.

**430-1** = 693-4, 8. 28-9.

**433 ἀναπρήσας:** 'letting tears burst forth' (ἀναπρήθω). Alongside the perfect form, περιδείδια 'I am in great fear for', we find in Homer the imperfect περίδιε, always in tmesis περὶ . . . δίε, in the same position in the line.

**434 ff.** *The Speech of Phoenix.* This contrasts with that of Achilles (an older man tells stories, utters parentheses, is discursive rather than intense), and also with that of Odysseus (a personal and emotional appeal after an 'official' one). Phoenix addresses Achilles repeatedly: 437, 444, 485, 494, 496, 513, 601 by name and as φίλον τέκος. Unlike Odysseus, but like Achilles, he refers to his own sufferings and appeals to his love; and the less predictable course of what he says suggests that he, like Ajax, (624-42) is thinking out his speech as he goes, not delivering a prepared address. He speaks of his attachment to Achilles and tells his own life-story (434-95); appeals to the universal power which should be possessed by prayer, and appeals to Achilles to relent (496-526); and tells the story of a hero, Meleager, who yielded to prayer only too late, rounding it off with a last appeal (527-605).

**435 οὐδέ,** not μηδέ, in an if-clause: not uncommon in Homer where the emphasis is less on the hypothetical than on the fact: 'If it is really the case that you will not help . . .'. K–G ii. 189; cf. 3. 289, 4. 160, 15. 215.

**438-43** Odysseus also tried reminding Achilles of his parting from his father, but less tactfully (ὣς ἐπέτελλ' ὁ γέρων, σὺ δὲ λήθεαι, 259); Nestor will use it on Patroclus with effect, 11. 765ff., quoting what was said by Patroclus' father. The two narrations complete each other interestingly.

**438 οἶος.** Emphasized by the enjambment: 'Alone in the world.'

**440 f.** Cf. *Od.* 4. 818 νήπιος, οὔτε πόνων εὖ εἰδὼς οὔτ' ἀγοράων. That line, which preserves the older and more Homeric form ἀγοράων (*Il.* 2. 275; ἀγορέων appears only here), looks like the model of this passage (Hoekstra, *Homeric Modifications*, 40 f.). ὁμοιίου πτολέμοιο: from the older ὁμοιίοο πτολέμοιο; strictly, ὁμοιίου does not scan. With the disappearance of such genitive forms in -οο, the inherited words were re-interpreted. See on 64, ὀκρυόεντος. Cf. e.g. *Il.* 2. 325 ὅου κλέος; 5. 21; *Od.* 10. 36, 60; 14. 239.

**443** The theme of 440-1 (fighting and speaking) is summed up in one lapidary line. The excellent man has both capacities. Cf. what Odysseus says to Achilles, 19. 215-9, and the rebuke of Polydamas to Hector, 13. 726ff. Great prowess is not necessarily accompanied by excellence in βουλή and speech, especially in a young man, and Diomedes, who speaks well for his age, still needs to be criticized by old Nestor, 52-62; while older men can speak but not act (3. 149-51). Achilles in the end is forced to admit that others are better at ἀγορή than he (18. 105-6). The claim of Archilochus to be a warrior and also a singer (fr. 1 W) is related, (R. Harder, *Kleine Schriften*, 177); here too Achilles leads the way (186ff.).

**444** ὡς introducing a wish, cf. *Od.* 1. 47 ὡς ἀπόλοιτο καὶ ἄλλος, ὅτις τοιαῦτά γε ῥέζοι; with the modal particle ἄν, cf. *Il.* 6. 281 ὡς κέ οἱ αὖθι | γαῖα χάνοι.

**445** οὐδ' εἴ κέν μοι. Homer freely puts the modal particle κεν into εἰ clauses with the optative. It makes no difference to the sense (K-G ii. 482).

**446** ἀποξύσας. The image is of scraping away calluses and wrinkles, to restore the smoothness of youth. It recurs at [Hom.] *h. Ven.* 224, *Nostoi* fr. 6D. Related is the idea of old age as a skin which, ideally, we could slough off, as snakes do (a cast snakeskin is called γῆρας), or remove by boiling, as Medea does for Jason's father Aeson.

**447ff.** Old Phoenix, like old Nestor, likes to tell stories of his youth. The point of this autobiography is to show Phoenix as having no other love but that for Achilles; and, like Achilles, Phoenix threw everything away because of a woman. A quarrel with one's father was a frequent motif for leaving home in the heroic age. 2. 629; *Od.* 15. 254 (πατρὶ χολωθείς). Anger, however, and supplication, are key motifs: the story is calculated to reflect Achilles' own actions and position. Some of Phoenix' narrative reads almost like a burlesque of Achilles' story: the quarrel over a concubine, the sulking, the attempt to prevent him from going away, his undignified departure (R. Scodel in *AJP* 103 (1982),

128-36). This is what the choice of long life without κλέος could be made to look like; Achilles cannot behave like this.

**447 Ἑλλάδα καλλιγύναικα.** The epithet is used again of Hellas (2. 683), and of Achaea and Sparta. It is a formulaic adjective and not to be pressed; but here it is particularly appropriate.

**449-50** This sort of domestic unpleasantness was avoided in the better run family of Odysseus' father, who never laid a hand on the maidservant Eurycleia, 'and avoided his wife's indignation', *Od.* 1. 433.

**450-1 φιλέεσκεν . . . ἀτιμάζεσκε . . . λισσέσκετο.** The concentration of 'iterative' verb forms brings out the duration of this family crisis and the cumulative pressure under which it placed the young Phoenix.

**451 γούνων.** The mother abased herself, crouching and clasping her son's knees in supplication, cf. Thetis before Zeus, *Il.* 1. 500-13. That produced in the person supplicated the feeling of embarrassed constraint which the Greeks called αἰδώς. See J. Gould, 'Hiketeia', in *JHS* 93 (1973); D. Cairns, *Aidos* (Oxford 1993). The genitive is influenced by fuller descriptions of the gesture, as 1. 500 (Thetis) λάβε γούνων, 1. 512 ὡς ἥψατο γούνων.

**453 τῇ πιθόμην καὶ ἔρεξα.** Prudery led one ancient scholar to rewrite the line: τῇ οὐ πιθόμην οὐδ' ἔρξα, 'and he was praised for preserving the hero's virtue' (Σ ad loc).

**454** The Erinyes particularly avenged breaches of respect within the family: cf. 571; 15. 204 οἶσθ' ὡς πρεσβυτέροισιν Ἐρινύες αἰὲν ἕπονται; *Od.* 11. 280.

The father's curse—childlessness for his disloyal son—has some appropriateness. It is expressed in a way which looks forward to 488: the child whom Phoenix *did* put 'on his knees'—Achilles. A baby is put formally on the knees of his grandfather: *Od.* 19. 401-2, the young Odysseus in the lap of Autolycus, who gave the child a name. The occasion was thus one of accepting the child as one of the family. In another ancient tradition Jacob cursed his son Reuben for having intercourse with his concubine (Genesis 49. 4): the situation must have been all too common.

**457 ἐπαινὴ Περσεφόνεια.** The epic word ἐπαινός seems to have arisen from mistaken division of the phrase καὶ ἐπ' αἰνὴ Περσεφόνεια 'and too the dread Persephone' (Leumann, *HW* 44);

compare English *a norange* (Spanish *naranja*)—*an orange*, etc. The process was perhaps helped by the observation that the verbs αἰνέω and ἐπαινέω both exist (C. J. Ruijgh, *L'Élément achéen dans la langue épique* (Assen, 1957), 103).

**458–61** Four lines absent from all the manuscripts but quoted by Plutarch, who says that Aristarchus deleted them, φοβηθείς: alarmed by the mention of parricide. Normally Aristarchus' deletions did not mean the disappearance of lines from the standard text, and it is tempting to disbelieve the story. 458 is composed of two half-lines which occur in different places in the *Odyssey*: 9. 229; 4. 700. 460 does not look Iliadic, but it resembles lines in the *Odyssey* like *Od.* 14. 239 χαλεπὴ δ' ἔχε δήμου φῆμις; *Od.* 16. 75 εὐνήν τ' αἰδομένη πόσιος δήμοιό τε φῆμιν. In the *Iliad* public opinion is not so expressed: cf. 6. 350–1, 22. 105–6. Probably, despite D. Cairns, *Aidos* 51, they are not original but derive from a marginal note by some learned ancient reader. Cf. S. R. West in *LCM* (1982), 84–6. However, they present a striking similarity to Achilles' own impulse to kill Agamemnon, 1. 188ff; cf. Heubeck, *Kleine Schriften*, 135; and as such they might be seen to have a function in a speech in which Phoenix is trying to assimilate his own career to that of Achilles. The lines are 'good enough to be genuine': Janko, *Commentary*, iv. 28.

**462** ἐρητύετο: 'would not be restrained'.

**θυμός:** Achilles is repeatedly urged to control his θυμός in *Iliad* 9: 255, 496, 639. Phoenix' story is less irrelevant than it might seem.

**463** πατρὸς χωομένοιο. Word order makes it impossible to choose clearly between 'the house of my angry father' and 'while my father was angry'.

**464–9** Fourfold repetition of πολλά . . . πολλά . . . πολλοί . . . πολλόν holds this sentence together and gives it rhetorical force; cf. 581–5, on the same subject.

**464** ἔται καὶ ἀνεψιοί: 'Kinsmen and cousins'. The whole extended family crowded round (ἀμφὶς ἐόντες) in this crisis.

**466** εἰλίποδας ἕλικας βοῦς. This formulaic expression is traditionally explained as 'shambling cattle with crumpled horns'. The shambling gait of oxen is contrasted with the high-stepping horse (ἀερσίποδες); ἕλιξ is perhaps a shortened form of a compound epithet like *ἑλικοκραίρους.

**468 φλογὸς Ἡφαίστοιο.** Hephaestus, god of forge-work, was also god of naturally appearing fire like that on the island of Lemnos. His name can be used for fire itself: 2. 426 σπλάγχνα . . . ὑπείρεχον Ἡφαίστοιο. The bristles were singed off the hogs' skin.

**470** Sc. παρίαυον ἀμφ' ἐμοὶ αὐτῷ ἐννέα νύκτας: 'for nine nights they slept close round me all night'. Things often last for nine days before a decisive change on the tenth: 1. 53 f., 6. 174 f., *Od.* 9. 82 f., etc; cf. the nine years of the siege of Troy and capture in the tenth, 2. 329 f. It is a good epic number.

**472-3** Two fires were kept burning, one in the colonnade, the other outside Phoenix' room.

**477 φύλακάς τ' ἄνδρας.** The addition of ἄνδρας follows such Homeric phrases for a class or occupation as ἰητρὸς ἀνήρ, 11. 514; χαλκῆες ἄνδρες 4. 187; Schwyzer, *Gr. Gramm.*, ii. 514. The men then naturally suggested, by a 'polar' expression, women as well, cf. *Od.* 4. 142 'I have never seen anyone, man or woman, with such a likeness as he has to Telemachus', οὔτ' ἄνδρ' οὔτε γυναῖκα; and even *Il.* 8. 7 μήτε τις οὖν θήλεια θεὸς τό γε μήτε τις ἄρσην | πειράτω, and note on 36. These slave women doubtless slept in outbuildings: cf. *Od.* 20. 105 ff.

**478** In the accusative case Hellas is 'of fair women' (see on 447); in the genitive, for purely metrical reasons, it must be 'of wide dancing floors'.

**478-9 φεῦγον . . . ἐξικόμην.** After the single acts of escaping described by the aorists ἐξῆλθον, ὑπέρθορον, the imperfect φεῦγον ('I was on the run') contrasts with the aorist for the act of arriving in Phthia. Included in ἐξικόμην is the idea that on his arrival he was a ἱκέτης: a stranger arriving suddenly must throw himself on the mercy of his host.

**ἐριβώλακα μητέρα μήλων:** formula used of Thrace at 11. 222.

**480-2** The simile expands the idea of the second half of 480; and 482 in two stages (μοῦνον τηλέγυτον, *Od.* 16. 19), expands and exaggerates the idea cf. 481 ('He welcomed me—he loved me like a son—like an only son—like an only son and heir to property—'). We can see how the singer can at will extend or abbreviate his narrative in every detail. With such love cf. 15. 432-4, 13. 176, 5. 534-6.

**482 ἐπὶ κτεάτεσσι.** Cf. 5. 154 υἱὸν δ' οὐ τέκετ' ἄλλον ἐπὶ κτεάτεσσι λιπέσθαι, 'in possession of his property'.

**483 πολὺν δέ μοι ὤπασε λαόν.** Phoenix was made a subordinate king. So Agamemnon is forced to offer towns and their people to Achilles, 149–56. Without λαός a man cannot be great: cf. 2. 675, the handsome Nireus was feeble, ἀλλ' ἀλαπαδνὸς ἔην, παῦρος δέ οἱ εἵπετο λαός.

**484** The Dolopians, only here mentioned by Homer, lived to the west of Phthia.

**486 ἐκ θυμοῦ φιλέων.** Phoenix echoes Achilles' language about Briseis, 343. The phrase does not occur again in Homer, though we find such expressions as θυμῷ φιλέουσα, 1. 196, and ἐκ θυμοῦ πεσέειν, 23. 595, 'to fall out of somebody's affections'. Surely here a deliberate echo of a striking phrase: Phoenix' claim on Achilles is founded, as Achilles says that his own grievance is, on love. In the myth, Achilles was brought up and educated by the centaur Chiron (traces still in the *Iliad*, 11. 832, 19. 390): Homer has humanized this non-human figure completely, replacing him with a man, and a very affectionate one.

**487** The imagined scene with sons appearing at the men's dinner is like that which Andromache imagines at 22. 492.

**488** There is an understandable illogicality about this: 'You would not go into dinner until I held you on my lap.'

**γούνεσσι**: see note on 454.

**489** 'I gave you your fill (ἄσαιμι from ἄω), cutting up your meat for you and holding the wine to your lips'.

**491 οἴνου ἀποβλύζων.** 'Spirting out (some of) the wine.' These loving services entitle Phoenix to a return from Achilles.

**νηπίῃ ἀλεγεινῇ.** This curious phrase seems to be modelled on 6. 156 ἠνορέην ἐρατεινήν (Leumann, *HW* 110 n. 7).

**492 ἔπαθον, ἐμόγησα.** An answer to Achilles' resentful claims to have suffered and toiled, 316 ff. (321 πάθον ἄλγεα).

**494 θεοῖς ἐπιείκελ' Ἀχιλλεῦ.** Cf. 485. This formulaic address (×6 in Homer) is used by Phoenix with special poignancy: 'I *made* you the godlike man you are' (485); 'Having no son, I thought to take you as my wonderful son.' An old man, even a king, needs a young man to defend him; cf. what Priam says of Peleus, 24. 488–9—in Achilles' absence doubtless his neighbours are oppressing him.

**495** In antiquity there was no coyness about the idea that children were the only insurance for men and women in old age. The obligation on children to support aged parents, in return for being reared when they were themselves helpless, was absolute and enforced by law.

ἀμύνῃς: cf. note on 99.

**496 θυμόν.** See note on 109.

**496-7 οὐδὲ . . . στρεπτοὶ δέ.** Greek verse often adds supporting grounds, where we might have expected γάρ, with δέ—'and it is also true that . . .' Cf. Denniston, *Greek Particles* ii. 169, K–G ii. 230f., 274. This is akin to the simple style in which elements are added ('parataxis') rather than grammatically subordinated ('hypotaxis')—'and another thing . . .'.

**499** Plato, *Republic* 2. 364d7 quotes this line in the form καὶ τοὺς μὲν θυσίαισι καὶ εὐχωλαῖς ἀγαναῖσι (for θυέεσσι, εὐχωλῇσ’ ἀγανῇσι). The Athenian philosopher's memory has transposed the words into Attic forms: an interesting example of the difference between Homeric and classical Greek.

**500** 'With libations and the smoke (of burnt offerings)'. Cf. Exodus 29. 40, simultaneous drink offerings of wine and burnt meat offerings 'for a sweet savour, an offering made by fire unto the Lord'.

**502-14** *Allegory of Prayers* (for forgiveness and harmony). Ἄτη is personified by Agamemnon as a daughter of Zeus, 19. 91: a way of saying that its power is great. Atē is what 'comes over' a man and makes him act in a way which later he sees to be disastrous and can no longer understand. Agamemnon falls back on blaming Ἄτη for his own role in the quarrel: 9. 115-6; 19. 90-136. The frankly allegorical character of this passage is clearer and more elaborate than any other in Homer; it is less surprising in a speech made by a character than it would be in the poet's own narrative. Atē is strong, because she overpowers her victims, and quick, because they act hastily and rashly. The Prayers come along only when the damage has been done, and so they are lame and aged (like Phoenix and Nestor); they look askance, 'because they wish to steer the stubborn man away from his unbending path' (H. Fränkel, *Early Greek Poetry and Philosophy* (Oxford, 1975), 63. Agamemnon rejected prayers in Book 1 and is now suffering for it; Achilles has been warned.

**508f. αἰδέσεται.** Short vowel subjunctive; it is followed by 'gnomic' aorist tenses, ὤνησαν and ἔκλυον, as is regular to express a proposition generally true in specified circumstances: cf. 1. 218 ὅς κε θεοῖς ἐπιπείθηται, μάλα τ᾽ ἔκλυον αὐτοῦ, K–G i. 160; Schwyzer, *Gr. Gramm.*, ii. 283. 'Whoever, (having been offended), is prepared to be talked round . . .'.

**509, 511 δέ.** Cf. note on 167.

**515f.** Phoenix leaves no doubt possible: by heroic standards, Agamemnon's offering is sufficient.

**520 λίσσεσθαι.** Cf. 501 λισσόμενοι, 511 λίσσονται: the echo underlines the connection 'prayers and gifts to the gods—prayers and gifts to you; gods accept, so should you'.

**522f. ἐλέγξῃς.** 'Expose to contempt their message or their journey'; cf. *Od.* 21. 424 for this sense of ἐλέγχω.

**524–6** Phoenix makes it clear that such attacks of χόλος were one of the familiar themes of heroic song. Outside Homer, where it half appears in connection with Paris (6. 326: denied by him, 6. 335f.) and with Aeneas (13. 460), the theme is in fact surprisingly hard anywhere to find in oral poetry. The simple pattern is outlined by Athena to Achilles, 1. 213f.: the hero withdraws, proves his value by absence, forces recognition and reward for returning. The *Iliad* represents a more complex and sophisticated development of that simple plot. We remember that Achilles himself was singing the κλέα ἀνδρῶν when the envoys arrived: 189.

**525 ὅτε κεν . . . ἵκοι.** This usage is peculiar to epic; ordinary Greek has no κεν or ἄν in indefinite statements in past time.

**527 μέμνημαι τόδε ἔργον.** Verbs of remembering and forgetting originally took an object in the (partitive) genitive; the reason for this was felt less clearly with time, and, as here, the accusative came in.

**529–49** *The Story of Meleager.* This is full of difficulties. Meleager kills his mother's brother (567), and she curses him, calling on the lower gods to bring him death; so he will no longer fight for his city of Calydon against the besieging Couretes, but lies sulking in bed. All his dearest connections beg him to return to the battle and deliver them: the chiefs and priests (574f.) offer gifts, his father, his mother (!), his dearest comrades, all implore him—in vain; until his wife Cleopatra (whom her parents called Alcyone) finally persuades him. And so he came back and rescued the city—but after all he did not get the promised reward. The role of the mother is baffling, and it is clear (despite Bremmer in *Metamorphoses du mythe grec*, ed. C. Calame (Paris, 1988)) that the original story about her was that in her anger she burned a log of wood which she had heard from the Fates at her son's birth was his 'external soul', the talisman of his life; and so he died. That version, too uncanny for Homeric taste, is memorably told in the Fifth Ode of Bacchylides, 37–56. Here her curse is clearly a secondary motif, and it has no apparent effect; a fundamental breach of the nature of such a story. Meleager is defending the city, not attacking it, and yet we hear that 'as long as Meleager fought, things went badly for the Couretes, and they could not stay outside the wall' (550f.); that is language appropriate to the situation of the *Iliad*, where it is the champion of the besiegers who leaves the battle: as long as he took the field, the besieged could not come outside the wall to fight (352f.). The reverse does not make sense—and yet we observe that now the Achaeans have built themselves a wall and virtually become the besieged; the situation is thus not so clear as is often alleged by critics. Homer also prefers to get rid of so peasant-like a notion as that of Fates who can be eavesdropped on, filling the story as far as possible with chivalrous warrior motivations. J. T. Kakridis (*Homeric Researches*, 1949) showed the existence of a regular pattern in stories of supplication, in which a hero's connections plead with him in ascending order; it is normally the wife whose persuasion succeeds where the others fail (cf. Hector's words to Andromache, 6. 450–5; but in Rome, characteristically, it is not the wife but the mother who prevails on Coriolanus); but the high position here given to the 'dear comrades'—above the parents—is exceptional and anomalous. It seems to be produced in order to reflect the *Iliad* situation, where it is comrades who are doing the pleading. The name Cleo-patra, for a woman who was clearly better known under another name—a name with a real story to explain it—looks very much like an invention based upon Patro-clus, the person who in the *Iliad* will succeed, where others have failed, in persuading Achilles to return to the fighting. It is a very bold step to say (R. von Scheliha, *Patroklos* (Basel, 1943, 247)) that Homer himself invented Patroclus and named him as 'The glory of his father', i.e. of Homer himself. The wife is clearly not part of the log-story, and she is slightly awkward in the *Iliad* version, too: therefore she must have been present in some version of the story before the *Iliad* (under the name Alcyone). The motif of Meleager 'not getting the reward' also seems out of place in a story where a curse should lead to his death. Again, it looks like a reflection back into the Meleager story of the situation in the *Iliad*: Achilles should not miss his reward. All this has involved transformng the central meaning and content of the Meleager story. From a grim tale of the clash between parenthood and the tie of blood with brothers, it has become a more complicated story of anger, withdrawal, supplication, reward, and love (Heubeck, *Kleine Schriften*, 134f., H. Petersmann, 'Homer and Matriarchie' *WS* 15 (1984), 57–61). It has been shown (Heubeck) that the Meleager-story as told by Phoenix has many motifs in common with Phoenix' narrative about his own youth: family quarrel, curses, anger, withdrawal, prayers; and the Homeric poet has left the death of Meleager like that of Achilles himself in the *Iliad*: foreshadowed but not narrated. W. Kraus (*Kleine Schriften*, 37) compares, with the original mother of Meleager, the grim figure of Kriemhild in German legend. The appeal to a parallel story from the past is a regular Homeric way of persuading: it will be by such a story that Nestor will work on the feelings of Patroclus (11. 670–762), and that Achilles will constrain Priam to eat with him (24. 602–20).

**529–47** A neat example of ring-composition (Willcock ad loc.):

A 529–32   the Couretes and the Aetolians were at war;
B 533–4     Artemis had sent an evil thing on Oeneus;
C 534–7     Oeneus had omitted to sacrifice to Artemis;
B 538–46   so Artemis sent the Boar: its career and death;
A 547–9     the Couretes and the Aetolians were at war over the trophy.

Line 549 closely echoes 529 and closes the ring.

**530** Calydon: a city of Aetolia. The Couretes were a neighbouring people. The slaying of the Calydonian Boar was a great mythical story, represented on the François Vase (illustration: P. E. Arias and M. Hirmer, *A History of Greek Vase-Painting* (London, 1962), plates 40–6) and amusingly told in Ovid, *Metamorphoses*, Book 8. Many heroes took part. Meleager, son of King Oeneus of Calydon, killed the boar; but the first wound was given by a woman, the huntress Atalanta. Some heroes resented Meleager's giving her the trophy of honour; hence the fighting.

**534 γουνῷ ἀλωῆς.** γουνός probably means 'high ground' (akin to γόνυ) rather than 'most fruitful ground' (akin to γονή)—another ancient guess; contrast οὖθαρ ἀρούρης, 141.

**535 θεοὶ δαίνυνθ' ἑκατόμβας.** Normally Homer avoids saying that the gods *eat* the offerings made by men, preferring such expressions as 'the goddess came to meet the offering', ἱρῶν ἀντιόωσα, *Il.* 3. 436, or Zeus 'received the offerings', 2. 420; it is not made clear why the gods insist on receiving them, cf. Kirk, *Commentary* ii. 10-12. This uncomplicated assertion is put in the mouth of Phoenix, not that of the poet himself, and refers to the past.

**537 ἢ οὐκ,** one syllable ('synizesis'). Absence of bad intention— whether Oeneus 'forgot or did not intend to do it'—made no difference to the anger of Olympian gods at a slight; and Artemis was particularly irascible.

**540 κακὰ πόλλ' ἔρδεσκεν ἔθων.** Traditionally translated, 'did damage regularly, making a habit of it' (ἔθων present participle of the verb ἔθω familiar in the perfect, εἴωθα, cf. 16. 260 ἔθοντες). But perhaps more plausibly ἔθων means 'ravaging': cf. Leumann, *HW* 212f.

**542 αὐτῇσιν ῥίζῃσι:** cf. on 194.

**546 ἐπέβησε**= 'made them mount the funeral pyre', cf. 4. 99. βαίνω, too, can be used transitively, e.g. 5. 164.

**547 ἡ δέ:** still Artemis.

**552** On the difficulty of this line see note on 527. The resemblance of Meleager's to Achilles' position is exaggerated, and 550-2 echoes Achilles' boast, 352-5.

**554** Looking back on his quarrel with Agamemnon, Achilles will curse 'anger which urges on even a sensible man to quarrel; sweeter than honey that drips from the comb, it expands like smoke in the human breast' (18. 107-10). So here it 'swells the heart' in the breast. What is meant is perhaps the great gulping breaths taken by a man swelling up with rage: cf. 646 ἀλλά μοι οἰδάνεται κραδίη χόλῳ. At 4. 24, 'Hera's breast could not contain her anger.'

**555 φίλη.** The scholia say the epithet 'is used generally, as his mother was not dear to him then'. Cf. *Od.* 11. 327: Eriphyle took a price for the life of her φίλου ἀνδρός. φίλος in Homer does not primarily mean 'dear' but something more like 'related to oneself', by some link of blood, or community, or ownership. Cf. E. Benveniste, *Le Vocabulaire des institutions I-E* (Paris, 1969), i. 337ff.; J. T. Hooker, 'Homeric φίλος', *Glotta* 65 (1987), 44-65; D. Robinson, 'Homeric φίλος', *Owls to Athens* (*Festschrift K. J. Dover*) (Oxford, 1990), 97-108.

**556** κεῖτο. Compare 2. 688 (of Achilles): κεῖτο γὰρ ἐν νήεσσι . . . κούρης χωόμενος.

**558** Ἴδεώ θ'. However archaic the story of Idas and Marpessa may be, the Ionic form Ἴδεω (for Ἴδαο) suggests that this line is not very ancient. The story is allusively and incompletely told here. Euenus, Marpessa's father, has the name of a river in Aetolia, where the story is set. Idas sometimes has a twin, Lynceus: the two are then rivals to the Dioscuri, Castor and Polydeuces. But here Idas alone challenges Apollo, and with success. An early version of the tale said that Zeus let Marpessa choose between Apollo and Idas, and that she chose the mortal, for fear the god would leave her when she was old, (Simonides 563P). Here, too, she is carried off by Apollo against her will. Εὐηνίνη, cf. Ἀδρηστίνη, 'daughter of Adrastus', 5. 412.

**562** It seems clear that the name by which this heroine was really known was Alcyone: her second name, Cleopatra, is then an invention by the poet to make her resemble Patroclus (note on 527), but he has expressed it in such a way as to suggest the reverse, cf. 6. 402-3 and Kirk ad loc. Later myth said the woman Alcyone was actually metamorphosed into the bird; perhaps Homer knows but understates this story.

**563** The halcyon (kingfisher) was known for its mournful cry.

**565** τῇ ὅ γε παρκατέλεκτο. Closes the ring opened at 556, κεῖτο παρὰ μνηστῇ ἀλόχῳ. χόλον θυμαλγέα πέσσων: a half-line applied to Achilles himself, 4. 513. The situation of Meleager is made to resemble that of Achilles as closely as possible.

**568** πολυφόρβην. Compound adjectives generally but not always have two terminations in Homer; that is, the feminine form is identical with the masculine (but ἀθανάτη; ἀπριάτην 1. 99). At 14. 200 and 301, πολυφόρβου (from πολυφόρβοο) πείρατα γαίης shows such a declension of this word; but πολύφορβον χερσὶν ἀλοία is not accepted by Homer because hexameter poets avoid closing the fourth foot with a naturally short syllable lengthened 'by position' ('Wernicke's law', cf. M. L. West, *Greek Metre* (Oxford, 1982), 37). Beating on the ground (in ritual: Pausanias 8. 15. 3) had the point of attracting the attention of the chthonic powers.

**571 ἠεροφοῖτις.** The ancient commentator on 19. 87 quotes as a variant the form εἰαροπῶτις 'blood-drinking'. The Indo-European word for 'blood', in Greek εἶαρ/ἦαρ, seems to have been avoided as taboo; it was replaced in Greek as in other languages (αἷμα; Latin *sanguis*, etc.). The word εἰαροπῶτις perhaps was originally applied to the Erinys, the avenging spirit of the curse, and subsequently either became unintelligible or was felt to be too crude for a god and was replaced by 'roaming the air'. With this theory (A. Hoekstra, *Epic Verse Before Homer*, (Amsterdam, 1981) 87) cf. the redefining of βοῶπις and γλαυκῶπις, epithets of Hera and Athena, not as 'ox-faced' and 'owl-faced' but as 'ox-eyed' and 'sparkling eyed'.

**572** 'A mother's Erinyes' are mentioned at 21. 412, *Od.* 11. 277. Telemachus fears his mother's curse, *Od.* 2. 134. Despite the impressive scene here, we are not explicitly told of any consequences for Meleager. His story is dramatically Homerized: like Achilles, he is left still alive but under sentence of death.

**ἀμείλιχον.** The point made at 158 is repeated: only hellish creatures refuse to yield to supplication.

**573** The Couretes (τῶν) are on the point of storming the city: ὅμαδος, shouting; δοῦπος, the sound of missiles. ὀρώρει: note on 13.

**576** The Aetolians offered gifts—but not on the scale of Agamemnon's offerings.

**577 τέμενος.** A royal estate of his own; cf. 6. 195ff., the τέμενος given to Bellerophon. The word is akin to τάμνω (6. 194 τέμενος τάμον): 580, ταμέσθαι.

**579 πεντηκοντόγυον.** Apparently 'as much as a man could plough in fifty days'; half vines, half arable.

**580ff.** Meleager's closest connections try him in turn. Kakridis (*Homeric Researches* 19ff.) points to a folk-tale motif,·the 'ascending scale of affection', the wife normally succeeding where the others have failed (see note on 527). Repetition of πολλά (581, 584, 585) adds rhetorical shape and emphasis.

**583** The father supplicates his son, as at 451 Phoenix' own mother did to him (and as Phoenix, who claims to be virtually a parent, does to Achilles).

**584** The mother was so regular a figure in the 'scale of affection' that she appears here, incongruously after her curse.

**585f.** The ἑταῖροι are promoted to penultimate position, irregularly, to suit the present occasion. When Achilles' dearest comrades fail, only Patroclus (note Cleopatra's new name) can succeed.

**586, 589 ἔπειθον.** Repeated attempts failed. βαῖνον, ἐνέπρηθον: all imperfects: the sack of the town was on the point of beginning.

**592** The *Iliad* does not tell of the sack of Troy, but the horrors of a sack are not omitted. That of Troy is anticipated: 22. 59–71 (Priam), 6. 448ff. (Hector), 24. 728ff (Andromache). Cf. *Od.* 8. 523–31. The audience of Homer can have no illusions about war.

**593–4** This was and remained the normal Greek practice when a city was taken. βαθυζώνους wearing the girdle low, above the hips. This word, like βαθύκολπος which describes the effect of the girdle ('with deep folds in the dress') is restricted to non-Greek women in *Il.* and *Od.*; the Homeric *Hymns* use it of any women (Richardson on *H. Dem.* 95).

**595 κακὰ ἔργα.** Such expressions as this, and ἀεικέα ἔργα (15. 97, 21. 19, 23. 176; 22. 395 = 23. 23), mean rather 'disastrous for the sufferer' than 'wrong for the doer', cf. Griffin, *Homer on Life and Death*, 85 n. 9. We are to think of Meleager as most moved by the thought of the fate of his wife; cf. Hector in 6. 450ff. Tacitus says of the Germans of his own time that they were far less anxious about their own fate than that their womenfolk might be enslaved after their defeat (*Germ.* 8).

**598 εἴξας ᾧ θυμῷ.** The parallel at 109 suggests that this means 'after yielding to his anger', sc. and refusing to fight, rather than that he now gave way to his own impulse and not to the prayers of his wife, a distinction which has no point.

**600** 'Do not have such thoughts' and 'let not a δαίμων turn you in that direction' are clearly two ways of saying the same thing; cf. 702–3 'when his heart bids him and a god arouses him', and note on 636. On this 'double motivation', human and divine, in Homer: E. R. Dodds, *The Greeks and the Irrational* (1951), ch. 1; A. Lesky, *Göttliche und menschliche Motivation im hom. Epos* (Heidelberg, 1961).

**601 δαίμων.** Often used by speakers in the *Iliad*, who do not share the omniscience of the poet about divine interventions, this vaguer expression conveys sudden and, sometimes, rather sinister impulsion; cf. 4. 420, 15. 418, 15. 468, 21. 93; *Od.* 10. 64, 24. 149. Cf. H. Erbse, *Untersuchungen zur Funktion der Götter im hom. Epos* (Berlin, 1986), 259–68.

**602 ἐπὶ δώροις,** the reading of most of the manuscripts, means 'for, in return for, the gifts', cf. 10. 304 δώρῳ ἐπὶ μεγάλῳ. The genitive δώρων of the OCT would be unparalleled in this sense. ἶσον . . . θεῷ repeats the promise of Odysseus, 302 f.

**605 τιμῆς.** Metrical contraction of τιμήεις, cf. 18. 475 χρυσὸν τιμῆντα. The point is not merely economic: the gifts will be visible tokens of respect and position.

**607 ἄττα.** A child's word, 'Daddy'; cf. μαῖα, used in the *Odyssey* to address elderly women.

**608 τιμῆς.** Achilles immediately picks up Phoenix' word and crushingly rejects it. Here a noun, in 605 it was an epithet: it is the identical sound that the poet wanted.

**Διὸς αἴσῃ** 'by the will of Zeus', visible in my status in the world. Agamemnon uttered a similar boast in the quarrel (1. 174–5), but he was mistaken.

**609 ἥ μ' ἕξει.** Cf. *Od.* 1. 95 κλέος μιν ἔχει: 'My superiority will stay with me among the Achaean ships.' Achilles is not thinking of his threat to sail home in the morning.

**612** Achilles is aware that the emotional appeal of Phoenix has had more effect on him than the cool speech of Odysseus.

**σύγχει θυμόν,** cf. 13. 808, 'shatter my resolution' (not 'confuse my heart', as Macleod, *Commentary on Iliad 24*, p. 27).

**614–16** Achilles presses the point: Phoenix should be on *his* side. 614 has a threatening tone; 616 is unexpectedly lavish (cf. Bellerophon being given 'half the kingdom', 6. 193)—*if* Phoenix is on the right side. Heyne and others have deleted 616 as an later insertion, plausibly.

**617** The unexplained and odd position of Phoenix, away from Achilles—because the poet wants him as part of the embassy from Agamemnon—will now be rectified.

**618** Achilles recedes considerably from his first reply.

ἅμα δ' ἠοῖ φαινομένηφι: Originally ἠόι, giving a dactyl in the fourth foot. φαινομένηφι = φαινομένη; cf. note on 58.

**620-1** Only now is it made clear that Patroclus has been present throughout, listening to the discussion which will decide his fate as well as that of Achilles. The unobtrusive touch opens a profound vista. The datives: he nods *with* his head *to* Patroclus *in* silence to prepare *for* Phoenix (Leaf); ἐπὶ . . . νεῦσε = ἐπένευσε.

**622** μεδοίατο. 3rd person plural (μέδοιντο in Attic): 'So that they should think of going back immediately.' Achilles reacts as if he were anxious to get rid of his visitors before they make even more of an emotional mark on him; but to do so with courtesy.

**624** After so heavy a hint it seems that Ajax will not after all be able to make a speech. With great skill, he is shown accepting that and addressing not Achilles but Odysseus: 'Let's go!' (ἴομεν, subjunctive). Ajax as a warrior is the last hope of the defence and 'virtually never leads an attack' (Kirk, *Commentary* ii. 53); here too he intervenes when all seems lost.

**628** ἕαται. 'Are sitting' (Attic ἧνται); also Homeric are ἧατο (11. 76) and, with short vowel, ἕατο (3. 134, 7. 414): Chantraine, *GH* i. 476.

ποτιδέγμενοι = προσδεχόμενοι: see on 191.

αὐτὰρ Ἀχιλλεύς: the speaker begins to work round to Achilles.

**629-32** ἄγριον, σχέτλιος. The strongest terms of condemnation in the Homeric vocabulary. 'He has made his proud heart savage, he is so unreasonable . . .'

**631, 641** ἔξοχον ἄλλων. The repetition, with the superlative, abnormally, in the second place, seems consciously contrived: *we* honoured *you* most, and we claim to be *your* dearest friends. Ajax' argument, that we are friends and all in the same boat, is reinforced by this device.

**632** The kinsmen of a murdered man were bound to avenge his death, unless the killer left the community: hence the wandering homicides in Homer (e.g. Patroclus, 23. 85ff.; others, 13. 696 = 15. 335; *Od.* 15. 272; *Il.* 24. 480f.). At some times or in some places it was possible to come to a financial arrangement, cf. 18. 497; Ajax complains that much closer losses than Achilles has suffered can be so compounded. Similarly at the end of the *Iliad*, for his treatment of Hector's corpse, Achilles is said to have 'destroyed pity' and to have a heart as savage as a lion's; even after the death of a brother or a son, mourning does not last for ever (24. 40-49).

**636** Ajax turns on Achilles, with admirable effect: 'Men who have suffered worse losses do this—but *you* . . .'. At 629 he said Achilles hardened his own heart; now he says that the gods have done it. It is clear that these are not different statements but only two ways of speaking of the same thing, a clear instance of the 'double motivation', human and divine, regular in Homer, cf. note on 600.

δεξαμένῳ. After τοῦ we expect δεξαμένου, but the construction drifts into the dative because of the close connection between the verb and the subject: cf. 14. 139-41.

**638** οἵης. The Homeric enjambment allows emphasis to fall crushingly: *one* miserable girl! For the bluff mind of Ajax, seven girls are obviously better than one; but Achilles loves Briseis.

**639f.** The appeal of Ajax is again different: to the solidarity of comrades in a team. 'We are your friends, and we represent the whole army.' Similarly blunt and forceful speeches by him: 15. 502-13; 73. Such an appeal has weight with Achilles and leads to a further stage of relenting from his original decision. Achilles will bitterly regret failing to help his friends; 18. 101-5, cf. 18. 128-30, 19. 61-4.

**640** αἴδεσσαι δὲ μέλαθρον: i.e. 'let the fact that we are under your roof add to the moral pressure on you (αἰδώς, cf. note on 451) to yield to our appeal'. Cf. Cairns, *Aidos*, 91 n. 133 on this use of an emotive feature of a relationship to stand for the relationship as a whole. So Hecuba asks Hector to respect her breasts; that is, her motherhood (22. 82).

**641** Cf. note on 631.

**645** The adverbial τι slightly softens the adjective: 'pretty well everything'. Cf. 523 πρὶν δ' οὔ τι νεμεσσητὸν κεχολῶσθαι, 12. 9 οὔ τι πολὺν χρόνον, 'not really for long'. κατὰ θυμόν 'in agreement with my own feelings': not 'according to your heart' (as Martin,

*Language of Heroes*, 40, 142). Achilles admits that Ajax is right, but insists on following his own anger.

**646** Cf. Achilles' words at 16. 52 ἀλλὰ τόδ' αἰνὸν ἄχος κραδίην καὶ θυμὸν ἱκάνει: Achilles' anger continues to be fully roused by remembering his grievance; the passage in 16 resembles this one and looks like a conscious echo (Lohmann, *Komposition*, 274f.). Too late, he will curse χόλος (18. 108).

**648 ἀτίμητον μετανάστην.** (Attic, μέτοικον). Like a landless man who arrived on the run and has no legal position.

**650ff.** A second stage of relenting from his original announcement that he would sail home in the morning. Achilles refers to these lines at 16. 60–3 (but cf. Janko ad loc.). We remember that Achilles originally threatened the Achaeans with Hector: 1. 240–4; and the words of Zeus, 8. 473f.:

> οὐ γὰρ πρὶν πολέμου ἀποπαύσεται ὄβριμος Ἕκτωρ
> πρὶν ὄρθαι παρὰ ναῦφι ποδώκεα Πηλείωνα . . .

Human will and divine plan echo each other and work together (Motzkus 64f.).

**655 σχήσεσθαι.** Passive, 'will be checked'. μάχης, both with μεμαῶτα and σχήσεσθαι: 'eager though he is for fighting, he will be checked in it'.

**656-7 οἱ δὲ ἕκαστος ἑλὼν . . . σπείσαντες . . . ἴσαν.** Each man took a cup, and all poured libations and went. Cf. Chantraine, *GH* ii. 15.

**657 σπείσαντες.** It was customary to pour a formal libation to the gods at the end of a meal, cf. 712; *Od.* 3. 332–4 'mix the wine, so that we may pour a libation to Poseidon and the other gods and think about going to bed.' Gods receive meat offerings and drink offerings, like the God of the Hebrews (Leviticus 23: 37, etc.) and the gods of all their neighbours (Deuteronomy 33: 37–8). The plurals here must refer to the two envoys, Odysseus and Ajax: another difficulty for the problem of the duals at 168f.

**661 ἄωτον.** The 'nap', the softest surface of cloth; but according to J. L. Melena 'plucked wool' (not sheared): *Minos* 20–22 (1987) = *Studies in Mycenaean and Classical Greek presented to John Chadwick*, 404f.

**663 μυχῷ κλισίης.** The dative without preposition, indicating place in which something happens, is a poetic feature. It shows the dative replacing the Indo-European locative case: K–G. i. 441 f. Achilles feels no need to sleep alone in the absence of Briseis.

**668** Achilles is here imagined as having raided the island of Scyros, as he raided Lesbos (128 f. = 271 f., 664): cf. 328 f. on his expeditions while at Troy. Another tradition told of his being hidden there by his mother, dressed as a girl, to keep him from the war. There he seduced the princess Deidameia, who bore him a son. At 19. 326–333 we hear that he has a son, Neoptolemus, who is being brought up there; that seems to belong to the second tradition.

**670** Achaeans are not described as having much gold with them at Troy (except in the funeral of Patroclus, 23. 92, 196, 219, 243, 253). Nestor's famous cup in 11. 632 is only decorated with gold. It seems to be only Agamemnon who has a complete set of gold cups with him (E. Bielfeld, *Archaeologia Homerica* I C (Göttingen, 1968), 64).

**671** A lively line of δ and α.

**673** μ': μοι
πολύαινε: only of Odysseus; traditionally 'much talked of', but another explanation, going back to antiquity (Hesychius s.v.): 'with many tales (αἶνοι) to tell'—perhaps rightly.

**676 ff.** Scholars have wondered ever since antiquity why Odysseus reports only Achilles' first and most hostile speech, not the much more encouraging things which he said at lines 618–19 and 650 ff. Some resorted to the superficial expedient of deleting 682–4. Another popular line was that only Achilles' first response was an 'official' reply to Agamemnon's overtures, a line which leaves us with a low opinion of the intelligence of the wily Odysseus. Psychological explanations have been tried, e.g. that Achilles' first, intemperate speech was the only one which really impressed the envoys (Spiess 110). Or: Achilles here as elsewhere indulges in exaggeration, the emotional immediate response being as usual followed by a cooler and more rational one; the rational Odysseus knows that this will happen (Lohmann, *Komposition der Reden*, 279 n. 118). Or: Odysseus wants to emphasize the perilous situation of the Greeks (Schadewaldt, *Iliasstudien*, 135 n. 1). Or: Achilles has disappointed the envoys, and Odysseus deliberately presents him in a bad light (C. Ulf, *Die homerische Gesellschaft* (Munich, 1992) 93 n. 18). The point is that the Achaeans in the following books must be fighting on in despair of Achilles' return, and so envisaging complete defeat and destruction; it would be poetically disastrous to make them confident that he will return to the fighting in the nick of time. Cf. R. Scodel in *CP* 84 (1989), 91-9. In a way which recalls the technique of the opening of the embassy (see notes on 182, 223-4) the poet leaves a rough edge in the interest of his general conception. It is deftly blurred by the fact that Diomedes (702-3) speaks as if Achilles were still to be there in the Troad.

**676 πολύτλας δῖος Ὀδυσσεύς.** The epithet πολύτλας must refer to Od.'s sufferings on his way home. This formulaic phrase is regular of the hero in the *Od.* and no doubt antedates that poem.

**680-7** Cf. Achilles' words at 347, 357-61, and 417-20.

**684** In *oratio recta*, καὶ ἂν παραμυθησαίμην . . .

**690-2** Cf. Achilles' words at 427-9.

**693-6** = 29-31, with the addition of 694 (= 431). 694 was ejected by the Alexandrian scholars; unexpected here, it suggests the whole army was present, see note on 17-27, and κρατερῶς is hardly the right adverb for Odysseus' speech. The speech of Achilles himself could well be described in this way, but hardly Odysseus' résumé of it. Without 694, the parallel—obviously deliberate—between the beginning and end of this sequence of scenes is perfect. The brave and uncomplicated Diomedes again steps in.

**698 μὴ ὄφελες.** 'I wish you had not', cf. 22. 481 ὡς μὴ ὤφελλε τεκέσθαι; 17. 689 ἢ μὴ ὤφελλε γενέσθαι.

**700 ἀγηνορίῃσιν ἐνῆκας.** 'Made him haughty'. Homer often uses plural forms to express abstractions, as if instances of haughtiness were a more natural way of thinking in a period not much at home with 'pure' abstractions. Cf. 6. 74 ἀναλκείῃσι δαμέντες, 'defeated by their cowardice'; 2. 792 ποδωκείῃσι πεποιθώς, 'trusting in his speed of foot', etc. ἐνῆκας, from ἐνίημι; cf. *Od.* 14. 183-4; (in the past sequence, with optatives, *Od.* 15. 300); Chantraine, *GH* ii. 295.

**702-3** Cf. note on 600.

**705 τεταρπόμενοι.** Reduplicated aorist middle of τέρπω: 'having satisfied ourselves'.

**709 καὶ δ' αὐτός.** It is natural to regard this singling out of Agamemnon as preparing the way into his spectacular role (ἀριστεία) in the first half of Book 11: another indication that Book 10 was not originally, or not always, part of the *Iliad*.

# GENERAL INDEX

Roman figures refer to pages of the Introduction, italic figures to line numbers of the Commentary.

# GREEK INDEX